D0951945

HEARTH

HEARTH

A Global Conversation
on Community, Identity, and Place

Edited by Annick Smith and Susan O'Connor

with contributing editor Helen Whybrow

MILKWEED EDITIONS

Published 2018 by Milkweed Editions
Printed in Canada
Cover design by Mary Austin Speaker
Cover illustration by goodwin_x / Shutterstock
18 19 20 21 22 5 4 3 2 1
First Edition

Milkweed Editions, an independent nonprofit publisher, gratefully acknowledges sustaining support from the Jerome Foundation; the Lindquist & Vennum Foundation; the McKnight Foundation; the National Endowment for the Arts; the Target Foundation; and other generous contributions from foundations, corporations, and individuals. Also, this activity is made possible by the voters of Minnesota through a Minnesota State Arts Board Operating Support grant, thanks to a legislative appropriation from the arts and cultural heritage fund, and a grant from Wells Fargo. For a full listing of Milkweed Editions supporters, please visit milkweed.org.

Library of Congress Cataloging-in-Publication Data

Names: O'Connor, Susan, editor. | Smith, Annick, 1936-
    editor. | Whybrow, Helen, editor.
Title: Hearth : a global conversation on community, identity, and place /
    edited by Susan O'Connor and Annick Smith ; with contributing editor Helen
    Whybrow.
Description: First edition. | Minneapolis, Minnesota : Milkweed Editions,
    2018. | Includes bibliographical references and index.
Identifiers: LCCN 2018011459 (print) | LCCN 2018033315 (ebook) | ISBN
    9781571319890 (ebook) | ISBN 9781571313799 | ISBN 9781571313799
    (cloth ; alk. paper) |
Subjects: LCSH: Hearths--Social aspects.
Classification: LCC GT420 (ebook) | LCC GT420 .H43 2018 (print) | DDC
    392.3/6--dc23
LC record available at https://lccn.loc.gov/2018011459

Milkweed Editions is committed to ecological stewardship. We strive to align our book production practices with this principle, and to reduce the impact of our operations in the environment. We are a member of the Green Press Initiative, a nonprofit coalition of publishers, manufacturers, and authors working to protect the world's endangered forests and conserve natural resources. *Hearth* was printed on acid-free 100% postconsumer-waste paper by Friesens Corporation.

For those who have lost their hearths
and those seeking new ones

Contents

ART

HEARTH

Rain Light
W. S. MERWIN

All day the stars watch from long ago
my mother said I am going now
when you are alone you will be all right
whether or not you know you will know

look at the old house in the dawn rain
all the flowers are forms of water
the sun reminds them through a white cloud
touches the patchwork spread on the hill
the washed colors of the afterlife
that lived there long before you were born
see how they wake without question
even though the whole world is burning

from *The Shadow of Sirius* (Copper Canyon Press, 2009)

Keeping the Fire Alive

Annick Smith and Susan O'Connor

O ur idea for a book about hearth started on the rim of the Kīlauea Volcano on Hawai'i's Big Island. Pualani Kanahele's extended family was dancing a traditional hula at the edge of the vast crater. The dancers moved with rhythmic steps to the powerful beat of the *ipo* and Pua's booming ritual chant. This was the opening ceremony for a gathering of environmental and cultural leaders that Susan had helped to organize.

Known throughout the islands, Aunty Pua is a revered elder, a teacher or *kumu*, and a friend to both of us. A few days after the hula ceremony, Pua spoke to the gathering and described her hearth as the volcano itself. Kīlauea, she said, is a living, creative, and continuous force tying her and her kin to earth and ocean and sky, to myth and tradition, to generations past, present, and future—"the chaos that begins and ends life over and over again."

Pua suggested ways to discover our own hearths. "Invite guests to your home, and over a generous offering of food ask them where their hearth is." Where do they feel the pull of the earth? Where do they return over and over in body or in mind? What is their sanctuary—their centering ground?

Months later, after a sumptuous meal at Susan's home at the Valley of the Moon Ranch, we began the conversation that launched this book. "I've got a project for us to do," said Susan. "Let's make a book about hearth." Annick warmed her hands over a blazing fire in Susan's fireplace. Why, she wondered, do we need a book about something so obvious and good?

Remembering Pua's instructions, Susan asked Annick, "Where's your hearth? Mine," she explained, "is an ancient grove of larch and pines in the heart of our valley. Small wooden signs tacked onto the oldest guardian trees by the original settlers are what drew me to this refuge. They turned out to be Stations of the Cross. I've walked those woods almost every day for the past twenty-five years, and they've given me a sense of kinship with the moose and mountain lions, the squirrels in the forest, and the trout in the streams." Susan was talking about her connection, through place, to the entire biosphere.

Turning again to Annick, she asked, "What's your hearth of hearths?"

Annick pondered a moment. "I guess it's the log house we built in the meadow off Bear Creek Road—that's my home." But home is not necessarily a hearth like Pua's volcano or Susan's ancient grove. Annick shrugged. "Maybe it's the Red Rocks beach along the Blackfoot River, a kind of sacred place where I want my ashes to be scattered.

"No," she smiled, "I think it's my grandmother's recipe for *csirke paprikás* (chicken paprika)." This is her Hungarian–Jewish family's traditional meal—a recipe passed down to her mother, and to her and her sisters, and now to her four sons, and even her granddaughters, who love to make the *galuska* (dumplings) that are served with the chicken at family celebrations. The recipe is not a place but the symbol of a moveable feast upholding culture and identity and relationship through generations—a portable inner home.

We ended the evening determined to continue on the track of hearth. A conversation that began with a volcano, entered into a forest, and concluded with a grandmother's recipe could, we decided, be the impetus for a most intriguing book.

❖

During the following weeks, the two of us talked about the multiple meanings of hearth and questioned what the idea might mean today. How has it changed? Is it still important? Is it even a possibility for many people? We wondered how different cultures and generations would define the notion of hearth, and started making a wish list of writers who might enlighten us. Then we named the people we'd like to enlist in helping us to craft our dream anthology.

It did not occur to us that the project we had started so casually would take years to complete, but once we got going, we could not stop. We had embarked on a long and intensive collaboration with consultants and editors and publishers, and most importantly with writers from all over the world—famous and not-yet-famous or never-to-be-famous—friends and strangers who would become our intellectual partners in a mutual quest for meaning.

Our starting point was the connection between *heart* and *earth* embedded in the English word *hearth*—a place like Pua's volcano or Susan's forest or Annick's meadow with its elk and coyotes and migrating birds: the natural world as home. But that was only a starting point. We soon understood that nature was not the only heart place to explore. The notion of hearth began in caves—stone dwellings that were part of nature, but also a stave against its cold, darkness, and dangers. Such shelters were where our earliest ancestors discovered how to use fire for heat and food preparation, found refuge, and evolved as social beings, developing tribal identities—to say nothing of language.

Hearth is still associated with fire, warmth, and cooking, as well as with family and the homes where families gather. But as time passed and cultures diverged, the concept grew to include public squares, markets, and mosques—destinations where larger communities come together. The word also came to embrace symbolic centers such as belief systems and ideologies that people cling to as identities. Hearth could be understood as a defining story or mythology, an electronic network that ties vast numbers of people together, or a vital creative center. Hearths, in this broad sense, may be communal and traditional, personal and idiosyncratic, or all of these at once.

✶

As editors, we believe that the writers included in this collection have created a diverse, thought-provoking, and utterly original cacophony of voices to explore the meanings and uses of hearth in a world that is changing rapidly. Some, such as Barry Lopez, Bill McKibben, Natasha Thretheway, and Terry Tempest Williams, are well known in the United States. Others are distinguished writers in their homelands: Zoë Strachan in Scotland, Chigozie Obioma in Nigeria, Pualani Kanahele in Hawai'i, Gerður Kristný in Iceland. Still others are emerging writers whose powerful voices make a deep impression: Angie Cruz from New York and the Dominican Republic, Andrew Lam from Vietnam, Sara Baume from Ireland, Boey Kim Cheng from Singapore and Australia, and Yvonne Adhiambo Owuor from Kenya—to name just a few.

Their contributions, written expressly for this anthology, explore ideas about what, if anything, takes the place of hearth in the lives of refugees and immigrants, and how ideas of hearth have evolved for a young generation in a globalized world. With passion and care, these authors celebrate natural and spiritual hearths, or mourn hearths that are being destroyed—never to be replaced—in our increasingly endangered, highly populated, but still natural world.

In addition to these essays, poems, and stories, the Brazilian photographer, Sebastião Salgado, has contributed compelling images of traditional peoples and natural wonders that continue to exist in Africa's cradle, and on the frozen tundra, or within the Amazonian delta. Such images remind us of our human journeys and of the earth that endures with us or without us.

The world is in flux because of climate change, wars, refugees, migrants, and constantly evolving technologies. Traditional centers of home and personal affiliation are being destroyed and fragmented, leaving millions bewildered and suffering. We are tempted to wonder whether the very notion of hearth has lost all meaning. But our species is irrepressibly adaptable. New ways of experiencing identity and interconnection are in process. Science offers proof of a universe created through infinite interdependencies. It offers clues about the evolution of human consciousness—where we come from and why we are here. As Mary Evelyn Tucker suggests in the essay that concludes the book, the whole cosmos may be our centering place.

❦

From the beginning, we editors knew that a single volume could never cover every meaning of hearth and home. But we believed a collection of diverse voices and stories might spark a necessary conversation—that it might serve as a virtual hearth where disparate minds could come together in a global discussion.

We hope this book will expand our readers' thinking and imaginations in the same way its creation has expanded ours. If readers are inspired to identify, protect, or reimagine their home places, the book will have done its job. If it leads some folks to join with others in revitalizing and rebuilding communities, it will have done more. And if it opens hearts to deeper understandings of the values, needs, and desires of others, engendering empathy, we will have achieved our highest goal.

Finally, we offer thanks to the people who have made this book possible. Thanks especially to our consulting editor and associate, Helen Whybrow, and to our invaluable project manager, Minette Glaser, who were full partners in the making of this book and worked closely with us and with our writers over several years. Also to poetry consultant Sandra Alcosser, whose good advice we treasure. And to our fine publisher, Daniel Slager, and the great staff at Milkweed Editions.

We give special thanks to Pualani Kanahele, William Kittredge, Christopher Merrill, Barbara Ras, and Frank Stewart. They led us to expand our vision of what the book could and should be, connected us with many international writers we would otherwise not have known, and offered criticism and support unstintingly. Barry Lopez has been an inspirational guide, an impeccable critic, and a strong supporter from the start, and his foreword sets a high standard for the authors who follow. Most of all, our thanks go out to all of the authors who so generously contributed their experiences, thoughts, and words to our anthology.

It seems we humans, like whales and monarch butterflies, are programmed to return to, or to seek, places of refuge, nurture, and deep connection. But unlike butterflies and whales, we also keep asking questions about who we are, why we are here, where we came from, and where we are headed. All around the world, individuals, families, friends, and neighbors gather around a campfire or a computer, a kitchen table or an auditorium stage to share ideas, and warmth, and often food. This book, we hope, may become one such gathering place where questions are asked that have no answers, but where the talk goes on and on, connecting us in peace and trust. Keeping the fire alive.

Annick Smith and Susan O'Connor
January 24, 2018

Finding the Hearth

Barry Lopez

It was summer, and years ago. I'd been staying in a small Nunamiut Eskimo village in the central Brooks Range in Alaska, Anaktuvuk Pass, with my friend Bob Stephenson. We'd left this small settlement of 110 behind and were walking north through the Anaktuvuk River valley, camping as we went, headed toward that river's confluence with the Colville River. We were trying to find active wolf dens, a part of Bob's summer work as a field biologist. The weather had been good. Clear skies, temperatures in the fifties. Our search was concentrated on an open tundra plain west of the river, especially along a series of creeks where we might be able to locate paw prints on the banks and sandbars. These creeks carried late-season snowmelt down to the river from valleys in mountains farther to the west of us.

At this time of year there was no night that we needed to plan our days around; we ate and slept according to another rhythm, the rhythm of our own energy. In this valley, far north of the tree line, planed smooth thousands of years ago by a glacier the size of Delaware, we enjoyed panoramic views, like those from a ship's bridge in midocean. The air was so clear I was able to study the slow drift of caribou grazing on a mountainside six miles away with my spotting scope. Astonishing, but it was easy to verify the distance on a topographic map we were carrying.

When we decided to rest, to drop our packs, make a meal, and perhaps sleep a bit, we built a fire of dry arctic willow twigs. We didn't need the warmth, and it would have been quicker and more convenient to cook on our portable, single-burner stoves; but we built a fire every time, without discussing it. A patch of bare ground, shavings from the willows for tinder, a wooden match cupped against the breeze, encouraging the first flames with a human breath. Carefully feeding the burn to grow it.

Small and assertive, the fire centered us every time, defining a space temporarily ours in an enormous and indifferent expanse of country. The flicker of the fire's flames within the boundary of a stone perimeter urged us toward quiet thoughts of the day's events. It reeled us in out of a vast silence, the absence of any sound in the air over the tundra, a silence inflected by the murmur of a fire, slowly devouring bits of wood.

One night, after we'd eaten and settled in back-to-back behind our spotting scopes, Bob told me a story. A few years before, he'd been traveling with three Nunamiut men in country to the south and east of where we were then, in the drainage of the Anaktiktoak River. They'd halted for the day, had built a small fire, and put an aluminum kettle on for tea. It was a chilly evening. The four of them were standing around the fire hunched in their parkas, not saying much, waiting for the water to boil, when Bob noticed a man named Simon Paneak moving his walking staff back and forth in a gesturing way, as though signaling for someone to come closer to the warmth of the fire. When Bob shifted his eyes, he saw that Simon was welcoming a porcupine.

Whenever we sat next to the fire scanning the tundra plain, always alert for wolf howls, the aluminum kettle nestled down in the embers, we felt the security of our friendship, of the work we were doing together, and the embrace of the vast landscape beyond the ambit of the fire, a fire not much larger than the battered kettle.

The absence of darkness during our journey sometimes reminded me of a phrase I had learned in high school. Roman soldiers, halting for the night to make camp, referred to the shadowy area between the ground lit by their fires and the outer dark as *inter canem et lupum*, the space between the dog and the wolf. It was the sort of locution that stuck in my mind as a boy, a suggestive and succinct thought. The outer dark. Where we were on the tundra, no such situation would arise before the coming of fall. Here, though, we were certain that there were wolves out there, aware of us. Once we caught three of them at it, a mile away, studying the two of us. The five of us then—traveling, resting, and hunting in the same, sunlit world.

The geography that surrounded Bob and me on those July days was so immense we felt less than incidental when standing up in it. It was the fire each evening that gave us definition and meaning. Here was the mark of our arrival and departure. Here was our reassurance, and a faint reminder of what Prometheus had stolen from Zeus to make human life less anxious, less beleaguered, more independent. A tiny memorial, then, to our very old and particular hominid ways.

Wolves don't make fire. They do not have the need.

With that fire at my back, it seemed I was able to see farther into the outer world. And whenever I poured hot water for tea, I was always careful to hold the mug away so steam wouldn't fog the eyepiece of the spotting scope, disturbing for some moments the camaraderie I felt with the resident animals I watched in those days—a fox, a ground squirrel, ducks rising from a tundra pond. Tundra grizzly.

The Nunamiut people we were staying with at Anaktuvuk Pass had lived and hunted in these mountains and valleys for centuries. We knew because we came upon the remains of their old fires once in a while, evidence of how they had once paused in a certain place to regain control of the vastness through which they moved.

❖

What one thinks of the word *hearth* depends both on the range of whatever a contemporary human mind might imagine and on the informing experience of one's own life. Many people who grow up in dense urban environments today have virtually no experience of hearths in the historical sense—the stones that contain or carry a fire and form a physical space that defines the locus of a domestic life, a setting in which food is prepared and eaten, a quarter from which warmth emanates, and around which conversation occurs. This universally appreciated spot is, for us in the cultural West, the domain of Hestia, Zeus's sister and the goddess ritually honored by Hellenistic Greeks at the beginning and end of every meal. Every Greek home had its hearth, every Greek town its ceremonial hearth, a shrine tended by virgins. In Roman mythology they were the vestal virgins, the women who served Vesta, Hestia's Roman counterpart.

The hearth Bob and I established each day on the tundra comes, of course, from a different tradition than the hearths of Hestia and Vesta, but the values they symbolize overlap—the freedom of thought afforded by the presence of like minds, shelter from the storm, unguarded socializing, even the opportunity to welcome strangers, to express one's capacity to be generous. Against these sustaining values, however, must always be considered the divisive aspects of tribalism, its wariness of the outer world, its resentment or hostility toward other ways of knowing, its impulse to banish its own if they do not conform.

Some of the contributors to this volume offer us eloquent evocations of what it might feel like to perceive, maintain, and cherish a personal hearth. Others, perhaps more acutely aware of what lies behind the bombed, strafed, and bulldozed hearths of the Middle East, wonder what might symbolically replace the traditional hearth, especially in modern urban settings where the notion of a hearth seems quaint. The question that underlies virtually all these essays, then, is: What is the hearth of the Anthropocene? What, now, is the symbol of our allegiance and our concern for one another's fate? Or, is a concern for the fate of others, especially the fate of the stranger, now naïve? Has it become impractical and dangerous?

Perhaps it's fear that urges me to recall those days years ago in the Anaktuvuk River valley with my friend, who has since passed away. Perhaps this is a past I have grown nostalgic about, a poignant or even romantic situation with little relevance to the modern predicament. I can't easily imagine what might replace the actual fire in a modern reification of a hearth, although the essays in this volume suggest there are ways. What concerns me even more, though, is the loss of those values the fire precipitates and reinforces. The comfort that can arise from shared history, from shared ancestors, a comfort so deep it can be understood in complete silence, as it was in that situation around the fire where Simon Paneak welcomed the stranger. Where will the opportunity for intimacy come from now? What will replace this answer to the human longing to be known? How will the affirmation by others of one's own necessity in the world be validated? What will be the opportunities for profound courtesy and for ceremony, of which there is such a dearth in the modern world?

We can lose the communal fire and survive, but survival without the values of the hearth—a complex of associations cited throughout these pages—seems a brutish prospect, a retreat into intolerance.

❖

Most of my experience of hearths outside my own culture has been with friends or acquaintances gathered around a fire to partake of food, to pursue long conversations, to experience together the unplumbable mystery of the world beyond the firelight, and to sleep close on cold or weather-beaten nights. Traveling with seminomadic people and camping in tents, I became acquainted with the notion of "portable hearths," though my mostly benign experience here does not compare well with the experiences that several writers in this volume have had with what could be called impermanent, symbolic, invented, or even abandoned hearths. I've no experience, either, of the pulverized hearths of Palestinians living in the West Bank, of Syrian hearths desacralized by warfare, or the temporary hearths of refugee camps in the Horn of Africa. I've been fortunate to have been able to travel widely, to have shared meals at the hearths of many different types of homes, permanent and temporary; but for most of my adult life I've returned to the same domicile in the woods of Oregon to rekindle, literally and figuratively, my hearth. When I do, I feel secure once again in the turbulent world of my time. And I wonder, often, what it means today to not have a hearth.

The editors of this volume offer us, in addition to a range of thought about an idea, "hearth," a prompt to consider—at a specific time, a time of environmental emergencies, of a sixth biological extinction, of economic violence, and of social disintegration, all on a scale unprecedented in our history—what it might mean to lose one's spiritual footing in the time ahead. Heroic tales from numerous cultures in both hemispheres, stories with an eerie timelessness, consistently tout the wisdom of maintaining a hearth. In them, the maintenance of a hearth, real or symbolic, is not merely a strategy for survival. It is the foundational condition from which human courage arises, from which wisdom emanates, and where a belief in the idea that all storms pass, no matter how disruptive or terrifying they might seem, is anchored. To not be done in by "the enemy," however one might define that, one traditionally councils with one's allies at a hearth, shares sustenance, and then departs fortified.

Or so the tales say.

❖

Prompted by essays in this anthology, particularly by Boey Kim Cheng's "Reflections of a Returnee," Ameena Hussein's "A Staircase with a View," and Kavery Nambisan's "The Rent Not Paid," my thoughts have too often, I suppose, gone off in the direction of those who might dismiss as antiquated or inconvenient the values of the hearth.

The *Hearth* essays expand our conception of hearth, but many of them also make obvious the position of those for whom the idea of a hearth does not resonate. If the reader considers what it might mean to survive in the world without even a figurative hearth, they will understand better, I think, what their life stands for—politically, socially, and economically. They will locate that refined and particular sense of justice that compels people to take a stand. Each true hearth, it seems to me, produces people who live in opposition to those who have lost a sense of empathy with others, those for whom the sacred is a nuisance, an impediment to cultural progress, those who value personal success over human companionship.

❖

I look back on those days in the Brooks Range with my good friend, at the simplicity of our lives, at the purity of my emotions as a young man, and know how very far I still have to go to answer the question this collection poses: What is the modern pivot for these values of love, comity, and the courage needed to face the outer dark that I have touted?

I know that during those days along the Anaktuvuk River I experienced an enthusiasm for life, felt the pleasure of a friendship and shared meals, and held a belief that we would find what we were looking for in that nearly unbounded geography, and I know that all of this was elevated to palpability for me by the small fires of dry arctic willow twigs we constructed each day and lit.

HEART

Meditation at Decatur Square

Natasha Trethewey

1.
In which I try to decipher
the story it tells,
this syntax of monuments
flanking the old courthouse:
here, a rough outline
like the torso of a woman
great with child—
a steatite boulder from which
the Indians girdled the core
to make of it a bowl,
and left in the stone a wound
forged to hold; here,

the bronze figure of Thomas Jefferson,
quill in hand, inventing
a language of freedom,
a creation story—
his hand poised at the word
happiness. There is not yet an ending,
no period, the single mark—
intended or misprinted—that changes
the meaning of everything.

Here too, for the Confederacy,
an obelisk, oblivious
in its name—a word
that also meant the symbol
to denote, in ancient manuscripts,
the *spurious, corrupt,* or *doubtful*;
at its base, forged

in concrete, a narrative
of *valor, virtue, States' Rights.*

Here, it is only the history of a word,
obelisk,
that points us toward
what's not there; all of it
palimpsest, each mute object
repeating a single refrain:

remember this.

2.
Listen: there is another story I want
this place to tell: I was a child here,

traveling to school through the heart of town
by train, emerging into the light

of the square, in the shadow of the courthouse,
a poetics of grief already being written.

This is the place to which I vowed
I'd never return, hallowed ground now,

a vault of memory, the new courthouse enshrining
the story of my mother's death—

her autopsy, the police reports, even
the smallest details: how first

her ex-husband's bullet entered
her raised left hand, shattering the finger

on which she'd worn her rings; how tidy
her apartment that morning, nothing

out of place but for, on the kitchen counter,
a folding knife, a fifty-cent roll of coins.

3.
Once, a poet wrote: *books live in the mind*
like honey inside a beehive. When I read
those words to my brother, this is what he told me:
Inside the hive of prison, my mind lived in books.
It was a small library, he said: several Bibles,
a few dictionaries, lots of dime-store fiction,
some good novels too. He'd spend hours reading
until he could read no more. What he wished for,
he said, was to get through an entire book,
but each one ended before the story did—
the last pages ripped out so someone could roll
a cigarette. At first he hated missing the endings,
the not knowing, but then he began to write,
in his head, a book of the lost stories—each
ending a possible outcome. He wrote all year
until the day he walked out of the prison
into a story he could write from the beginning.

4.
I have counted the years   I am
a counter of years   ten twenty

thirty now   So much gone and yet
she lives in my mind like a book

to which I keep returning   even
as the story remains the same

her ending   the space she left
a wound a womb a bowl hewn

published in the *Georgia Review* (2016)

Heaarth

BILL MCKIBBEN

L iving in the north, in the woods, I've of course spent much of my life in front of an actual hearth, or at least a woodstove. For decades it was the main way of heating our house, and my body clock reset to the point where I'd wake at three in the morning to stoke the fire as easily as a mother to nurse. Every night from October to April finds us in the few dozen square feet in front of the stove, our house collapsed into that narrow envelope of warmth. The dog can sit for hours looking into the flames: the "fire channel," we call it.

But honesty requires me to say that in recent years we haven't really inhabited that space. We've been there physically, but we've been staring into the small and portable hearths resting on our laps, staring into the mesmerizing blaze of light that now enthralls people everywhere. Enthralls them, or at least my wife and me, more powerfully than the TV ever did. Television we happily did without—its din and clamor easily enough forgotten the minute you stepped away. But this? Not so easily avoided.

To say that the Internet—something that did not really exist till my life was half over—is now where many of our lives are lived is almost an understatement. Twitter is the center of our political life, Facebook the replacement for the newspaper and the newscast, and Amazon where we go to shop. Spotify offers a catalogue of every vaguely musical sound emitted everywhere on earth, yours for ten dollars monthly; Wikipedia delivers a roughly reliable guide to our collective knowledge. I've spent the last decade helping organize a global grassroots movement to fight climate change, and we literally could not have done it before the Internet. We live in a nation governed now by someone who could not have been elected before the Internet's advent. But no need here to tally all the Internet's terrors. Suffice it to say that the Internet is now our collective hearth, the place where our species addictively turns. We tilt toward the screen the way plants twist toward the sun. Orthopedists report that our characteristic posture has shifted from all that staring downward, bringing us new aches and pains. If we were the ape that walked upright, we're now the ape that looks at its palm most of the time.

So let us think not about the manifestations good and bad of this technology but instead about the basic nature of this new world we inhabit, and compare it to the hearth around which we've gathered since the start of things.

Life on the Internet means two opposing realities. One, the bedrock solipsism of the experience. This is for you, and you only. You follow your own series of clicks down your own warren of trails, a path no one else will ever follow exactly. You've shaped your own feeds to reflect your own beliefs and persuasions, and hence they now reflect that back at you. Even the TV was a river with relatively few channels—three, in my youth. There was unavoidable sharing and overlap. But the Internet is a delta with endless braided rivulets and streams. You are by yourself.

And yet you are also never alone, never unoccupied. The clicking never ceases—I follow nine hundred people on Twitter, which means that never more than a few seconds elapses before some new idea pops up on the screen. One never reaches Facebook only to find a notice saying "nothing interesting has happened." There's always more. And our brains seem to crave that endless flow of novelty—not looking at the unread e-mail in your inbox is at least as hard as not eating from the open box of chocolates in the pantry. Stimulus, reward, dopamine, something something—that's how it seems to work.

My fear is that we're losing—that I'm losing—the two crucial things the hearth, or the campfire before it, provided. The first is commonality, the shared community built by the gathering of several souls in the same place. Think about the creation stories passed down by millennia of oral repetition. Or think of the gossip exchanged nightly. Both served to ground us in particular communities, instead of the literal nowhere we now spend our time. There's still plenty of gossip, but it's about worlds we don't actually inhabit. We are truly by ourselves, and for a socially evolved primate that is a strange experience; it wasn't that many generations ago that we were sitting on the warm savanna grass and picking lice out of each other's fur. The closest we've got now is the moment when something goes viral, and for a moment there's a connection between us, until the next click kills it.

But at the same time, we're never alone. At night, when the fire dwindled, the talk did too. People drifted toward sleep, or into their thoughts.

Throughout human history, one of the characteristic experiences of *Homo sapiens* has been to stare into the dying embers, one's mind wandering. But that, I think, rarely happens anymore. There's something to fill every moment, something new and different even if it's essentially the same.

All this is a way of saying: thinking consciously about the hearth—about those places and activities that center us in community and also in our own minds—is now crucial in a way it's never been before. I miss, a great deal, those experiences that have always marked our lives, and there are times when I feel as if I'm living inside an experiment, an experiment going wrong. That's why this book is important. If we're to keep the chain of deep human contact intact, we need to actively seek out those experiences. For most of human history, rattling on about community and about focus would have been like having a considered opinion on breathing, or offering advice on bipedal locomotion. But all of a sudden our default is in the opposite direction. The Internet, whatever its other vices and virtues, is an anti-hearth, and it is winning. Where our time is spent, there also is our heart.

Codex Hogar

LUIS ALBERTO URREA

"Why should love stop at the border?"
—PABLO CASALS

Uno.

You'd think
a desert teemed with heat, churned
volcanic with dusted daylong baking: precious
little warmth beneath the pyramid of night those hard
Christmas eves: we gathered before a kerosene heater burning
within its glass tower, blanketed and huddled on bare floors with the dogs
in chemical smell not at all like pine boughs: and aunts who did not decorate trees,
exhausted from long days working American bowling alleys, American
tuna canneries, smoking
and giving us American gifts that my father would not allow: a teddy bear
was not a gift for a Mexican
boy—and my aunt taking it back and giving me instead a cheap plastic
pinball game I did not want, but
received in a stoic fashion though years later, all of them dead, I wish I
had that ridiculous Woolworth's
bear
to remember
anything soft
from that world
before the walls
loomed
over us.

Dos.

Your house might have perched on the side of a hill
miles south of the border, whatever that was. Somewhere
up there by the riverbed. Past the sidewalks where spray-
painted donkeys played the roles of zebras
for beer-drinking Americans calling everyone "Pancho"
and "Mamacita." You could have been a child
who thought wonderful things: that Americans were
always drunk and were the ones who wore big sombreros,
that zebras came from Mexico. You might have been a skinny
girl whose name meant "Daisy" in translation. A girl who lived
in that house perched on that hill, where the neighbors had
outhouses and tuberculosis, but a girl whose roof looked out
across a small canyon to the city and its dusty trees
with whitewashed trunks and gazebos with old men too fat
to button their uniforms and too slack to blow their
trumpets well, but their bleating as sour as tamarind juice
was somehow beautiful with the sounds of old buses and
police whistles and the ten thousand insouciant
street dogs barking at children playing soccer in the park.
You might even have had that girl's mysterious power
to hold out her fingers and attract wild birds
to tumble from the sky and grip her knuckles as if
they were her feathery rings. And you might have seen
when the family went to a rare restaurant meal together
the poor people from some dark South begging on the street
called Revolution. Seen how all modern nations only love
dead Indians and make for their ghosts tales of noble mystics
who are played in films by handsome Italians and Mexico City
rich kids in spray tans and $5,000 wigs, but send machine cavalries
after their living children: four-wheel drive Hemi horses
chasing Aztecs and Mayas and harrowing them to pens
in Wonderland. You might have walked beside my cousin
with her birdy fingers, and my aunt, after that plastic American

Christmas, smoking her Newports like a power station burning
cheap sulfury coal, already seeding the cancer in herself,
and the living *India* standing outside the chicken diner as beautiful
as anyone I had ever seen. Seeking alms like a gospel sojourner.
Almost black, she was—braids brilliant in that winter sun, rebozo
over her shoulder and slinging her dark child at long breast,
suckling in the long smoky crèche of the avenue—
and my aunt suddenly turning on her
and kicking her
and shouting,
"Dog!
Get away from us!"
You might have felt the world,
like we children did, spin away and become something
made of iron
and bullets.

✦

Tres.

You'd think a desert
would be hot. But
away from sight
there were beds
made of paper
in boxes of cardboard
on hilltops of wraiths
and ghost walkers
where gulls haunted
the sleep of dogs
too old and sick
to run the streets
where trucks
dropped all the

broken things
both countries
threw at the border
like toys like boots
like plastic chairs
like cans of peaches
like televisions like
laptops like tables
like porn magazines
like Bibles like rotten
fish like run-over cats
like rabid raccoons like
worn-out zebras like
canisters of blood
from abortion clinics
like underwear like
burning horses
and Indians
from impossible lands
where it stayed hot
but trucks came
at any hour
and the sound of engines
meant dying time
had come 'round again
and there was nothing left
to eat
those Indians
slept on plastic
spread over mud
in their boxes
and blessed America
for the old blankets
born-again conquistadors
dropped from above

and their babies
coughed in the night
because they had never
felt such cold
as they found in the shadow
of the Great Wall
coughed until blood
fell from their lips
fell like beads
from some ancient raiment
and I know
because I was there
the year fourteen
of these small ones
died
on Christmas Eve
on a hill
where their mothers
could watch
the lights of California
where it was always warm
and where kings in golden planes
moved around the brilliant
hive like
magnificent
wasps.

Hearthland

I have often and long written about the borderlands. Having been born and bred there, I consider myself as somewhat of an expert. Though no place on this earth reveals all its history and wonders to any observer, it does help to have lived there. And it gives any writer a great place to stand, that old dirt and shadow. It has been my experience, especially in the age of the Trumpion, that there is a shocking freakishness to the Mexican, Mexican-American, and borderlands narrative. New York editors, for example, need to be reminded that we are actually human beings. Washington politicians need to be reminded that we might actually love something south of the Great Wall.

I have said before, and I will say again, that Tijuana was a wonderland for me. I didn't know we were not well-off. (I won't honor our struggles with the word *poor*. Anyone who has read my early works will know all about real poverty.) I did nearly die of tuberculosis. And you could not drink the water. However, Tijuana was where the music was, and the dogs, and the food, and the colors, and that sacred summoning of spirits called Spanish. All the stories were there. All my ancestors.

There came Biblical failures of Eden, as they always do. Mine were twofold, and I tried to meld them in this poem. The first was my first encounters with the meek who shall inherit the earth. The invisible poor— invisible because we would not look at them. So the day I saw my beloved aunt kick an Indigenous beggar, I knew two things profoundly—yea, three things did I see. One: I was with that poor woman and loyal to her forever. Two: I was with the Indigenous people, whoever they were, and knew I would learn who they were. And the third lesson was witness. I would never look away. Selah.

The other lesson that the recent toxic election reminds me to suffer over and over, with women and Latina/os and Black citizens and people of good heart and will, was that once I came to the United States (my mother was American, so this, too, was home), I was suddenly called things I had never heard of. Greaser, wetback, pepper-belly, beaner, taco-bender. I learned that we were not human. We were Other. Because of some line that a commission decided to etch on some map (not smart enough to draw the boundary a few miles south so they could steal the mouth of the Colorado River and the top of the Sea of Cortez, thus costing the United States a potential powerhouse port system and utter control of the river). And this mythos of wall-building was just more calling of names. Names in brick and mortar and wire and steel. And thus, my fourth lesson in home: I am and will be Other. Until I write you into my heart and make you see my home as what it is. Just another extension of your own home. For there is no them; there is only us.

Enchantment

Andrew Lam

When I was six or seven, and living in Dalat, a small town in Vietnam's central highlands, my mother told me that my umbilical cord was buried in the garden. Afterward, I walked among the guava trees, daffodils, and overgrown lantana bushes in wonder and awe.

Not long after this, I witnessed Mrs. Lau, the wife of our servant, whose family lived in the small compound in the back of our villa, dragging herself out of bed only a few hours after giving birth to bury her newborn's umbilical cord in that same garden. Something in her mysterious gestures among the grasses, flowers, and trees—the mumbling of prayers, the burning of joss sticks, and the offerings of mangoes and rice—stirred a deep sense of belonging in me.

I was part of the land, and it was part of me. Which is to say, our ways were very, very old and I lived once in awe of that hallowed land, gripped in its powers.

Where ties are permanent and traditions practiced daily, and where the land still holds one's imagination, there exists a deep sense of mystery and enchantment. It is normal that your ancestors' ghosts talk to you in your dreams, that they inhabit all sorts of corners of your house, and that you should answer them in your prayers, in your offerings, in the incense smoke you burn nightly. A butterfly that lands on your shoulder at night may be a sign that your long dead grandfather has come for a visit. The wind that blows through your window that topples the old vase portends a bad omen; someone close to you has died.

My grandmother talked to my dead grandfather often in her dreams. Once she lost a precious jade bracelet and we searched and searched to no avail. A few days later she was all laughter: "Your grandfather came in my dream and told me where to find it." It had fallen through the small space between the bathtub and the wall and was stuck there. No one doubted Grandma that Grandpa came back to help.

I can still see myself as a pious child climbing that desk above which was the family altar. In it, faded black-and-white photos of the dead stared out into our living room from high above. It was my role to put incense in the bronze urn. The smoke wafted amidst solemn chants. There was a war then and we prayed for safety, for peace.

The Vietnamese word for country is Đất Nước: Land and Water, the combination of which is mud, the rice field. I remember standing in line before class with other classmates—white shirts and blue shorts, all—singing at the top of our lungs the national anthem each morning. "O citizens, let's rise to this day of liberation," we would bellow. "Let's walk together and sacrifice our lives. Blood debts must be paid by blood." I had believed in the lyrics, every word, felt that shared patriotic fervor among my young, bright-eyed peers. We swore to protect the land. We swore to live and die on it.

But then, at the end of the Vietnam War, all that changed. The old way of life gone.

Indeed, nothing could have prepared me or my family for the mass exodus that followed the end of the Vietnam War. We fled; my family and I, in an army cargo plane with many other refugees. From the plane's window I saw the land giving way to a hazy green sea and the border was suddenly porous.

I remember a refugee camp in Guam made of khaki tents and barren ground and long lines for food, for rations. I remember adults weeping upon news of the fall of Saigon. I remember myself, curling up on the army cot, crying to sleep each night, wondering about my dogs and neighbors and classmates and cousins and, above all, the fate of my father, who had stayed behind. (He managed to escape by boat and made it to America a few months after us.)

Almost half a million fled Vietnam at the end of the war, followed by countless others out to sea.

When I reached America I was almost twelve years old and in a few years I had become someone else. I stopped praying to the dead, stopped believing in old fairy tales, stopped, for that matter, speaking Vietnamese altogether.

The short version is that I stopped wanting to remember—not that I could forget—that lost homeland, no longing to mourn who we used to be, what we used to own, and how we used to behave in the old world. I couldn't bear that enormity of loss. None of it had helped me in the new world, so it seemed to me, and in fact my memories were like a heavy stone around my neck—they threatened to drown me each night. Often nostalgia renders many an exile helpless: failing to overcome his grief, his losses, he becomes an enemy of history.

Our first home in America was a crowded apartment at the end of Mission Street in Daly City, shared with my aunt's family who fled after us. In it the smell of incense wafted at the new makeshift altar and in it echoed adults' voices arguing and reminiscing. Vietnamese was spoken there, often in whispers, and occasionally they exploded in heated exchanges when the crowded conditions became too much to bear.

Vietnam, the lost country, ruled that apartment. It ruled in the form of two grandmothers praying in their separate corners. It ruled in the form of my mother's muffled cries late at night when she thought no one was awake. It ruled in the quiet way my father watched the evening news each night, his eyes glued to the images of people sailing out of our homeland seeking freedom and shelter, the ones Walter Cronkite called the "tragic boat people."

To stave off the past, my cousins and I would escape to the nearby library. Or else we would walk the hills behind our house. Or we would watch *Popeye the Sailor* and *Scooby-Doo* and *The Monkees* and laugh at *The Carol Burnett Show* and "ooh" and "ahh" at the amazing feats of *The Six Million Dollar Man*. We practiced our English. We played along with *Let's Make a Deal*. We recited commercial jingles—

My bologna has a first name, it's O-S-C-A-R
My bologna has a second name, it's M-A-Y-E-R

We pretended amnesia and saved ourselves from grief.

After all, if I was old enough to remember Vietnam, I was also young enough to embrace America, to let it seep into my dreams, bend my tongue, define my sense of humor, my outlook, let it feed my vision of the future. I was willing to be reshaped by newness.

Even my voice shattered upon speaking English, having gone through puberty a few months after coming to America. English, I felt, was changing me inside out.

"What do you want to be when you grow up?" Mr. K., the eighth grade English teacher, asked. Such an American question. But I did not hesitate. "I want to become a movie star," I answered, and he laughed.

Perhaps I understood it without fully knowing that to swear allegiance to the lost homeland was to bond to an exile identity dictated by impossible longings. Indeed, the Vietnamese refugee child learns quickly that there's no returning, that he, like his family, is an exile and an enemy of history; that he must venture into the new world alone, as he, being young and embracing newness, is a better navigator than his parents. I understood that in order to have any control over my life I had better embrace the American narrative. I needed to go down that road as fast and as furiously as I could, betraying memories, and go wherever it would take me.

And it's not just me, of course, who changed. My father, after twenty-five years in the South Vietnamese army, got an MBA and became a banker. My siblings, too, found their American Dreams, moved into well-placed professions in American society. Even my traditional mother became an accountant and found humor in it—an upper-class woman of the old world selling earthenware for an import-export company. Even my paternal grandmother, until a stroke put her in a convalescent home, studied English into her midseventies.

My community transformed too. The diaspora sent a people scurrying and subsisting elsewhere but in time we became a global tribe. Soon enough many prospered. We bought houses, found jobs, opened restaurants, built malls, temples, and churches, owned our own TV and radio programs and newspapers. Ours is a community whose roots burrowed, slowly but deeply, into the new loam.

If exile is spiritual amputation, then the pangs of longing and loss are dulled by the necessities of living and by the glory of newfound status and wealth. And the refugee-turned-immigrant (a psychological transition) becomes a naturalized US citizen (more or less a transition of convenience) and finds his memories and longings insist a little less as he zooms down the freeway toward a glorious chimerical cityscape to work each morning.

How did this happen? Perhaps only a loser knows real freedom. Forced outside of history, away from home and hearth, the migrant can choose to remake himself: one night, America seeps in, and out slowly goes the Vietnamese soul of sorrow.

Some years ago a friend who worked for the United Nations at the Palawan refugee camp in the Philippines sent me a poem he found carved on a stone under a tamarind tree. Written by an unknown Vietnamese boat person, it tells how to escape tragedy. "Your mind is like a radio that you can dial to a different voice. It depends on you. So do not keep your mind always tuned to sorrow. If you want, just change the channel." It occurred to me that I, too, switched that dial in my teen years.

As did my family: didn't I see America invade the household when the dinner conversation in our new home leaned slowly but surely toward real estate and escrow, toward jobs and cars and GPAs, and over time to vacation plans to Europe and Disneyland—the language of the American Dream? Exile identity quietly slips away in America, giving in to the immigrant optimism.

The traumas of the initial expulsion and the exodus and memories of reeducation camps under communist rules, thirst and starvation on the high seas, years languishing in refugee camps, the horror of Thai pirates and unforgiving storms are slowly replaced by the jubilation of a new-found status and, for some, enormous wealth. A community that initially saw itself as living in exile, as survivors of some historical blight, gradually changed its self-assessment. It began to see itself as an immigrant community, as a thriving Little Saigon, with all sorts of make-it-rich narratives.

And so, in between, the boy who once wandered in his mother's enchanted garden of Dalat and the man who writes these words witnessed the slow but natural demise of the old nationalistic impulse. The boy was willing to die for his homeland. The man had become circumspect. The boy who once cried singing the Vietnamese national anthem had believed that the borders, like the Great Wall of China, were real demarcations, their integrity not to be disputed. The man discovered that borders have always been porous. The boy was once overwhelmed by the tragedy that has fallen upon his people, resenting history for robbing him and his family of home and hearth and national identity. The man, though still sometimes ruled by the primacy of his childhood emotion, has become emboldened by his own process of individualization.

Many years passed.

I didn't become a doctor like my mother had wanted. The youngest member of my family, I rebelled. After I graduated from UC Berkeley with a biochemistry degree and started working with a team of cancer researchers at Cal, I was suddenly plagued with a deep yearning to make sense out of my Vietnamese memories. My fledgling scientific career thus came to an abrupt end: two years into research I put down the test tube, picked up the pen, and began to write. I struggled and, after some years, became a bona fide journalist and writer. I traveled the world.

But what of the old enchantment?

If I am American now, this much is true also: were it not for the Vietnamese people, their suffering, their tribulations, my American individuality would be shallow. In a sense, writing about the past makes me the kind of American that I'd like to become, someone who owns his past rather than flees from it.

Indeed, in adulthood and as a writer, I grew intrigued about my own inheritance, the old land-bound ethos, the archaic rituals, and my childhood vision in my mother's garden of long ago, that first sense of wonder and awe, the war and the tragedies that befell my people. I hunger for the lost enchantment. I hunger for memories.

Edward Said, the cultural critic, once suggested that if one wishes to transcend his provincial and national limits, one should not reject attachments to the past but work through them. Irretrievable, the past must be mourned and remembered and assimilated. To truly grieve the loss of the nation in the robbed history of a vanished people, and through the task of art, through the act of imagination, that old umbilical cord, long buried, could be unearthed and transmuted into a new transpacific verse, a new living tapestry.

So I wrote and wrote.

A child forced to flee. The long line for food under a punishing sun. People weeping themselves to sleep. The family altar, where faded photographs of the dead stared out forlornly, the incense still burning but the living gone. A way of life stolen, a people scattered, uprooted, a way of life gone, all gone.

And I began to go back.

The man who sees the world with its many dimensions simultaneously can be a blessed man if he practices alchemy. To be defined by incongruous history is not necessarily an impediment these days. A border-crosser, the multilinguist builds bridges to otherwise disconnected, seemingly opposed ideas and civilizations. He takes his reference point across time zones and often from two or three different continents. Old traditions revive, transformed: Grandma's old recipes turn into new-world fusion dishes; the traditional zither plays jazz songs; memories of war and exodus become—in another language, another country—poetry and novels.

I once met a woman in Belgium who lived in a castle. She had been a boat person. She and her sister, close to death from starvation and thirst on a crowded boat, were saved by a Belgian merchant ship, and they ended up living in the basement of a church in a town an hour by train outside of Brussels. One day the local baron saw her while praying there. He fell in love. They married. Now she's a baroness living in a castle with two children of noble blood. Listening to her story one summer evening many years ago while eating her Vietnamese cooking in the castle's gigantic kitchen where once deer and boars were roasted for the local nobility, I remember thinking to myself: there's tragedy but also marvel for those who cross the border. And who is to say the old enchantment is lost?

Instead, it has been synthesized. My sense of home these days seems to have less to do with geography than with imagination and memories. Likewise, I no longer see my identity as a fixed thing, but something open ended.

Home? Home is human connections, ambition, imagination, and memories. And it dwells in particularities: I live in San Francisco, but I am connected to different parts of the world. I have relatives in Ottawa, Paris, Hanoi, Saigon, Miami; friends in Rio, Dallas, New York, and yes, even Dalat. Over time, I've learned to navigate and live comfortably with these multiple nodes of connection, crossing back and forth over the hyphen that connects dissimilar spheres, different sensibilities and languages and practices, different senses of the self.

And more: Home becomes anywhere and everywhere, its logistics translated into a beatific vision of freedom. I feel most at home when I have a sense of direction, a purpose. If my work, my words, evoke enchantment, then I am home. I carry worlds within me; home is portable, if one is in commune with one's soul.

The Fire in Ten: Elements Necessary to Build a Hearth

YVONNE ADHIAMBO OWUOR

I

Hearth of home, home the hearth. Hearth, where heart and earth and fire merge to summon souls into a stillness that is a window into tales that refract human beingness: Nairobi (sometime home), Kolwa, Chiga (where Daddy was born, where he dreamed impossible dreams while herding resplendent beasts and studied, into which he brought his cherished bride, my mother, and would later build a road and a house large enough to shelter all his loves, and where he would reveal the real color of stars to his children, and chart the progress of his slow-growing pawpaw tree, and then after time broke our hearts by coming for Daddy so unexpectedly, where we buried him, and once a year light a fire to remember him, and sometimes when the light is right we see his fire-cast shadow floating among us, contented, and where the bones of other ancestors molder). Hearths in a Zanzibar Stone Town beach among tellers of worlds, and the hearth of hearths (any fire lit by Mother). A confession: I have sought out fire as a doorway through which to peer at the soul of God and imagine myself a spark dancing among well-lit stones that can disappear the night in a million light sprinkles.

II

Crossing thresholds. I roam the world. Planes, trains, and vehicles. A ship, too, I hope. Soon. I encounter souls and eavesdrop, gathering stories, hearing about vulnerabilities that might heal, or triumphs that humble. I receive those previously unmet friends, and they receive me. My passing of time is not always marked by birthday parties now, not because of a desire to cling to an illusory eternal youth as much as it is about the awareness of the inexorable march to literal and figurative decrepitude. At some point in my future, parts of my body shall crumble into plant manure—I hope. So, what endures out of this mysterious adventure called life? What endures, so one can announce with the certainty of a president's press officer that *this* lasts forever and will never sputter away like the fire in a hearth struggling to keep the Nairobi July chill at bay? But not for long, not for long.

III

Azure, cobalt, sapphire, cerulean, navy, saxe, ultramarine, lapis lazuli, indigo, aquamarine, turquoise, teal, cyan: dominant shades of the blue of our exquisite earth from outer and inner spaces. Hues of earth from the view of intergalactic birds. No one needs to remind me that "this is beautiful." It just is, as if perfect beauty is a preternatural memory intrinsic to the blood and knowing. The made-in-China globe on my dark brown fire-stained table—candle burns—is also mostly blue, but the shapes of the continents are deformed to make Africa—zoom in—seem smaller, makes it small and not threatening and not so immense that it might consume every other by its age. Hue of home, Nairobi, Kenya, is blue-blue, blue like the earth's new day.

IV

There is a literature of dark nights (look to Ra'abia, or Tagore, or eavesdrop on a mother's whispering passed-down tales to her granddaughters, or even retrieve Mwana Kupona binti Msham, who long ago off the East African coast created words with which to fill the spaces of night: "*Negema wangu binti / Mchachefu hasanati / Upulike wasiati / Asaa ukazingatiya*"). Listen, we are here around a single fire in an old valley in the northern Kenyan desert gossiping about illusions, and how bodies curl into themselves and move toward one another seeking heart warmth. Dissolution of certainties. And boundaries. True. There are nights when no fires are lit, no fires are to be found, a literature of cold hearths (there are so many tales of absences and loss, of cold bodies on cold slabs, of ice floes and suddenly cold-hearted lovers who must leave) and poetry made in the memory of those shadows that certain fires cast upon certain walls.

V

Three years ago I heard the story of certain earth birds. It was murmured to me by a lean, lined elder draped in a red *shuka*. His more than two hundred cows seeking pasture in a dry Kenya spring season browsed close to him. It was an October that was as this October 2016, when the short rains have failed and the land is golden and red stained with dust, an elegiac beauty. Passing by, as passers-by can still do in a land such as ours, we paused to greet each other. And then we stood in silence, the wind in our soul. A Ngong Hills' sunset is the substance for poets and a site of contemplation for mystics.

The birds.

A moving cloud weaving this way and that, a grayish sky accordion, like a song set free. On any other day this would have been a reason to rhapsodize.

Except the elder's gaze is bleak.

They are beautiful, I say, trying for shared delight.

He answers. *They are lost.* He indicates westward. *Someone has cut their trees. For a road.* He gestures. *That was a forest . . . over there.*

I squint. I do not see.

When?

January.

The birds have been lost ever since?

He looks at me. He glances away. *They come from far. This is the season of visitors. Now there is no hospitality left to offer. Someone has cut their trees.* He uses his chin to point at the birds. *Been like that since yesterday. What a struggle. To what home do they now go?*

Stillness. Except for the churning, restless wind in our souls, the orange fire of the evening glancing off our faces, and off the wingtips of so many tired, home-seeking birds.

VI

As a people and a nation we might have saved a thicket of shrubs for fellow travelers. The Kenya Ministry of Planning or the National Environment Management Authority or any one of our chief roads engineers could have deigned to ask to whom the trees belonged. I am told these birds are a species of swallow, and every year at about the same time, for eons, they have shown up after battling distances across seas and storms. They start their journeys in northern Europe. They leave fledglings behind. In an act of splendid mystery, these little ones, weeks later, follow hidden song trails written in the skies and their valiant hearts to find parents who, earlier, had come to Eastern Africa for warmth and to build summer nests. But here in Kenya, their homes have been turned into a winding tarmac road. If only we had not been deafened by our delusions, the cacophony of so-called progress. We might have asked, as citizens: *To whom else do these trees belong?* Any one of the herdsmen who traverse these lands often would have told anyone who had bothered to ask about the meaning of the trees. Anyway, would it have cost anything to let just one tree remain standing? It would have sufficed as a resting place for the little weary, wandering feet of twenty thousand songbirds.

VII

Several months ago, I bumped into a priest from the Eastern Congo. He was wrestling with the phantoms ploughing through his soul. He was battling knowledge: meaning, vocation, reality, and what it means to be human. You see, weeks before, having heard rumors of a village on fire, he rushed to look, traveling a long distance, slipping past military roadblocks. At the site he found charred ruins, unpaired shoes—icons of futile escape, the stench of smoke. He wandered surreal homesteads calling out, and climbed a small hill that descended into a sprawling blood-deluged field, turned by humans into earth's main outpost of hell. He would tell me that he touched the debris from human hypocrisies, and the blood of souls-made-invisible by willful public relations plans. He counted human souls on a thousand earth altars. In exchange, coltan, sapphire, hardwood, titanium, gold, and silence now flowed into the bloodstream of the world unimpeded by a moral stance or an ethical imagination. The many now-dead had been reluctant to leave their mineral-replete ancestral fields; they were obstacles to "social and economic progress." The priest had counted the broken human body parts scattered on earth's dust hearth in that place that is the center of the world. He counted until he stopped counting.

The priest had fled. He stripped the clerical collar off his neck. He crossed national boundaries by boat, road, and on foot until he halted inside a small, dark, almost-invisible Nairobi sanctuary in Westlands. I saw him there. A big, broad, beautiful ebony-stained man of our continent, with three thousand lines crisscrossing his face, eyes red with tears, half-prostrate. He was kneeling on one leg before the tabernacle with its solitary red light. His tears were a puddle on the floor. When he rose, his body had sculpted itself into a form that evoked the *Pieta*; the hollows, the harrowing, the sorrow. "Are you OK?" I asked this at-first stranger. The answer in his eyes was tears that were unfalling globules. Later, in French-accented crackling words, he cried, "Are *we* doomed to be ghosts? We the peoples of this continent? Are we the ghosts written into life with such contempt that our slaughters must remain unseen, unmourned, unheard? Tell me, sister, are we ghosts?" Silences in the shrine. Sliver of evening sun, like an arrow gesturing outward. We follow the sign. Outside, dark blue sky. An echoing bell. Behind us, the tabernacle light shines red; like blood, like fire, like memory that burns.

The priest. His hands shook as he tried to light a cigarette. Flare of match. We watched it burn down and die. He whispered. "Look. Even the flames we relight our vices with are not drawn from the forge of our hearth."

Please note: I understand that some answers for some questions can be spelled out only in tears.

VIII

Dear Fr. Aurelien,

I have not yet heard that ghosts weep tangible tears. Still, I do not know yet that I am not a ghost (in answer to one of your questions). I do know, however, that I am now a reluctant audience to that unhappy grace that shook you with its horrifying presence, its eldritch truth. Your fate is to be witness of what is most abysmal about humanity and its willingness to invest in horror, lies, and death to try to purge the evidence of the human suffering it relishes, for which it designs monstrous machinery. The only epitaph for (y)our beloved, already-forgotten murdered is the shelter, refuge, and hearth that your witness has made of your memory. The terrible flame in your gaze is the repository of evidence against our human senselessness, the banality of our evil. It is not given to many to stumble through a field strewn with a thousand murdered men, women, and children and wail a prayer as the only acceptable language, until even that prayer dries up. It is not given to many to glimpse its horrifying sequel: a casual parade of the world's representatives, its global businessmen, its sheep-clothed lupine humanitarians driving past innocent corpses, trucks laden with the bounty of the land, this, the great vestige of Eden, still desired, still coveted, its treasures craved, but its people loathed and in the way. Ever since I saw and heard you, I have been unable to speak (we have not yet constructed a lexicon for this type of inferno, have we?). But I have sought to listen to whispers traveling through fireless nights. Last evening, to my initial horror, I heard arcane susurrations that are the voice of the blood of Abel crying out to Eternity and demanding it to ask of Cain: "Where is your brother?" (Did Cain, that cursed wandering ancestor of humanity ever find a hearth before which to stop and warm his fratricidal heart?) For our hundred thousand slaughtered and lost siblings who are nameless (for now) is there a Supreme Judge to whom their blood may appeal? I have sat in stillness with that question. I am certain we shall each have to respond to this question in one way or another, if not now, then later when we cross that darkest of thresholds. I recognise the dreadful gift you bear, that of seeing the world as it is and then being asked to love it, starting with its toxic wounds including that of indifference. What a weight, that of forgiving our own continent for not protecting our people better, and the world for its pathological lust for the blood of our most vulnerable, for their child-eating, fire-breathing, ghastly gods of war. (You are going to have to teach me how to forgive God for these and other things.) Anyway, dear Fr. Aurelien, with this note I enclose a pack of matches. They are made in Kenya. I checked. The hint of phosphorus on their tips is also African. I asked. Your vice can now be set alight with something of the fires of home.

In gratitude.

For your immolation.

For the wail in your heart,

Sincerely,

PS: Mother confirms that the tears of ghosts do not quell flames. She knows such things; you understand?

IX

I am seeking ingredients. I must learn to create a hearth and build a fire that might warm the iced hearts of a universe that cannot see those siblings in a corner of the earth who were slaughtered by the weapons these others have created and sold to grow their economies, reassure their citizens about a shining future, become rich, do good things by making donations to the poor of the world that their seven deadly sins have gutted, while also aiming to live a long and complacent life deaf to the sound of the gnashing of teeth embedded in the melody of the merry ring tone of their coltan-fed cell phone. Anyway, the fire that feeds my hearth should be capable of flowing through and sealing with warmth the fractured heart of a red-eyed cleric:

Earth. For the sanctuary. The dust of stars and souls, earth in Kenya can be red, brown, black, gray, and beige. Earth can be white in places of Kenya. And there is a place, I hear, near Tana River where it is rather blue. The soil from home where antecedents have rested is always the most beautiful because there is something of the fragment of their souls lingering to offer color and new life to future fire.

Stone. Heat resistance without repelling fire. So many choices: Nairobi bluestone, black granite, Mazeras natural stone, limestone from Kitui, soapstone from Kisii, and Athi River marble, or make your own with baked clay from Kisumu like my late grandmother Aduda used to. Clay is good, they say, if chewed, for storing and restoring memory.

Enclosure. Best if a shelter encircles the hearth, a shelter with walls so that the secret messages in and of fire can be cast as dancing shadows.

Fuel. Like wood. But not in this age. The tears of homeless traveling birds now soak into rare wood and cause fire to spit in offence. Wood, only if it has fallen of its own accord, and has desired a destiny as food for fire.

People (and other creatures). To imagine, to create, to gather, to draw in, to sit still and watch and witness and wonder, and hope together that the demons that lurk within are exorcised by the sight of flames (bad memories of their inevitable fate). To blend and ignite the wood so that there will be fire, and inside the fire there will be the presence of the many—the ones who have gone before, the ones to come, the unseen, the watchers. When people talk and cook and dream near fire, they may laugh, they may cry, and they may also fall into silence. Some of their unanswered questions might be soothed into stillness, and maybe on the night of fire, they may sleep better, because fire is another way of prayer. Not all fire is the same. The fire in Kenya is not the same as the fire in Thimphu. Every fire has its own fragrance, and look, and feel, and sound, and grammar. The fire in Kano Kolwa is not the same as the fire in Frankfurt.

Darkness. Wait. Wait until the deepest of darknesses emerges before setting the night alight. One *matchstick*, one matchbox. Strike, light.

Murmurs. Ghosts, souls, and other night beings (mostly shy), murmurs interspersed with *silences*, for fire stutters, fire plays, fire has music, fire is music.

An enflamed hearth requires a mother. Every hearth has a *mother*. A mother is not *people*. A mother upon whose face fire shines is a picture of one of the most beautiful shades of God.

X

Her breasts now skim the top of her belly, gently pulled down by the years of suckling by her eight separate children, the ones she summoned, sought, and willed into life. Her eyes are tinged with the cataract gray of inexorable age, this scientist, this headmistress, this matriarch, this woman of many worlds who has also carried the world on her back in order to make it safe for her children. She is not as tall as we once believed and the omnipotence of the past is strewn with the truth of vulnerabilities that time has allowed us to see had always been there. And four years ago, when her husband—our daddy—died we saw her crumble and splinter into four solid pieces. Unlike Humpty Dumpty, she put herself together again (the king's horses did not help). Her skin is still honey-sun, warm-soft brown, and her voice rings clear across grasslands and causes four dogs to race toward her—tongues lolling, eyes grinning. There is a place beneath her heart, surrounded by her ribcage. A hearth. Here is the site of home, a map of belonging in the life-story lines etched into skin. Here is the center of this woman's well-worn body, above caesarean war wounds and mounds and marks and a womb that opened as a pain portal to urge renewed life onward. Beat, beat, beat, still it beats, my mother's heart beats and in the place where it beats is a fire. I am warmed by her name—Mary—and loving her is also who I am. Loving her is a fiery glow in my heart.

"Mummy, what do you know about hearths?" I tilt a pretend microphone toward her mouth. She gives me her sideways "you are menacing my tranquility with your generation's brand of insanity, child" look. Part impatience. But she is a still a teacher and a mother of eight children who tormented her with a billion urgent questions so now she is an adept at accommodating all manner of strangeness. She purses her lips. She thinks aloud. "Mhhh . . ." Then she says, "All hearths are created outside of time."

We Will Wait for You

Chigozie Obioma

Dim, since you left,
we have been waiting for you.
We've lived here for long,
so long the thatch has turned gray,
—for we have been waiting for you.

I am not waiting alone.
Your father, Yee Emeka, sits on his stool outside his obi every day, waiting.
Da Ndali, your mother, crouches beside the hearth on which she cooks,
    waiting.
Ikenna, your son, crawls about killing ants with his hands, waiting.
And I, the woman on whose breasts you slept every night, lie here
—waiting for you.

Our people say that a goat cannot lose its voice to bleating.
Although it has been long, my strength is being weakened
by the violent fear that ravages me every night,
leaving me naked as the horn of a cow.
Because it is what you asked me to do,
—I keep waiting for you.

Last week the wind blew the frightful braying dust toward our house
and I knew that the harmattan had arrived, the third since you left.
Night has begun to fall earlier again.
This, too, is the third of such changes.
Even now from my cooking hearth, I see that the moon
has become an angry eye peering down at the hills of Nta,
for perhaps the thousandth time since you left.
When it darkens more, the way it now does,
bleachless, visceral gloom, and I lie down in our hut to sleep,
perhaps my dreams will again be peopled by strange men.

But when I wake up at cockcrow, and the hymen of darkness is torn,
—I will continue to wait for you.

But then, strange things began to happen recently:
It began to feel as though you had returned,
that you were here, but I merely could not see you.
Nkechi said I'm hallucinating, that these were mere illusions.
But then I ask, "What about the voices I hear?"
"Those, too," she says, "are not real.
You are a troubled woman."
Then I tell her that I saw you in the lobes of the kolanuts
we broke at Uli shrine last Uli festival.
But she said you were not in them.
She said I should be strong,
—that I should wait for you.

For long I was strong and was waiting until last moon
when a sparrow made its way into the hut while I was napping
and perched close by my head,
and began watching me with the sure and steady gaze
you often gave me before we made love.
But, while we were seated around the hearth later that day,
Nkechi said it was not you. She said you were away in Burma,
in the white man's land, fighting for the white man.
She said you were a member of the African Frontier Force.
She said you were not the sparrow, that it was not real.
Then she said she would take me to Agwoturumbe, the diviner.
I know that you and I converted to the white man's religion, and that you
    might not support my decision to go with her to a sorcerer,
but I thought it was the only thing I could do to stay sane
—while I waited for you.

We went yesterday to Agwoturumbe's shrine.
It was in the heart of the Eluama forest,
beyond the brown hills.

Agwoturumbe jumped about in his regalia,
speaking in the rapid language of the gods.
Then, like a tiger, he danced around a point,
exerting a centrifugal energy, his bells rattling
as he made incantations into what looked like the empty shell of a turtle.
Then finally, he faced us and in plain language said,
"He whom you seek is no longer alive.
I saw him fall in a cloud of smoke, near the house of white-skinned men.
Then I saw men carrying him away, somewhere."
I returned yesterday, envenomed with Agwoturumbe's words
and the words, "cloud of smoke," "alive," "white-skinned men"
orbiting the burning ring of my heart, as is the question that will not desist:
—should I continue to wait for you?

❖

I conceived this poem while working on my debut novel, *The Fishermen*.
Before it became divided into nation-states, Africa was for long a place
where the various European powers "dumped their wastes." Those wastes
ranged from ideologies to actual indoctrination that would lead to the
replacement of our civilizations by those of the West. But also, they took
men and women out of the continent during the transatlantic slave trade,
and in the context of this long poem, soldiers. In "We Will Wait for You,"
the unnamed woman is waiting for her husband who has been drafted
as a member of the African Frontier Force to fight for the colonial army
of the British in World War I. In a time when there were fewer reliable
means of communication, *waiting* was even more difficult. The one place
where she is able to wait, which offers some symbolic signification of
hope, is the cooking hearth. For not only does the open fire signify life in
the Igbo imagination, it is a life created by her hands, and every time it is
lit, her hope is awakened, and when it is quenched, despair returns.

As her hope continues to wane, we see the impact it has on her
well-being, and the penumbral visitations that drive her to the edge of
sanity. It is this same phenomenon that drives her to the shrine of the *dib-
ia*—a shaman who must return to the gods of her people and attempt to

reach him who cannot be reached. It is here that her last effort lies, after which she must resolve whether or not to keep waiting.

For me, the poem embodies what I think might be the hope that is dying in Africa today as nations continue to descend lower and lower into impoverishment, lack, and misery. The world holds few answers, and the preeminent question remains: "Should we continue to wait?"

My Mobile Home

Pico Iyer

The minute I stepped into the little room high above the Pacific Ocean, I knew I'd come home. A rabbit was scuffling through the undergrowth in my small walled garden. The sun was burning on the flat blue plate of the ocean, extending for fifteen miles far below. Birdsong rang out in the silence and then within me, as it never seemed to do elsewhere. For someone who had always found his deepest home alone—recovering whatever lay deeper than the chattering self that skittered through the world—the simple retreatant's room in a hermitage high above the sea became the truest hearth I could imagine.

I know that solitude is not where we are meant to find our richest fulfillment. But I also recognize that one can't bend the truth to fit one's sense of right and wrong. I'm an only child; I grew up on planes, traveling between my parents' home in California and monastic, medieval boarding schools in England. My nearest relative six thousand miles away, I came to find all the fun, the diversion, the sense of company and adventure I needed, alone. So to discover a place where solitude appeared to involve a dissolving of self, rather than a consolidation, and where isolation opened out upon a horizon as wide and radiant as the blue ocean all around, felt like coming upon the home that had been waiting for me since birth, thirty-three years before.

Eight months earlier, my family "home" had burned to the ground in a forest fire. I'd sat in a car, trapped on our mountain road, and watched the flames systematically pick apart our living room, our library, my bedroom, everything I and my parents owned. When I walked up the road the following day, past exhausted firemen scattered along the sidewalk, I'd come upon a wasteland of ash—cars reduced to hubcaps, bronze statues nothing but debris—and then a vast emptiness where my life had been.

Fire is an antagonist, I came to feel; the devastation of everything I understood by a physical home made the flames associated with a hearth seem threatening, malign. There was a "he" at the center of "hearth," and an "art," but I could not for the life of me find a "we."

Now, though, stepping into this simple room, which pulsed with everything that wasn't there, I forgot about the past. The future, too. The many arguments (with myself and others) I'd spun out on the long drive up, my anxieties about next week, this ambition and that little idea: I was seeing the world with a transparency that felt like original sun. This is what I was when all thought of "I" was gone. And this was what the world looked like when I was truly inside it, wholly present, not clouding the scene with thoughts or projections.

I warmed my heart at the monastery—returning again and again— and knew that this was a hearth I could carry with me wherever I went. On a broken castle wall in Ethiopia one bright day at the end of December, I saw in my mind the Pacific Ocean stretched out, quite motionless, in Big Sur, California, a candle flickering in one corner of the chapel I visited when nobody was there, and felt restored and anchored.

＊

And then, fully twenty years on, long after I'd grown used to seeing my private hearth, the monastery, as sanctuary and hermitage, the strangest thing occurred. To celebrate the twelve hundredth anniversary of their Camaldolese order, the fifteen white-hooded men within the cloister convened a small assembly, along the sea, thirty-five miles or so north of where they live, and invited maybe a hundred and fifty of their friends to join them. Old men, young ones, women, girls flew in from Santa Fe and upstate New York and Singapore and down the road. We heard the future prior give a concert, singing infectious Hindu chants, accompanied by tabla and sitar, to honor the fact that the order maintains an ashram in southern India. One of the fathers, from South Africa, spoke with luminous intensity about how the entire Camaldolese congregation had shrunk to barely thirty a century before, yet still the fire kept sparking, refusing to give out. As the most contemplative order within Catholicism—so committed to silent prayer and meditation that sometimes the brothers are hard to tell from the Zen monks with whom they often sit—the Camaldolese have always been radical and on the edge. They are watched over with vigilance by Rome and largely overlooked by the world.

And as the days in community went on, something began, at a monk's slow pace, to shift inside me. I saw that what I had taken to be singular was in fact shared, a collective practice that brought me closer not just to friends but to strangers, too. Our whole large group took one long lunch in silence, and when we met afterward, along a sandy path, we found ourselves exchanging smiles or wishes for loved ones far away in pain.

I'd never quite seen how solitude in unison becomes a network greater than the sum of its parts. I'd never quite fathomed that everyone I met in silence was there for the same reason as I. Very soon, it became irrelevant to talk of "he" or "she" or "you" or "me." Identities dissolve if the hearth is strong enough and the night is dark and deep.

I stopped off at the hermitage on my way home and noticed that I was looking at all my old friends in the new light of bodies gathered around a hearth. I realized that shy Joshua had been bringing lunch to the kitchen since before my father died, a generation earlier. I'd seen Father Robert serve out his time as prior, and move to another monastic house in Berkeley, and then come back, in his late seventies, to encourage his brothers to friend him on Facebook and join him for a Sunday night screening of *Henry IV, Part 2*.

I'd grown old with these men, lost hair, seen mutual friends die. I'd come here more than seventy times, through a hundred seasons, sometimes for three weeks on end in a silent trailer overlooking the sea. And yet the quiet I sought, the truth that is the deepest kind of hearth, was never quite so solitary as I had foolishly imagined.

A few days after I wrote those words, I found an e-mail in my spam queue from a name I didn't recognize. Either an offer of expensive virtual sex, I assumed, or a scam from West Africa. Not long before, I'd suffered through a whole lost day by clicking on a message from a stranger that led to courteous Indians on the other end who called themselves "David" and "Michael" and, after helping me almost repair a computer they'd all but destroyed with their virus, asked me to fork over $270 for their pains.

This message, however, came from @contemplation.com, so I clicked on it, and found a letter from the ninety-year-old woman I'd occasionally seen at Sunday lunches in the hermitage. Thirty years before, she and her husband, both French-Canadian, had been permitted to live out their lives in a little hut in a valley beside the monastery, to see if fresh blood might open out the community a bit. After her husband died, the monks had honored their promise to protect their old friend by tending to her, day and night, wheeling her into the chapel for Mass, coming down on hot September afternoons to fix her screen door so the flies wouldn't attack, joining her at Christmas as she placed lanterns in the trees around her house to create a festival of lights.

Now, suddenly, she was writing, with graciousness and humility, to say that she'd come across an old book of mine whose very title seemed to speak to her: *The Lady and the Monk*. She would be so happy, she wrote, if I might stop by to say hello on my next visit.

A few days later, that next visit evaporated—my bedridden mother had to go into the hospital again for surgery. But if I didn't move soon—the fire had reminded me—my new friend, even less young, might disappear.

So I drove along the narrow coastal road, and turned off at the narrow path that snakes up the mountain, and asked my way to the very back of the "Enclosure," where a rough road leads down to a little trailer in the forest.

My hostess was waiting for me, with ginger cookies that she'd baked for the occasion. She urged me to take some cookies home for my mother. She handed me a cool, moist towel to refresh myself after the long drive. She'd set out a chilled little bottle of water and a glass for each of us. She'd gathered two CDs to share, and two diaries she kept.

On a yellow legal pad, she'd written down all the points she wanted to share with me, so she wouldn't forget.

As we began talking, she glimpsed the prior through the window, hastening down the slope, white robes flying all about him, to join us. Somewhat briskly, she told him, "We have a project!" as soon as he came in, and sent him on his way. Later, a withered-looking worker from the Enclosure, unsteady on his feet, and flashing a grin with no teeth, came down to help with a plugged toilet, then disappeared again.

"When I got your message," my elegant friend said to me, eyes shining

under her bright red Alice band, "I felt as if I was being pierced—pierced!
I haven't had a very turbulent spiritual life; I'm not an emotional person.
But when I read your book, I felt, 'God knows me. He understands me.
Someone sees me.' And when I got your e-mail, it was like a sword of light
coming through me. That's never happened before."

She looked up at me, eyes moist.

"I'm sorry. You're a busy man, I know. I don't want to take away from
your time in silence. But I felt I had to say this, and I couldn't say it in an
e-mail. This morning I had my English, but now . . ."

"Nothing could be a greater gift." I didn't know if I was talking about
the sense of being known—understood—or what she'd just said, and the
way something in my life had touched something in hers.

"You can have a lifelong love affair without touching," she said. "A
liaison"—her native French gave the word a lovely timbre—"of the heart."

"Yes," I answered. When I'd found myself at the same table as her
at Sunday lunch, the simple truth of her few sentences, drawn from the
silence in which she lived, had struck me as one of the great teachings this
community of men had to offer.

"I'm sorry," she said again, eyes brimming. "I don't want to keep such
an important man . . ."

"You're the important one," I said. "Or we all are."

She didn't try to say anything else, but I realized that what she had
wrought in this solitary place was a kind of quiet revolution, and now
she was giving me a fresh set of principles by which a hearth could be
defined. She was reminding me how women were traditionally kept out
of monasteries, even though—or perhaps because—they could warm the
place up and bring a different kind of light. How male hearths are often
very isolated and can leave you shivering a little. How the white-bearded
former prior, nine weeks from his death, had seen that having a woman
live near the community might be a godsend, not a threat, since he caught
the spirit of belief and not just the letter.

I took my leave of her—"My health is well balanced," she said, with a
bright flash in her eyes, "but I've had falls. I don't know when I'll be in my
next home"—and I clambered up the rough slope toward the prior's office. My portable hearth, I realized—the "heart" in it at least as important

as the "earth"—was durable precisely because it contained so many others, with the same loves, the same losses, the same flames. I'd never thought, sequestered in my little cell, that many hands reaching in the same direction may in the end become one. Even—especially—if they never touch at all.

Völuspá

GERÐUR KRISTNÝ

Translated from Icelandic by Victoria Cribb

They appear
from the east
an unknown horde

riding out of hell
on hidden highways
from the burnt regions
to a fertile haven

Driving their horses
till they drop
on the bridge

Now they're beating
at the gates
and begging us
to open up

Age-old fear
runs hissing through the ranks

Our knuckles whiten
on axes and swords

❋

The word *hearth* has a deceptively familiar ring to the Icelandic ear. It sounds like *hirð*, meaning "a court," and also *hjörð*, meaning "a herd," but the real meaning turns out to be the home itself, a place sacred to all of us. Of course its literal meaning is "a fireplace," and it was around the long hearths in

Viking halls that our ancestors used to recite their verses and tell their tales. In this way the Eddic poems and sagas were passed down from one generation to another for hundreds of years before being recorded in writing in the thirteenth century on white calfskins with ink made from crowberries.

Völuspá, or *Seeress's Prophecy*, is one of the greatest of the Eddic poems that are preserved in medieval Icelandic manuscripts but draw on earlier traditions of Norse mythology. In it, a seeress responds to questions by Óðinn (Odin), the chief of the gods. She tells him of the creation of the world and goes on to predict its impending destruction in Ragnarök, the doom of the gods. Hordes of giants will muster from land and sea to storm the bridge into Ásgarður, the world of the gods, and kill both gods and men. As it says in Carolyne Larrington's translation:

Brother will fight brother and be his slayer,
brother and sister will violate the bond of kinship;
hard it is in the world, there is much adultery,
axe-age, sword-age, shields are cleft asunder,
wind-age, wolf-age, before the world plunges headlong;
no man will spare another.

The poem ends, "There comes the dark dragon flying." It swoops down on the earth and we are given our first hint that Ragnarök is beginning. The final words of *Seeress's Prophecy* are "now she must sink down."

There is no explanation in the Eddic poem of why the giants are coming; for all we know they may be fleeing war or natural disaster. That is why I drew inspiration from the *Seeress's Prophecy* in my poem. The creatures we fear are at the gates but are they as cruel as we think? There is an important modern twist to the old story since Norse mythology always has this idea of us and them, just as there is today when we talk of refugees. For, in common with other European countries, Iceland is currently facing the moral dilemma of how to respond to an unprecedented flood of asylum seekers and economic migrants searching for a better life. As an isolated island people, we have always been suspicious of outsiders, but this time we have opened our arms and bid our fellow earth dwellers welcome to our hearths. Yet, as the poem hints, we cannot quite shut out that lingering ancestral fear.

Hearths in the Highlands
ALISA GANIEVA

I went to school in 1992. Our Soviet textbooks proudly instructed: "Your motherland is the USSR; it occupies one-sixth of all the land on Earth." I knew that the USSR was already a shadow of the past and the world around kept crumbling. I was growing up in the republic of Dagestan, and neighboring Chechnya had already claimed its independence from Russia (in one year it would be bombed to ruins). Some of the dozens of Dagestan ethnic minorities also hankered after sovereignty. Makhachkala, the plain seaside town I lived in, wasn't native for my family, which had descended from different villages in the highlands. So I couldn't name my motherland. Was it Russia? Or Moscow—my birthplace and the capital of my freshly diminished country? I preferred to answer "Caucasus" or simply "mountains."

Both my parents were Avar by origin, but they spoke different dialects. Their forefathers belonged to different subcultures and political enclaves called free alliances, with elected leaders, primitive male parliaments, and customary laws or *adats*. Anyway, my ancestors were indigenous people of the Caucasus Mountains, their homes preserved in stony mazes and creases as samples of an archaic European race—matriarchal, brutal, and agricultural. Their settlements were single multistoried fortresses clinging to impregnable rocks. They regarded their houses as temples and easily died for them, even in recent times when they professed rather superficial monotheistic beliefs—first Christianity, which came in the first centuries AD from neighboring Georgia, and then a Sunni Islam dating back to the fourteenth century on my mother's side, and the sixteenth on my father's.

A hearth used to be the centerpiece of an open-spaced house, dividing it into a men's half and a farther women's half. The hearth was sacred, as well being the medial pillar of the house, and it represented a ritual fecundity of the clan. Fire burned incessantly, regardless of any practical need, which is how my forefathers' cult was eventually left without forests.

❖

My paternal great-grandfather's dwelling, with traces of centuries-old smoke, ran short of inhabitants and collapsed at the beginning of the twentieth century. I saw its hard walls and narrow loopholes drawn in the nettles. Only four people still live in this tiny mountain village of Gunukh, and I've lost the path to it.

My paternal grandmother lived in Tlyarosh—a bigger village down the slope. She also lost her hearth, and I hardly remember which of the crooked arched streets—or rather, tunnels—belonged to her family. Her father was killed in a blood feud when she was just one, her mother remarried, and no siblings were born. When my grandmother married my granddad, they moved from one mountain village to a bigger one again, and again, while his career kept rising. Finally they rooted in a town apartment, which adopted the role of our family nest for some time, though it wasn't my home. They also built a house in Tlyarosh and spent summers there on the banks of a rapid river running from perennial glaciers on the Georgian border. I've been there several times, adjusting to the local dialect and habits, milking a cow, and wearing a scarf, but I still felt detached from the locals, as if I were a tourist.

I wonder if I ever had a home. My mother didn't. Part of her kin belonged to Sogratl—the big and notorious medieval Sufi hub, a village of artful stonemasons, warriors, and Islamic scholars. Twenty years after the end of the Russian imperial war in the Caucasus a mutiny was roused there. Five rebels were hanged, the entire male population was fettered and sent to Siberia, and the village burnt to ashes.

Another part of my mother's kin dwelled in the idyllic and beautiful village called Nakkazukh, or "In Clouds." It was a territory captured by stonemasons from a local cult of half-Christian pagans who claimed the land was theirs in the presence of judges. They simply jammed the soil from native fields into their boots and swore on the Quran that the land they were standing upon belonged to them. Their youth started living and carousing in the village of In Clouds in bliss and felicity, though the elders repeatedly forced them to return to the main village, destroying their flimsy summer cottages. But the perky youth hid in caves and kept rebuilding the destroyed cottages until independence was gained.

Not for long though. The October Revolution of 1917 shuffled their fates. My maternal grandmother's family was dispossessed; her father was deprived of his herds, flocks, and lands, arrested, and sent to a work camp where he almost starved to death. Their house was turned into a public kindergarten, and after her father's return and according to his desire, the remaining rooms became a sanctuary for the poor and homeless who started appearing in abundance after the Revolution.

I have visited both villages—the big and austere Sogratl and the light-headed Nakkazukh. The first one is stately, with well-made ashlar, ordered architecture, and the graves of big theistic scholars. People in Sogratl are prim and somewhat haughty, unlike the simple, giggling, and unreligious folk of Nakkazukh. Sogratl is all about law, and pride, and tradition. I bet it's the only village in Russia that has its own monthly newspaper. They publish it in their own peculiar dialect (my mother tongue), which differs strongly from the literary language of Avar. Nakkazukh, on the other hand, is all about fun and vulgarity and nature. Once I decided to visit the Nakkazukh library—a small two-room house. They gave me the key and I was surprised to see the neatly filed Sogratl newspapers and freshly ordered Avar books. While I was reading, the villagers started to enter. They looked dumbfounded and awed and took off their shoes as if they were in a mosque. "Amazing!" they kept repeating. "We've never been here." It was my turn to get surprised. They acted so convincingly that I entirely believed it, but the next day they confessed that it had been a hoax and they had fooled me.

My maternal grandfather also lost his home. When he was ten he accompanied his father into the fields. Suddenly two mounted security officers approached them and took his father away forever, without any chance to prepare for a journey or say goodbye to his folks. He only had time to take an apple from his pocket and to hand it to his son as a farewell. Decades later my maternal grandfather discovered that his arrested father had died in the Siberian tundra at a tree felling. Two years after his father's arrest, my grandfather's mother died, and he and his brother became orphans and were regarded as children of the so-called people's enemy.

When my maternal grandparents married they moved to Gunib—the mountain village where the Caucasian War had ended and where its leader, Shamil, had been captured a century ago. In fact, the authentic Gunib had been destroyed after Russia's victory and the population had been forced out. So my grandparents lived in a new, nineteenth-century village founded by Russian officers on the picturesque slopes of the conquered mountain. There they raised four children, my mother among them. Their home was a modern hut that was constantly being reconstructed. It was always crowded with guests and dependents and offered no privacy at all. Their grandfather's outmoded hearth was superseded by a kerosene stove, and I remember a wood-burning stove alongside the kitchen range.

Although my family has no deep roots there, I think Gunib feels the most like motherland for me. Maybe that's because I spent early years living in its beautiful natural bastion, surrounded by breakneck precipices and Russian-fortified walls. Its motley population had gathered from all sorts of Avar villages, speaking miscellaneous Avar dialects and a common newly emerged Gunib dialect, which I used to know in my childhood. I spent much time near the neighboring spring where young women and grannies used to collect. There wasn't any water supply to the houses in those days and women stood in lines with ewers and buckets to water their gardens or to wash their clothes. I have to note that according to sustaining Dagestani pagan beliefs water was too sacred to allow men to collect it and bring it home. Only women were allowed at the spring and had to drag heavy buckets to and fro several times a day. I remember my uncle fetching the water surreptitiously at night so that people wouldn't see him and mock him for carrying water home.

So, there was much talk and laughter at the spring, and I remember the feeling of belonging to this village where everyone was relatively a newcomer. But then my parents brought me to town and I forgot the Gunib dialect and quickly turned into its summer guest. Now, against the backdrop of rapid Islamization, only a few regions in Dagestan remain free and secular. Gunib is one of these intelligent places. No one will say a word if a girl walks around in jeans and bareheaded. I love being there, but I don't have a hearth to lean on. Our grandparents' house is under eternal construction—my uncle has been building a second floor for the last twenty years (this obsession with building houses is common for all Dagestanis and seems to be the residue of their pagan cult of home). I don't feel completely relaxed there. It's my relatives' place, not mine.

My grandfather from Gunib also had his share of prison life. It may seem there are too many calamities in my history for one family, but in fact our story is very typical and basically normal for that period and geography. You can hardly find a Russian family without political prisoners in its past. If you lived in an imperial colony that suddenly turned into a part of the great totalitarian experiment, you don't wonder that bad things happened. In fact, my folks were lucky to escape mass deportations that dispelled not only hearths but lives. Several nations around Dagestan and some regions within Dagestan were forcibly resettled. In the 1940s the whole population of Chechnya was put in wagons, brought to Kazakhstan, and left there on bare steppes. Kazakh people helped them to survive, but being nomadic and used to centuries of changing habitations, they couldn't entirely share the Chechens' grief.

As for Dagestan, inhabitants of a number of villages were forced to leave their sacred hearths for Chechnya, which was now freed from the Chechens, and to do it on foot, with their possessions on donkey backs. But they were so attached to their stony boondocks that many of them hid and secretly returned home. But Soviet airplanes bombed their rocky nests to prevent them from coming back, so they moved to Chechnya. Some died on their way, others died of malaria in their new place. Then, fifteen years later, the Chechens returned home from Kazakhstan and the Dagestani had to leave again. Since their high mountain fortresses were now destroyed, they settled on plains in new villages that bear the old names, but all have the word *New* in them. Most of these settlers seem to have lost their previous culture and identity. They look like a marginal crowd stripped of national memory, of traditions and roots. No surprise that these are the places where most of the religious obscurantism, murders of honor, and sexism have been happening.

But I want to get back to my grandfather. He was an accountant who, while inspecting the kolkhoz economy, happened to detect and naïvely prevent some larceny schemes covered up by his bosses. Naturally they decided to get rid of him. And since nobody could find any criminal fault, he was eventually imprisoned for allegedly working in two places at the same time, which was prohibited in the Soviet Union. In fact, his second job wasn't even a job, it was just an occasional participation in labor squads, but who cared.

As for my parents, they got acquainted in Moscow, in a dormitory for PhD students, and I was born there. So Moscow was my sham motherland. I say sham, for a month after my birth I was delivered back to the Caucasus, where I spent seventeen years without a hearth or a sense of true home. During the first eight years of my life, living in a modern town, I moved five times (and I'm not counting years spent in Gunib). Finally, after perestroika my parents bought a temporary apartment in Makhachkala, for they were expecting to get a flat in a cooperative high-rise building. My brother and I grew up dreaming of a permanent home. But the building did not get finished for twenty years. My father died after taking out a mortgage in Moscow and a bank paid the rest of his debt, so my brother and his wife got something more or less permanent to live in. My mother lives in her old Makhachkala apartment alone, while I live in Moscow, renting my sixth short-term dwelling in a row.

This is why I still have no sense of hearth and home, or attachment and history. Our family's true home remains somewhere in the high mountains between several half-empty villages. As for Makhachkala, my native town in the Caucasus, it doesn't give me any sentiment. It is a new place—just several decades old—for mountain dwellers to live in. It's dirty and there are no cliffs or peaks. It's nothing but a flat steppe and dried swamps, a place historically harassed by nomadic tribes moving from Asia to Europe and vice versa.

The truth is that deep inside I'm glad to be a cosmopolitan. Sure, the rapid demise of my people's culture is a disaster. It would have been much better if they had slowly adjusted to the bigger world without any dispossessions or resettlements. Thus they could have preserved some of their archaic but unique worldview and would have been able to balance it with a modern one. The old and the modern don't disagree very much. Most of the *adats* are about the just self-regulation of a community. If somebody's house was destroyed with fire, the entire village gathered together and rebuilt it in several days. If a person was blackguarded in public, he had to hang a special sign of disgrace above his door, and so on. Now that all of these communities are scattered, the traditional laws don't work. Neither do the secular state laws of Russia, where bureaucracy, clan nepotism, and police lawlessness hold sway in the Russian Caucasus. And sharia law does not work either, since the Dagestani are very superficial Muslims. Instead there's a wild mixture of Russian norms, globalized consumerism, casual use of Islamic rules, and old traditions modernized by current fashion into a total absurdity.

Still, I'm glad changes did happen so that I'm now able to ignore the mountain community rules, to travel, and to think for myself. This would have been impossible without the destruction of ancient hearths and customs. My blood chills when I imagine living in the closed society of my ancestors. I know, most of them were very happy with their lives, but I'm an outsider with a different brain, and the distance created by passing time allows me to compare and judge. I'm not that attached to any hearth. My scoliosis wouldn't allow me to carry heavy ewes of water or to labor in the fields (fields used to be another sacred space, restricted for men). It's the same for millions of young people who left their native places and moved on. And not just in Russia. We all got rid of something warm and dear to be free in our decisions. But we got the entire world instead.

We former Soviets have several things in common: erased or warped memories, falsified or forgotten pasts, and unknown origins. Millions of Soviet people had to change their names, renounce their families, and hide their relatives—because knowledge of such facts could spoil their lives. Being a Russian German, or a Chechen, or a Jew, or a Crimean Tatar was dangerous. Being of noble descent was dangerous. Having relatives abroad was dangerous. Having enemies in a family was dangerous. Being a habitant of territories occupied by Nazis during World War II was dangerous, et cetera. So people got rid of their histories and heritage for safety's sake. In some cases they did it willfully. In others they were forced to. For example, Soviet authorities forced many Dagestani mountaineers to resettle on the plains under the slogan of emancipation and a better, easier life. Today, hoping to find lost identities, many Russians are delving into the past and looking to restore abraded family pedigrees. In Dagestan many old traditions and crafts still survive, but nowadays they have another big enemy—Islamic influence. Local wineries, dances, and carnival holidays are attacked by the Muslims as something hideous and contrary to the true faith. Looking at this painful reality, I realize that the only way to preserve the disappearing genuine history is to fix it in my fiction.

Perhaps my hearth lives only in my mind. Sometimes I feel a sting of happiness and a sense of hearth and home far away from my ancestors' lands—sometimes on another continent. It all depends on the ambience, on surroundings and people. The connection usually happens when I come across something similar to my motherland—a mountain village, a vernacular language, an old agricultural custom.

That's why I love old European towns with their narrow paved and covered streets and stony stairs—they remind me very much of Sogratl and other decaying mountain villages of the Caucasus. I love the American Midwest with its hospitable farms and prairies because rural simplicity is universal. I love old castles with antique fireplaces because stones and fire are things my ancestors saw every day. I adore everything hilly and irregular. Places where I make friends also turn into new little hearths for me. And I'm still hoping to get my own hearth someday.

Small Fires

Zoë Strachan

Once at Bay of Skaill on the west coast of Orkney, I saw a ring of wave-beaten stones, each one large enough to sit on, enclosing a pile of charred driftwood. Years later, on the beach at Maidens, not so far from where I grew up in Ayrshire, I caught the last shock of flame in a smaller stone hearth. People like building fires between the foreshore and the dunes, where the sand is dry but the wind still blows until your ears are numb and the tears and mucus are whipped from your eyes and nose. I am drawn to these embers and ashes, knowing that soon a high tide or gust of sand will sweep them away. I have never built a fire outside, or sat by one that burned on a windy beach, the whistle of salt in my hair.

At home in Glasgow, I'm used to laying a cast iron stove with scrunches of newspaper, constructing tepees of kindling, balancing lumps of smokeless anthracite brought in hundredweight bags by the coal man. Touching the match here, then here, then here, wedging the door ajar to draw the draught and coax the flicker and glow. Inside my body I feel a small surge, but primal, rising to answer the flame.

When I was seventeen, I moved from the Ayrshire town of Kilmarnock to Glasgow to study. It was the nearest city, but it felt as if I'd come a long way. There were days when it seemed more foreign than places I've traveled across the world to now. I lived for a year in a room in a house that had only an open fire for heating. I didn't have much skill in lighting it, and when it did burn, the soot coated my tie-dye dresses and second-hand textbooks while the warmth did not extend beyond the small rectangle of the rag rug in front of the fireplace. I remember being glad when someone visited, eager to singe marshmallows on the flames, and the muffled loneliness once they'd gone. It took me a while to learn how to make a home, and when I did it was for one person alone. Sometimes I'd lie in bed in that square, cold room and watch the reflections of the flames dance up to the dark ceiling.

When archaeologists find hearths, it is taken as an indication that domestic activity took place at a site. Keeping warm, cooking, storytelling perhaps. But Gordon Barclay, an eminent and much-respected scholar of the Scottish Neolithic, wrote that our "search for settlement is hampered by the limits of our understanding of the guises in which it will appear." Barclay was frustrated at times by the way in which the "luminous centres" of prehistory, Orkney and Wessex (where Stonehenge lies), attracted archaeologists at the expense of the underexplored areas of mainland Scotland. We don't know as much about how our Neolithic ancestors lived in these less glamorous places. For Kenneth Brophy, who I think might have been in some of my own university classes, one of the problems has been the failure of archaeologists to begin at the beginning, by trying to define what exactly we mean by *domestic* and *house*. These questions, of how we live and where, spool from the Neolithic to today.

The village of Skara Brae, which overlooks the Bay of Skaill, was built around six and a half thousand years ago. I went there first as an archaeology undergrad, drawn to the possibility of telling stories around our preliterate past, and have returned time and again in the twenty years since. At the center of each of the houses, surrounded by stone box beds and a shelved stone dresser, there is a hearth. It takes an instant to recognize where people slept, where they placed their belongings, where they knelt to touch flame to kindling. Orcadian poet George Mackay Brown imagined their "small fires and pots." Even on the wildest day, when the site is about to be closed to visitors for safety, it is possible to conjure a low roof, a smoky coziness.

A similar hearth lies in the middle of the Stones of Stenness, the oldest of all the ancient henges in Scotland. When it was excavated it was found to contain cremated bone, charcoal, and broken pottery. Stenness guards a spit of land that slices between the lochs of Stenness and Harray. Here, at Ness of Brodgar, archaeologists have found unique proof of painted decoration inside a Neolithic structure. As part of my studies I worked on a dig high on a hillside near Finstown. Our excavations overlooked a tiny island with a causeway leading to it. The site supervisor told us that the farmer who lived there alone had gone mad and shot the few cows that grazed by his home. I would look up from my trowel and brush to see curls of smoke rising from the farmer's chimney, glimpse a mud-encrusted car that seemed never to move, even when the tide was low enough to render the causeway passable. Above our dig was a chambered tomb, Cuween Hill. A torch was left just inside the entrance, and one day four of us, all girls, crawled the three long meters of the low passageway to reach the place built so that the bodies of eight people or more could be left to slip off their dead flesh. We had read our textbooks and knew that after decomposition others came to move the bones and rearrange them, alongside the skulls of twenty-four dogs. Death rituals always fascinated me, these Neolithic griefs that allowed people to return to their dead and, perhaps, their dead to return to them.

✦

When I was a child, a lot of adults remembered growing up with coal fires. The bunker out the back, the struggle to heat water in the back boiler, most of the heat escaping up the chimney. My Ayrshire family were coal miners. In the early part of the twentieth century, and beyond, the boys left school on their fifteenth birthday and went to the pit with their dads the next day. By the time I was born, most houses had a hissing gas fire that lit with a sudden whoosh of flame, or one with electric coils and fake coals, set on a fireplace made of tiles and colored breeze-blocks. Chairs and couch were angled toward the television. The fire wasn't used if there was central heating, but its bulbs would glow orange through the plastic nonetheless.

The distinction between domesticity and ritual may not have been as clear-cut in the Neolithic as it seems to be today. The quotidian might have been numinous, and the numinous, quotidian. The Scottish Archaeological Research Framework noted that "expecting to find wholly domestic activity may be inappropriate for Neolithic contexts." Daily life could have been chock full of ritual. A cooking pot might not have been just a cooking pot.

Hearths and cists look similar. It's hard to see one without thinking of the other, and perhaps that's the point. At Temple Wood in Kilmartin Glen, the twin stone circles have central burial cists. The nineteenth-century landowner planted trees around the circles to heighten the romantic sense of druidic worship, and today the woods lend an eeriness to the place. The positioning of the stones, plotted over five thousand years ago, is the earliest evidence we have in Scotland of an awareness of the movements of the sun. One stone is marked with a double spiral, another with a double oval. The first people to be called Scots were early migrants from Ireland. Kilmartin was a center of power for them, too; the rulers of the Gaelic kingdom of Dál Riata were crowned at what had been an Iron Age hillfort at Dunadd, to the south of the glen. This history resonates in different ways for modern-day Scots. The country debated—and voted against—independence in 2014. We can all sift through the past for the narratives we need.

My partner and I live in the attic of a converted late-Georgian townhouse in Glasgow. Behind our bed, the wind howls in the bricked-up chimney. Below us, the original hearthstone is embedded in the floor. There might have been a dozen fireplaces in the building when it was built; only two of the chimneys are safe to use now. The smell of smoke on the cold air as I walk home on a dark winter evening means my partner is in, and the house is warm. When I was a small child we visited Glasgow from time to time. The city was soot blackened, the red and blond of its tenements obscured, the pinnacled towers and sculpted figures of the art gallery and museum at Kelvingrove alluring but monstrous. The Clean Air Act was passed in 1956, a legacy of the Great Smog of London, which lasted five days and is now estimated to have killed twelve thousand people. The friendly warmth of Kelvingrove's Locharbriggs sandstone was revealed in the late 1980s. In 2016, Glasgow breached World Health Organization air pollution safety levels. These days the culprit is traffic rather than smoke.

Many of the later prehistoric buildings in Scotland can be made visible when their blanket of turf and soil is lifted away. When they could, our ancestors built with stone. One of the roundhouses at Aldclune near Blair Atholl had four hearths. People lived in extended families. When the Romans reached northern Europe they surmised that men may have had more than one wife; today we wonder if women had more than one partner too. It is possible that society was matrilineal.

As a family, we didn't travel north. The farthest we went together in Scotland was to Perthshire, where one Easter we rented a cottage that had been one of the gate lodges to a castle near Weem. Now, photographed in sunshine, with French doors and a picturesque bench outside, the lodge has all that is needed to secure four stars from Visit Scotland. Back then it was more rudimentary, and we didn't have the knack to charm many warm baths from the back boiler. I was studying for school exams and the chill of the bedroom numbed my feet and hands. But I could roam through the woods with my dog Nell and look across the fields to the castle. There was an open metal tank of water under the trees. It seemed vast, and frightening. At night Nell and I would sit so close to the coal fire that we'd risk scorching ourselves.

Like the early cathedral builders, some Neolithic people must not have expected to see their constructions complete. When we walk through their landscapes today, past their watch stones and cairns, the living are there alongside the dead. These places were built for the future, so that it would always hold the past. Rebecca K. Younger wrote her PhD on Neolithic henges, the earthworks that often contain stone or timber circles. She proposes that we think of them not as passive monuments but as "places of commemoration."

A few days before she died, my grandmother complained of feeling ill. She seemed to rally, but when I returned to Glasgow I wrote to her anyway. We corresponded often when I was at university; it was easier for me than calls on a shared telephone, which could turn long and difficult. I recall a pressing sense of things clamoring to be said, but the most important were simple enough to put into words. I loved her; she was important in my life. When she died a few days later and I returned to her house, I heard the postman's steps in the entry and saw my letter flap through the letterbox. We kept her in the house until the funeral, and that day I sat at her dressing table and brushed my hair with her ivory-backed brush, applied a dab of her No. 17 Toffee Apple lipstick. We asked the undertaker to place the letter in her coffin, to be cremated with her.

A friend in Orkney built a house next to the remains of a grain-drying kiln. It might date from medieval times; many do, according to local archaeologist Merryn Dineley. From my friend's garden you can look across to Cava and Hoy beyond, and watch the ferries carrying workers back and forth to the oil terminal at Flotta. A story that I never tire of hearing is that of two women, Ida and Meg, who were the only inhabitants of the small island of Cava for twenty-seven and a half years. They arrived on a motorbike and sidecar from the south of England in 1959, along with their cat. Their cottage did not have electricity or running water. They didn't mind visitors, liked religious songs and gin (or so I'm told), cut peat to burn on their fire. Prehistoric Orcadians probably gathered seaweed, braced it to dry in the high winds, and burned it on their fires. I have done this and can confirm that it stinks. Ida and Meg weren't a couple in the romantic sense, even if, as Andrew Greig wrote, their life together "makes marriage seem faint-hearted." Poets love islands even more than archaeologists do.

The Pevsner Architectural Guide describes the town I am from, Kilmarnock, as "the county's engine house, whose late nineteenth century–early twentieth century heyday took its name to every corner of the globe, on water hydrants, shoes, railway engines, carpets, and whisky. Those days are behind it now . . . and the town seeks to reinvent itself for the twenty-first century, and to forget the damage the late twentieth century wrought on its economy, communal psyche and built environment." Reinvention is not an easy business, and I wonder if our communal psyches benefit from an anchor to what has gone before. I find myself poring over old photographs, rewriting my hometown's past, sifting through the inherited narratives of family history in the service of fiction. In the absence of graves and chambered cairns, it's my way of crawling in to touch the bones and rearrange them.

Sometimes when I light the stove, I think of Nicholson Baker's novel *A Box of Matches*, which is about writing, and routine, and mortality, and perhaps most of all about the pleasure of lighting a fire. Prometheus didn't steal it from the gods for nothing. Most Novembers, in the tiny park just around the corner from our house, teenagers build a bonfire for Guy Fawkes Night. A strange thing to celebrate—the foiled 1605 plot to blow up parliament and the king for persecuting Catholics, and the execution of its perpetrators. Especially in the west of Scotland, where sectarianism teeters on. It is a few years now since I've been asked to contribute "a penny for the Guy," a mannequin representing Fawkes that is made by children to sit atop the bonfire, but it seems that a plastic refuse bin is a satisfactory substitute.

Sir Walter Scott was so taken with the remains of the sixteenth-century Old House of Sumburgh on Shetland that he named it Jarlshof and used it in his novel *The Pirate*. It turned out that people had been living there for epochs before the laird built his house. The earliest settlement dates from the Neolithic, about 2400 BCE. Two pits were found in the sandy floor of one oval house. One pit contained fragments of human skull, three stone clubs, and a stone knife; the other, the four feet of a cow. Another house became a smith's workshop in the Bronze Age, and by the Iron Age there was a farm, and then, still a couple of hundred years before the birth of Christ, a circular stone tower, known as a broch, and associated wheelhouses. The Picts, and then the Vikings, lived at Jarlshof. One of the earliest extant longhouses in Scotland is here; people lived alongside their animals, as many subsequent generations of highlanders and islanders would. As you walk through these buildings, you can look up to the lighthouse and World War II radar hut at Sumburgh Head, and hear planes land at the airport nearby. The road to Jarlshof crosses the runway. George Mackay Brown writes of "the old friendship of stone and man." No material is as evocative: the grain of it under our fingers, the marks where it was worked in ancient times. We recognize houses. The paved hearths with their stone curbs.

Madeleine Bunting's investigations into the Gaelic heritage of the Hebrides cause her to ponder whether people belong to places rather than places to people. We all want a center, a lodestone, a connection to the past that will write us into the narrative that leads to the future. As the only child of an only child, childless myself and an atheist to boot, sometimes my connections seem fragile. My family favors cremation. We don't leave behind sites of commemoration hewn in stone.

Landscapes change; what looks wild to our urban eyes is less desolate than we might imagine. At Machrie Moor on Arran some of the stone circles were built in timber first, then upgraded to what Anna and Graham Ritchie call "the designer version": tall sandstone slabs alternated with granite boulders. Many stones in this ritual landscape are missing, probably broken up to reuse in Moss Farm, a derelict stop along the moorland track where once my partner Louise and I saw a male hen harrier tumble and soar in his intricate sky dance. Three of the stones that remain are monumental, dizzying. One rises five and a half meters from the springy turf. The trees and the soil may have changed over the millennia, but the hills and the sea would orientate a time traveler. People lived and farmed here, and the ground received their dead. The stones align with the midsummer sunrise, when it peeks through a notch in the hills at the top of the empty glen. Lichen forms a patina like a lurid map of a long-gone archipelago. Close your eyes and lay one palm on the tallest of the upright slabs, turn your ear to it even, when it has a trace of warmth from the spring sunshine, and you can imagine a vibration, a pulse.

The Fire

JANE HIRSHFIELD

Again open
the book
of reds and golds.
Study the faces
of poppy and lion,
the bright-carpet
tapetum lucidum
of your own life.
What looks back
and seems to be burning,
is burning;
though not all the same:
in the moment
of turning away
from rain,
the day gives off—
red & gold—
the slightest scent
of peaches.
This too
so you might know things
as they are.
So you, who are
already walking within,
will come in.
Why else take up
the body's single candle,
if not to see
how everything is consumed?

from *The Lives of the Heart* (HarperCollins, 1997)

The most striking hearth fire I have ever gazed into was the aftermath of the 1977 Ventana Wilderness Marble Cone fire. I was living at Tassajara at the time, an inholding amidst steep mountains parched from multiyear drought. Most residents were evacuated as soon as the danger became evident, but a dozen of us went back in. I was in the final car to go over the fourteen-mile mountain dirt road, just before flames closed it completely. During what turned out to be almost three weeks of waiting, from dawn to dark, and sometimes beyond, we cut fire line and set up sprinklers and hoses to protect the compound's many small wooden buildings. One person would sit up alone each night to do fire watch, as the flames, still ridges away, embered down in the comparative coolness to a red glow.

The fire approached oddly slowly, at around the pace a person might walk that terrain—making uphill runs in the heat, crowning in the canopy, but pausing at night, or moving sideways rather than toward us. Its presence became an intimacy, a living thing. The days' light went from an initial deepening red to almost underwater blue green as the smoke thickened. Silence thickened also, as birds and squirrels left. We worked from first light to last and sometimes past, wearing soaked bandannas on our faces to screen some part of the smoke, and then another around our necks to temper the heat. They quickly dried. Our teeth were black, sieving soot out of the air. From time to time professional fire crews came through, helped for a day or so, then continued upstream—helpful apparitions we'd feed and give beds and showers to. A truckload of culled seconds peaches we'd just brought in to dry for winter was gradually eaten. I'd been in that truck returning from Fresno's canning lines, seen the first hint of the fire, a red streak in the wrong place on the horizon as we'd come over Chews Ridge at three in the morning.

When the fire finally reached Tassajara, three professionals from the Forest Service were there, showing a few of us how and when to use hand-held drip flares to light backfires outside the ten-foot scraped-bare line we'd cut. Others held hoses and shovels against any burning debris that might roll back downhill. Official CalFire policy has turned since then more against back-burning, it seems, but the technique protected us from the worst: our hand-set fires raced away and uphill to meet the main fire, taking its fuel before it could come down to us. We were lucky that year. It's strange now to ponder, but I don't remember ever feeling truly frightened.

What surprised most was the great beauty of the days and nights after. There was little left to do but look, holding shovels in case anything still burning flared up again. "Burning rolling yucca root balls" that might come down from the steep terrain above us was the awareness refrain, but fire can also travel underground, inside tree roots, or on the wind in sparks. Inside the preserved space, some patches of lawn remained eerily green. Outside, the hearts of trees burned for weeks, though the major smoke cleared enough after a while to leave visible the Pleiades' shooting stars in the mid-August sky. A few implausible surviving quail came through, their little family group pecking the ground. From what safety one could not imagine, given the scale of the Marble Cone fire: 178,000 acres, at the time the largest wildfire California had known.

A person walking inside a burning-down campfire of unimaginable scale finds herself speaking in the whisper of library or church. It is not a landscape living eyes were meant to see or can quite take in as actual and not dream. There was no sense of hell-like inferno in this realm of after, only exhausted awe at something so beautiful, so much larger than any experience I had yet known. A Grand Canyon of fire traveled all the way into, then lived inside of. A world whose long-familiar darkness had been turned into glimmer and glow.

The fire of this poem is not that fire. The poem's fire is held by hearth, by surround of stone that will not burn. The peaches of this poem hold mostly the color of sunset and eros. But those 1977 peaches are surely within them; such an experience does not vanish. The Lotus Sutra offers the parable of a burning house as a description of unawakened life; children play inside it, not realizing their situation, though the house is always on fire. In Greek mythology, the *penates*, pantry gods of family and household life, live on—perhaps in—the domestic hearth. Both traditions carry the same implication: we live within a blaze of transience both inevitable and complete. Life itself is a slow-burning fire, each cell's carbon turned by oxygen into cooking, sleeping, lovemaking, stories, laughter, grief. The same hearth fire that lights and warms the darkness consumes the night's minutes and hours. We feed it our lives' fuel willingly, to see and feel and know that we have lived.

A hearth fire, then, is a viewable, seemingly manageable self-portrait. We sit by it and tell stories and reflect, as bright flames murmur their way into the softer glow of charcoals. But the hearth-side sense of secured containment is deceptive. The held fire draws the body to its flickering warmth, the eyes to its fiercer, quicker version of our own passing and passionate existence, but it remains untouchable by our soft and vulnerable human hands.

EARTH

Kīlauea Caldera, My Hearth

PUALANI KANAHELE

Kīlauea caldera sits on the southeast slope of Mauna Loa
The southern mountain on the island of Hawaiʻi
Kīlauea means to spew out volumes of breath
Kīlauea is volcanically active and has been for thousands of years
It is the home of the volcano deity Pelehonuamea
Within the caldera of Kīlauea
Sits the crater Halemaʻumaʻu
Halemaʻumaʻu has been erupting continuously for the last thirty-four years,
Sometimes continuous for a hundred years
Other times barely sulfurous

I am from a family of dancers and chanters
Inheriting an archaic dance form
Our primary dances are about the erupting volcano
Composers of the chants describe the volatile earth
And the procreation of islands
It is humbling to know that you are part of a whole
While witnessing the eruptive phenomenon
Described in a chant composed over three hundred years ago
By an ancestor who observed the same kind of event
And eventually choreographed the dance and chant
I teach my children, grandchildren, and great-grandchildren
E komo ma loko o Halemaʻumaʻu
Welcome to Halemaʻumaʻu
He mauna puʻu e ʻolāʻolā nei
Lava gurgling, giving life to little mountains,
E Pele, e Pele, huaʻina, huaʻina kū
Pele, the fiery hostess, boiling, gushing up
Molten earth that grows
(An old chant extending welcome from

Pelehonuamea, the volcano deity
Part of the myth and the reality)

✦

Kīlauea is antitheses in nature
The east summit is a pristine wet native forest
Profusely endowed with native flora and fauna
The west ridge is dry and houses
Migrating geese and sea birds in the cliff of the caldera
The north rim holds fissures of vaporous steam
Rising from the depth of the earth
Depositing sulfur along the crusty crevasse
When honored with the north wind
An opulent waterfall of steam rushes down
From the caldera into the crater
Then exits on an updraft from Halemaʻumaʻu
Dissipating skyward choreography unequal
The south bank of Kīlauea is a barren lava field
From giant boulders to silk threadlike
Rocks, a vast land of pure untouched rocks

Kīlauea's presence acknowledges its effect on the weather system
Providing the knowledge that lightning and thunder
Originate from the earth as well as the atmosphere
That our water is recycled not only from the ocean and forest
But also from the heat of the volcano

Kīlauea represents a flux and flow of lifetimes
It is a place of wordless lessons
Cultivating a spiritual union with elemental deities
It is a reconnective portal with ancestral fire-folk
Producing generations of fire names
Therefore a link to ancestral genealogy

Kīlauea is my hearth my link to predecessors and progeny
To the past and the future

Kīlauea the source

Approach it empty, like a newborn
Sit quietly, patiently, no expectations

Myths are grounded, deciphered, and evolve
In eight strands according to the winds

Kīlauea
Comfortable, dependable, familiar always,

I sit on the west ridge with the sun on my back
Sit long enough you see it all

A misty rainbow grows on the sulfurous rim
To the north

Low-lying red rainbow over the cloud forest
In the east

And a steady stream of volcanic gas, uahi or vog
On the south bank moving toward the ocean

A rainbow appears in Kīlauea
Going through different stages of existence

Fading, bright, tall, wide
Recording the vitality of wind, sun, mist

Breath and life drawn into
And spew out of Kīlauea

Leave offering, breathe
A reciprocal process,

The cycle when one accepts it
Lives to direct the next

Kīlauea
The architect of island life.

Home Waters

SARA BAUME

1

December 2015, three days before Christmas. A woman walking along a strand on the southwest coast of Ireland finds a loggerhead sea turtle washed up on the pebbly sand. Wasted and exhausted, cold and confused, but still alive.

An adult loggerhead can outweigh an alligator and outlive a donkey. They have snub noses, sleepy eyes, and perpetually displeased expressions. The upper shell is ginger, amber, apricot. The underside is creamy yellow. The head is leopard print. The front flippers are long and wide and winglike; there is no creature more perfectly poised between dinosaur and angel than a loggerhead turtle. They swim in parts of the Pacific and Indian Oceans and the Mediterranean Sea, waters that are warm and calm. They have no business here in Ireland, where it is primarily wild and chilly. The displeased expression of a loggerhead sea turtle beached in the shallows of an Irish shore at Christmastime is entirely justified.

What a frightening derangement of nature, I think, when I hear the story. And a dreadful picture rises like bile in my head: a different strand, a different season. Under an ashen sky in autumn, on the brown shale of a Turkish beach, in blue shorts and a red T-shirt, lies the tiny, bedraggled body of a drowned boy. This is the photograph that made global headlines in the early days of September 2015. The boy is a three-year-old Syrian called Aylan Kurdi who perished at the mercy of an unseaworthy vessel in his family's attempt to cross the Mediterranean and reach the Greek island of Kos. It rises into my head—rises irresistibly, unsummoned—rises in spite of how reluctant I am to draw comparison between a turtle and a boy.

2

Winter 2011. A dark-sky morning, rain battering against our rented roof. The sound of clinking—softly, softly—like the rigging of a sailing ship, a wind chime caught in a draught. It clinks through my sleep; my dream-riddled mind registers it as unfamiliar—not the usual birdsong or barking or my boyfriend's breathing—its unfamiliarity rouses me. Cautiously, I descend the stairs to find our ground floor flooded. Soupy water shin deep, surface bog brown and rippled. But the water itself is deathly silent. It's the empty glass bottles usually placed in a cluster around the base of the rubbish bin that make the sound. They are floating about, colliding gently with one another. The table and chairs stand helpless in the flood. The dog's water dish has sunk beneath the weight of its load. My left Wellington boot has filled up and capsized. Its novelty polka dots seem suddenly, unbearably, ridiculous.

I was born with salted blood. When I was a child, I wanted—desperately, desperately—to be, when I grew up, an artist who lived by the sea. All of my brightest memories are backdropped by crashing waves and un-clouded sky: I am ankle deep in wet sand; I am bouncing in marram grass on a cliff edge; I am doggy-paddling against the current. In April 2011, I moved with my boyfriend from Dublin city to a shorefront village called Whitegate on the edge of Cork harbor. To a tiny, tumbledown house in a terrace with an oil refinery at one end and an electricity power station at the other. Admittedly, a somewhat compromised version of the child-hood dream. Trucks trundle through day and night, coating the parked cars and window boxes with dust. The water across the road is certified unsafe for swimming. The sea view out our front windows is obstructed by oil storage tanks. After our first flood, the locals tell us it was the worst for twenty years.

We've lived here for five years, and it floods every winter, and some-times again in spring, and once even in the middle of July. Storms can occur in any season; in this harbor, when they concur with high tides, it creates a flood. The water never comes over the wall and spills across the road; instead it arrives by way of the drains in the backyard, trickling un-der the skirting boards and up from the cracks between floor tiles. Every time it happens we camp upstairs and hope the flood doesn't creep high enough to infiltrate the lowest socket and shut the electricity off.

We develop new habits. Bringing the glass to the bottle bank before it accumulates, accumulating ragged old cloths and towels instead—donated by family members—for the soaking-up of floodwater, and after every flood, we wring out and rinse, dry out and fold, place them aside in wait for the next time. We pay particular attention to the elements. A booklet of tide tables lies ever open on the kitchen worktop. The weather forecast plays out over the radio once every hour. Sandbags are banked up at both doors—in half a decade we never feel safe enough to remove them. Instead we duck down and hop over, duck down and hop over, duck down and hop over. We adapt to the small threat that looms at the edge of our days, as our small house looms at the edge of the temperamental harbor. But with adaptation comes complacence. One evening I stand stubbornly over the electric cooker as the floodwater puddles beneath, bored of caution. Willing my potatoes to be roasted before I am electrocuted.

3

A memory from childhood that does not include any sea: I am gazing out the playroom window through a kaleidoscope of whirling droplets; I am chanting a rhyming couplet: *rain, rain, go away . . . come again another day . . .*

When I am home, it doesn't seem to me as if I talk about the rain all that much. It's only when I am away—elsewhere, overseas—that my susceptibility to the elements singles me out from those around me. I automatically quiz strangers about the precipitation in the place where they're from. Its frequency and strength, the shapes it takes and the shapes it leaves behind on the landscape. And then I compare and contrast their replies to the temper and nature of my home-rain. It's only when I am away and carrying out these tedious little exercises in rain study that I understand how much of a natural preoccupation—a national preoccupation—it is in Ireland. And I understand again as I return, as the airplane begins its descent. Dropping below the level of the ubiquitous clouds, my home island looms into view, and I see afresh, and freshly appreciate, its unequivocal, influential greenness.

In Ireland, we have numerous ways to recognize the coming of the rain: red sky in the morning, seated cows, horses stamping. When a cat settles down to wash behind his ears, there must be a shower approaching. Or when a dog eats grass, or soot falls down a chimney, or a yellow ring appears around the moon. And when the rain inevitably arrives, we have even more ways of describing it: as spitting, lashing, drizzling, driving, bucketing. Soft, fierce, showery, slanted. Localized, hovering, torrential.

There is an expression I tend to use nowadays: *I feel it in my waters*. As if there is a small sea enclosed inside me that I entrust all my decisions to.

4

Summer 2015. At night, on our television screen, between national weather forecasts, we watch scenes from a different sea, one we can rest assured will never infiltrate our sockets. A distant body of water that I have always imagined to be calmer, warmer, bluer: the Mediterranean. But these nights on our TV screen, in defiance of my imagination, these waters are persistently disturbed. By naval vessels and low-flying helicopters. By smuggling boats, sometimes floating, but more often capsized. Mostly timber, but sometimes only rubber—precarious as a polka-dot Wellington boot on a flooded kitchen floor. And the smuggled cargo of these unbearably ridiculous vessels: Syrians, Afghans, Eritreans. Men, women, and children, their first salted memories being formed as I watch. They are embarking upon a sea that represents a passage into safety. Behind them: the tumult of Africa and the Middle East. Before them: the sanctuary of Europe. And the only separation: a body of water not quite as calm, warm, and blue as imagined.

In May, the first Irish naval vessel is deployed to the Mediterranean to assist Italian authorities. It is called the LÉ *Eithne*, the LÉ standing for Long Éireannach, or Irish Ship. It is followed in the months to come by the LÉ *Niamh* and LÉ *Róisín*. Our ships generally seem to bear the names of girls with whom I shared a class in high school; all except for the LÉ *Samuel Beckett* and LÉ *James Joyce*—names chosen, inadvertently, in tactless recognition of the experimental poetry of their missions.

The base of the Irish Naval Service is Haulbowline Island, situated in the middle of Cork harbor. Though the island is hidden from our front-facing windows by the oil refinery's storage tanks, still we often sight its ships channeling through our obstructed view. They are squat to the water, missile shaped, painted bluish gray: a shade of the Celtic Sea in winter. Gradually it dawns on me that these are the same vessels I watch on the news at night, the ones that set forth to valiantly disturb the Mediterranean. On the TV screen, we are permitted to see them up close. Decks and rails and flapping tricolor. Life belts and life dinghies, the intense orange of life jackets. And outstretched arms lifting dripping infants, regulation blankets wrapped around shaking shoulders. The migrant crisis is reported in the Irish media from a peculiarly personal angle. Now we are taking some responsibility; it is our catastrophe too. Between May and November, Irish ships rescued 8,592 people from the Mediterranean Sea. And yet the ones I spot returning to harbor hold only crew; the rescued civilians swallowed somewhere along the way by European bureaucracy.

5

Winter 2015, the last one we spend in Whitegate. It rains and rains. Every morning I wake to listen for the prophetic pitter-patter, the tell-tale clinking of shipwrecked objects: our own personal flood-warning. The longest, largest Irish river—the Shannon—swells and swells, and bursts. Houses far from any seafront, unanswerable to any tide, flood too. The traces the weather leaves on the landscape aren't so much shapes as ravages. Fields become lakes; roads become rivers. Animals are drowned, displaced, disconcerted. "The cattle inside in the trailers are getting dizzy from going side to side over the potholes," a farmer in County Kerry tells a newspaper reporter. The blood banks appeal for emergency supplies.

The sandbags are still there on the day we finally leave. They are squashed down and split open and leaking. There are watermarks on the rusted chair and table legs. The low-down wall paint is warped and peeling.

We move—finally, finally—away from the harbor and to the west coast, the side of Ireland that faces the North Atlantic and is most vulnerable to roguish weather. We still have a sea view, but it is significantly farther away now, and much of the time obscured by rainclouds. When it does appear, it is always surprising, always tremendous. The house is on a hill; the rain runs down and away from us. Several of the properties in the surrounding countryside have a nameplate bolted into their front walls: *Radharc na Mara*, view of the sea—even though their views are just as far flung and unpredictable as ours. But people like to make this claim, whilst simultaneously maintaining immunity from the sea's force.

And yet if I walk down our hill and away for a distance, and up an opposite hill, and then turn around and look back, it appears every bit as if the ocean behind the house rises up above it—the level of the sea towering over the level of the land—as though at any minute, it will drop down and deluge, not just our house, but everything, my whole small island. Despite the salted blood and sea home, I swim only on the stillest days. My boyfriend angles from the rocks and I walk the cliff trails, but always, we are conscious, cautious. Love and trust are often different states, respect and fear often the same. We know we are safer onshore than off, that everybody knows this, in their waters; we appreciate that people don't choose sea over land unless they are already drowning.

6

May 5, 2016. The LÉ *Róisín* releases the loggerhead turtle beached in West Cork three days before Christmas 2015 into the Mediterranean. Since being rescued, she has been cared for in a turtle sanctuary in Dingle, County Kerry. On arrival, she had sores on the soft parts of her body and weighed only fifteen kilograms—far less than a healthy loggerhead should. She was put on a saline drip, her sores dressed. She was named Una, after the woman who found her. With the improving weather, a fresh gush of refugees are risking the crossing to Europe, and so it is necessary for the Irish navy to send ships again. Once the sanctuary staff have fed Una back up to a weight of twenty-three kilograms, to strength and health, they contact the Irish Naval Service and inquire as to whether it might be possible for one of the ships deploying to the Mediterranean for humanitarian duties to deliver the stranded, mended loggerhead turtle back to a suitable environment. Also onboard the LÉ *Róisín* in May is a consignment of two hundred woolen teddy bears knitted by members and friends of the Church of Ireland Mothers' Union. They are to be gifted to rescued children.

Una is lifted from a timber box on a rubber dinghy. Just for a second, she is held aloft at the edge of the rubber boat, as if in explanation of the situation, as if to ensure she appreciates the long way she has come and all she has suffered, and that what this represents is a passage into safety.

Splash, slap, slap, slap, sink; an angelic dinosaur is returned to her home waters.

Soul on the Tide

CARL SAFINA

Sometimes I get this image that my soul, anchored along the shore, floats in and out on the waxing and waning tides. In fact my actual house, between the shore dunes and the pines, anchors me on this coastal mooring. In metaphor, my life vessel swings in the tides of time. Sometimes gently. Sometimes inner storms rage and my vessel bucks, and this mooring-place is what steadies me.

Many a *house* could do—but it could scarcely be just any *place*. My place is on the eastern end of Long Island, New York, a hundred-plus miles closer to dawn than New York City and way out past where the island—which is named "Long" for a reason—splits into two forks that poke eastward for another forty miles. I'm near the east end of the south fork, the one that holds the ocean on its south and safe-keeps a bevy of bays and islands on its north in the scissored expanse between itself and its sibling northern fork. At night or during storms I can often hear the ocean surf along the south side of our narrow fork, but my little house is on the bay side, along the gentle shore facing Block Island Sound. So, like I said, not just any place. For me the meaning of home is the place where, when you arrive from wide wanderings, you can harbor your heart right where it wants to be. My place is a special anchorage—for some good reasons.

The light: that's one thing. The seasons, another. The haunts of varied waters—ocean, harbor, sound, marshes—another yet. Together, they sum to one place, this holy trinity of coast, season, light.

And what is it about the light here? Is it that the waters reflect light up into the clouds, which suffuse it back so that, between water and sky in the vapor off the sea, the light doesn't so much shine as glow? I'm not sure what causes it, but I'm sure that at times, usually in calm airs, the light here becomes glorious.

Other things—more obvious to me than the widely appreciated light—seem overlooked by others. "I've been coming here every summer for forty years," one summer-neighbor told me, "and I've never seen any of the things you talk about." I wasn't sure how to gently suggest that there's more to the place than wine and cheese. Visitors here to Long Island's water-borne east end come, overwhelmingly, for scenery and socials. Those who seem most outgoing seem least likely to actually go outside. For many, there is one season (summer), one acceptable forecast (sunny), one place (the beach), one animal (deer), one bird (seagull). It's not that I don't like spending time with people—some of my best friends are human—it's just that few people are more interesting than an hour spent outside.

Some people appreciate what they have and some don't, and appreciation seems to have a lot to do with going outside. At a recent dinner party the host complained of her dissatisfaction with her kitchen cabinets and the location of her stove (both of which looked spotless and perfect to me), and her fear of aging gracelessly. She fretted as though reordering her countertops might gain her some reprieve from time. I share, of course, her all-too-human fear. But I write myself a different prescription: never mind what you have; attend to deeper meanings and things that matter. Right outside her door a large and beautiful bay stood ready to grant as much timelessness as is available. She asked if we had herons around here, or maybe egrets; she'd seen a bird. There were herons visible right now from her dock, I replied. Great blues. And though I said nothing, I thought about how much more than with cabinets and countertops might she have enhanced her surroundings, how much more outer and inner beauty might she have summoned, if we'd simply sat on her dock watching those herons as the shifting daylight altered the blues and hues of their layered feathers, if we'd let them show us the grace in all living things, reminding us in their stately patience that life is its own affirmation.

As the sun went down, a beautiful full moon rose like a ripe peach. Oh, I could have done something with that moon! And with only three moons per summer I felt the loss acutely as I sat on her gorgeous patio listening to the list of complaints my host was lodging against her spotless cabinets and sturdy stove. The moon, I knew, was urging the ocean tides into fierce, powerful motion. The full moon of August creates perhaps the best tide of the year for hunting our greatest inshore fish: huge striped bass. The biggest fish feed when the tide runs hardest. During the many days between new and full moons when the current is less urgent, those big fish make themselves so spread out and scarce that they seem nonexistent. During the exceptional incoming current that occurs on the full-moon tide, though, the whole sea off the point runs over drowned boulder ridges like a mile-wide river. And then thirty- to forty-pound fish gather for their nighttime hunt. Such a big and meaty being surging and throbbing on your taut line in the darkness means feeling and stealing a little of that tide-stemming power; it means that for only one death inflicted one reaps many meals to share with a story behind them. This calm, moon-bright evening was among the best few nights of the short summer—of the year—to obtain some very good food in the oldest and most satisfying way: by the adventure of catching it.

But for me that night there would be no fishing, and the moon would remain just an object in the sky, and no amount of howling—were I inclined—could narrow that gap.

Had I been shrewder I would have declined the dinner party, sending respectful regrets. And then I could have headed to the boat, but not before sharing sundown with my across-the-street neighbors J. P. and Marilyn, who are the greatest aficionados of skies, cloudscapes, and sunsets. In their eighties, they live in a shack that J. P.'s father built in the 1930s for one hundred and fifty dollars' worth of building supplies. It's tiny—maybe four hundred square feet—crammed with mementoes and artifacts. J. P. and Marilyn happen to own what has been time-ripened into several million dollars' worth of land. But they are wise enough to keep their shack and sand dune and sky, where the spirit has unlimited room to roam and the mind to muse, and the sunsets are world class. Any material trade "up" would be a decisive spiritual downgrade. Smart people. Rooted, appreciative. Living in their tiny shack, their mansion of gratitudes.

❖

Ours is a locale of riches generously offered, seldom sought. The ever-changing light, the ever-shifting migrations of creatures of the waters and the skies, the woodlands and the wetlands; the place welcomes more intimate looks. Put in some time, surprises begin to come.

Because I like looking for things, I favor a calm overcast. Diffuse light, soft shadows, a low sun, the golds of dawn and dusk; these I prefer. As with painting or photography, so for the eye itself. For richness of color and the sightings of nonhuman beings, I look to both ends of the day while the sun is near contact with the horizon. Any season. There's a lot to see, especially because we live along the waterlines.

Water makes the world kin; its fluidity a great conveyor. And in addition to the coast, we have the luck of latitude. Our particular latitude is a kind of crossroads. In the span of a year here, arctic migrants and tropical animals cross tracks. One can see a snowy owl on a frigid dune in February, overlooking the same bay that by summer's end will float sea turtles and tropical butterfly fishes. Compared to almost anywhere, we enjoy wide possibilities.

So many animals are always on the move, that each month seems its own season. The birds and fishes, the turtles and whales, come and go in epic migrations. More than once, a spring morning has brought me one hundred loons along the beach; a summer morning one hundred whales far at sea; an autumn morning ten thousand swallows in the marsh. And even a winter morning on the "empty" beach finds sanderlings scurrying between the wipe of waves, in the narrow span of sand between tides.

✦

Like today. Mild day and a mild swell, a snoring surf. And there, scurrying along—sanderlings.

These sanderlings breed high in the Arctic in the short flare of summer. They spend winter as far south as Patagonia, but some winter this far north, keeping us Long Islanders company in the sparest time of year. So I see some in every season. They're usually busy probing food from the wet sand in the moments between waves, their bills bobbing like needles on sewing machines, working one of the thinnest threads of habitat on Earth.

Once, from my kayak, I was watching about twenty sanderlings mixed with a few dunlins and ruddy turnstones on the shoreline. Suddenly a merlin streaked meteorically past me. Despite all the flock's eyes, the alarm went up too late. Unlucky timing. The merlin struck the last bird rising, pinning it to the sand with its talons while steadying itself with wings and tail feathers spread tripod-like. But when a rushing wave threatened to inundate them both, the merlin let go and the sanderling achieved an unlikely escape. Lucky timing.

And so as you can tell by all these stories, here's a thing that makes it *home*: experiences connect time. What you've seen enriches whatever you see, even when you're not seeing much.

✦

Beyond the breakers, those ducks over there—they're called surf scoters. They, too, nest in the Arctic. No one knows how the word *scoter* originated. Yet two other scoter species, white-winged and black, live in the open ocean here all winter, never coming ashore, never taking cover of any kind—no matter the bitter gales or the long and frigid nights. Eiders, red-breasted mergansers—they all stay absolutely dry and adequately warm in their duck-down jackets, save their feet. And to save their bare feet the prospect of draining their core body heat into the insatiable frigidity of the sea, the blood vessels in their legs form a countercurrent heat exchanger. Blood going to their feet passes through an intermeshed system of capillaries so that before the warm blood from their body goes into their feet, its heat is transferred to cooled blood coming back from their toes. Warming the returning blood sends the warmth back into the body before it could drain away into the cold ocean through bare toes and webbing, conserving their precious heat of life.

Eastward off the tip of the beach at Montauk Point, sea ducks pile in by the tens of thousands for the whole winter. The food necessary to sustain thirty thousand ducks for months ... If each bird eats—I'll guess—a quarter pound of food a day for three months, that would be 675,000 pounds of mussels, little crabs, and the like.

A few harlequin ducks—stunning in their boldly harlequin-patterned blue and white and russet plumage—sometimes spend winter among the surf boulders at a place called Ditch Plains, though never on the open-sand beaches. Why? I'm not sure. The mysteries are many.

The big white birds flying a little farther offshore are gannets. They follow the herring of autumn. When they fold up and plunge, they send geysers of spray. Just like that one, yes; and sometimes a big flock, hundreds, will hurl themselves like thunderbolts, like white missiles into the sea. And when we're out in the fall fishing for anything that's chasing herring, from bluefish to tuna, gannets will be around us. Canadian breeders, they winter from here all the way down to the Gulf of Mexico. Hundreds got oiled in the BP Deepwater Horizon blowout, but there were plenty saved from that nightmare mess by the sheer vernal luck of having already started back north on the breath of lengthening days.

Recently we've been a bit concerned about the loons. Right before they travel northward in May, loons molt their flannel pajamas for plush new satin breeding plumage. Just beautiful. But in autumn they arrive when the fish are migrating and the nets are many, and we sometimes find them drowned and washed ashore. We'd like to do something about that. But you meet resistance when nets are all some people have spanning the continual gap between themselves and unpaid bills.

The challenges are many, yes. But not everything is getting scarcer. Animals that are much more abundant now than when I was a kid include, to mention a few, the long-winged ospreys, the sea bass, and the whales. In recent years I've even seen whales from shore. Falcons are back. Eagles are coming back—there's a lot of recovery going on.

Way up ahead—is that just driftwood? My binoculars reveal an almost horselike profile: gray seal. We usually see harbor seals. Thanks to legal protection that works *most* of the time, they're both recovering from the depletion brought by fishermen's enmity. Sometimes, our visitor will be a harp seal, having been born on Canadian ice as one of the famous white-coated pups so infamously slaughtered for fur by the hundreds of thousands. And still they come, as if forgiving us, or begging mercy.

✦

All seasons bring their triumphs and their tragedies. For me the most triumphal season is summer. Watching the world grow back, fill up.

Ospreys attending their huge stick-nests, so many fishes. Travel just a few miles from shore and the green water changes to clear blue in the realm of dolphins and shearwaters and sharks and turtles.

I think of them all—and I don't mean this just metaphorically—as my neighbors. That's who they are. It's who we all are. We live here and we all search for our food in the same waters. When I'm searching for fish I often seek the counsel of seabirds. They are professional fish-finders, and following them has allowed me to put many a fine meal on my table.

Following the terns also allowed me to catch my first inkling of how rapidly the ocean is changing. For a decade I studied terns formally and intensively. Their breeding, feeding, hatching, the growth and survival of chicks. For my graduate studies I put numbered leg bands on thousands of just-hatched tern chicks. Two were found breeding on Great Gull Island just across the Sound from where we're standing, *twenty-five years* after I banded them. Think of it: migrating each year from Long Island to South America and back, no shelter of any kind, for two and a half decades.

For studying them I'd earned the degree of Doctor of Philosophy in Ecology. I thought, why "Philosophy"? It took thirty years for me to realize how much philosophy there is in watching terns, to understand that in all of philosophy there is only one important question: How ought we live? These creatures provide answers that have withstood the test of deep time.

You don't sense the answers during ceaseless travels; you see them by coming home, and letting a few decades coil up in the same spot, giving your mind the room to consider what the world beyond our human borders all means, having the courage to ask whether it means anything at all, and having the humility to realize that it means everything.

❖

Each season brings certain rituals in specific haunts. As early as February we witness one of the strangest, most seemingly unlikely migrations. Even on frosted nights, and especially after rains, salamanders come out of woodland burrows and somehow navigate hundreds of yards to little freshwater pools, meeting other salamanders, producing and fertilizing eggs. Standing in nighttime woods amidst fallen logs, it's difficult imagining salamanders, at a cold crawl, successfully navigating to tiny half-frozen ponds.

Wearing warm boots and rainproof jackets we find marbled, blue-spotted, and tiger salamanders. Theirs is a strange life. And it gets stranger. Our blue-spotted salamander is a rare form of the species living in Montauk at Long Island's tip, and in Nova Scotia, and almost nowhere else. Blue-spotteds have a bizarre reproductive résumé. In most of their range, they're almost all female. To breed, they have to mate with a male—and any related species will do. But while they require sperm penetration of the egg cell to initiate embryo development, the egg usually *discards the sperm's genes*—and begins *cloning* itself. But the sperm's genome, not so easily jilted, is often incorporated into the fetus in the form of an added genome. Isn't that bizarre? And why? No one knows. Again, we may note, the mysteries are many. The result: animals with extra sets of genes, called polyploids. But sometimes the male genome may even replace part of the female genome. The scientists who managed to figure all this out termed this reproductive mode "kleptogenesis." Stolen beginnings. I'm not sure what's more amazing, the biology or the naturalists who perceived it all.

The salamanders of late winter are followed in those same ponds by the spring peepers whose chorus is surely among nature's most joyful noises. As Emerson said, each moment of the year has its own beauty. The seasons turn our one time, our moment here, into so many different times. The habitats turn this one place, our place, into so many different places. The migrants who span the hemisphere in their continual comings and goings let us travel more and more widely by staying rooted. We're so spoiled. And the more we look around here, the more we spoil ourselves.

On a good day here, a skilled birder can sight a hundred species and a skilled fisher can catch a hundred-pound fish and a practiced clammer can carry home a hundred clams. Not everyone from this place can do all these things. Skill and know-how is still required. But the *place*—this special, varied place—makes the people who can. Those are the people not just *from* but *of* this place.

I want to live up to the place, to honor it. And sharing helps to honor it, and by honoring I hope to help keep it. And if I help keep it, perhaps I've justified my existence a little bit. Is *home* the place where one justifies one's existence? Is that how one makes a home from a mere place? Is a *sense of place* the rooted relatedness to something larger that makes us better? Is it the feeling that comes when a place inspires us to belong to it as our home? Increasingly—after decades—I apprehend the miraculous in the mundane. The sparkle of water. Miraculous! Minnows in a bucket. Miraculous! The warmth ignited from a pile of cold wood as freezing wind shrieks across the icy bay—miraculous! Knowing during long, languid days and long, cold nights that seasons turn and tides flow in and out; that for now I am right here with my soul afloat, moored safely in this ancient feeling called home. Miraculous.

To Live

GRETEL EHRLICH

No longer safe anywhere, I don't care if I live or die, nor would I act only for my own safety, but I would like to visit a favorite place: the water-stained revetment, the copse of aspens, the small river flowing through a valley of willows filled with moose and birds. I will walk there and stay for a while. My family of one. The kelpie and me.

I take off as soon as the half-moon appears. Clouds dissolve and Venus is rubbed bright. I walk on dead leaves and crumbling grass—a charnel ground of mashed up beauty—up and up, past a cluster of wild raspberries, the fruit all gone, past the waterfall. Heat has drained couloirs of their plugs of old snow. I climb up to the open plateaus above and lie on spent wildflowers pillowing my head on pine boughs. When daylight comes, I sleep. There was no way to see when the dew arrived. It was just there. Gift of the night air, I harvest it because there's no water elsewhere.

When it's time to leave, I walk backward, a contrary clown, back, back, up, up, until, on a ridge where bits of glacier ice remain, I gnaw at a chunk and swallow ten-thousand-year-old meltwater.

Much later, maybe days or weeks, I descend. Welcome to the nightmare, the kelpie barks in greeting.

❖

We are born on a road or beside it or in some hospital near a big river that becomes a road, leading to smaller unpaved ones that reach into the heart of a mountain or a dry savannah or a plain of melting sea ice, places where it's said we have an innate longing to be.

In western Zimbabwe recently, I entered a parched world. The road to my friend's camp was covered with wind-blown coral-colored Kalahari sand, and the rivers were dry. A lid of smoke wreathed the sky: millions of hectares are burned each year—creating heat-absorbing bare ground and polluting the air.

Near my thatched-roof mud hut, great trees spread shade, but because of the drought, the seedpods were empty and the animals that came for that food went away hungry. A rock enclosure was made in the dry streambed and filled with fresh water from a borehole. Birds, bushbuck, kudu, impala, warthogs, baboons, monkeys, giraffe, water buffalo, and elephants came to drink. Only the primates and elephants had young. Most of the others not because they were unable to sustain a calf or baby with so little forage and water. The die-off had long since begun.

❖

An editor asked me to write about hearth—a flat place where a fire can be built. A floor. A solid space on which we can stand, sit, or warm ourselves, and cook food. How absurd the task seems now as the Arctic crashes, and we are being fast-tracked politically toward accelerated albedo loss and its many consequences.

The glaciologists I've talked to since 1997 understood two decades ago that the time to stop or mitigate global heating was limited, and that doing nothing was tantamount to suicide. The whole concept of home and hearth now seems like a cruel joke. We've run out of time to settle down, to make a place for the unborn, to plant a sequoia tree that will live three thousand years, to sire, mother, transmit, pass on. Forget Oxford and Harvard, forget the great libraries, forget we even heard about the burned Library of Alexandria with its five hundred thousand scrolls, its visiting scholars, lecture halls, and gardens. Forget discussions of a future. Erase all that. We are navigating our way toward ruin. At the Paris climate conference, the rapper Aku-Matu from Kaktovik, Alaska, sang: "I am the Ancestor of the future. Why is it so hot here?"

❖

In that delicious moment before waking before we can imagine we are still living in the interglacial paradise in which we were born and have thrived.

When we dare, we indulge ourselves and remember how it was. Then the Trumpian horrors that await us come into view.

I grew up in a modern half-glass redwood house in California. Its three fireplaces had raised hearths where, in winter months, we warmed ourselves by the fire. Much later, the ranch I lived on in the Bighorn Mountains was heated with wood. We burned ten or eleven cords a winter. The centrality of fireplace, woodstove, or cookstove shaped how we lived in that space. Time was measured in logs, not hours. The hundred-year-old house was made of gyp block—akin to a dissolving aspirin—and the floors, walls, and ceiling were uninsulated. Most important was the fire itself—the hearth—because those were the days when winter came hard and rarely was a night warmer than twenty below.

I lost that ranch after an accident and a divorce, and began traveling by dogsled with subsistence Inuit hunters in northwest Greenland. My Greenland friends became a family of sorts, and I spent months with them for twenty-three years until the sea ice had become unpredictable. At seventy-eight degrees latitude north their Wilsonian longing for home was not for green savannah, but for great expanses of white—of ice and snow-covered ice. Intense cold was not considered an enemy. They had no wood to burn. Hearth was a calm frigid place where sea ice could form, where the panting of sled dogs was the national song.

Earth House Hold, the poet Gary Snyder titled a book of essays. It could have been Ice House Hold. We lived on the ice for weeks at a time, eating what the men caught—ringed seal or walrus boiled in melted multiyear ice. Camp consisted of two dogsleds pushed together with a canvas tarp thrown over a ridgepole, and four of us: Jens, Gedeon, Mamarut, and me, squeezed together on frigid nights. In storms we slept in tiny huts with a haunch of walrus dripping blood by the *ileq*—the platform where we lay down caribou skins with our sleeping bags on top. Ice, snow on ice, the mounded, gleaming Greenland ice sheet filled our eyes and minds with delight.

But the ice didn't hold. That hearth—the culture of the extended family groups that coevolved with and was dependent on ice—is gone.

So is life as we have known it everywhere. First, ranch grief besieged me, then ice grief. I've been on my hands and knees pounding the floor and sobbing as the ice melts, as we lose albedo, as die-offs mount up, and though there's been no doubt that life is transient, chance, and change, I hadn't anticipated the scale of loss, of the many worlds, cultural and bio-logical—wholes within wholes—gone with no hope of return.

❀

I've moved a lot. It started slowly, then accelerated to something like twenty-three moves, as if mimicking the accelerated collapse of the Greenland ice sheet. Maybe that's why the Greenlanders said I must have been born on a moving dogsled, and why the traditional architecture of Japan has always appealed: the shoeless glide on tatami that still smelled like grass, and shoji doors that slid, opening onto emptiness.

The frail houses, shacks, and tents I've lived in have been more home than any house, and I've loved them all: canvas-wall tents fitted with foldable woodstoves; backpackers' tents, easy to put up, take down, and lightweight; tipis of sewn-together reindeer skins, raised on poles; or sheep wagons that can be pulled from place to place, ship tight and simple with a rounded top. Or a bivy sac perched on the ledge of a vast mountain.

Home is the horse I rode fifteen hundred miles a year, the cow dogs who traveled alongside, slept with me, and for whom I cooked scrambled eggs, elk steaks, and buttered toast. Or the sled pulled by three reindeer across the melting tundra of the Russian Arctic, or the Greenland sled dogs that often saved our lives.

Home is anywhere I've taken the time to notice. Where there is no "I." It shouldn't be called a sense of place, but a flat-out, intimate sensorium where Emerson's dictum suddenly makes sense: "I am nothing. I see all."

Intimacy requires time. Time requires devotion. Devotion demands surrender. Surrender means sponging in the whole: season, light, smell, moving shadow, every dark place, every one that is bright.

❀

Nostalgia is the ornament with which we decorate memory. Parent, house, car, horse, beach, sidewalk, school, sibling, boyfriend. We tangle with love and loss, injustice, disappointment, with inexplicable birth and certain death, with illusion. Finally able to drop personal history from our minds, it pops up again, if only to keep us on our toes, to make us laugh.

I was the night calver at the ranch and checked heifers on cross-country skis. Other years I moved through the seasons on the back of a horse, by sailboat across the Barents Sea, or by a pack canoe in arctic Alaska.

I spent three months in a tent on a glacial moraine where a friend was building a cabin for me and developed an aversion to "home" as I watched the walls go up, the windows arriving. When I told him that a closed-up house seemed like poison, he didn't stop to put the hammer down, just laughed and kept building.

Every camp, sled, tipi, or boat has been a kind of home, a place to perch, the wilder the better, with rocks holding down the edges of the sleeping bag to keep it from being blown away. Above tree line in the Brooks Range or out a New York City door, wildness shows itself. Cockroach and grizzly, the month-long hikes into the Sierras, Bighorns, Winds, and Crazies, the macadamia nut farm in the North Pacific Ocean, and the wind-shorn prairie homestead.

Every step outside is a complete meal. The old Navajo directive toward "beauty and harmony" has been there for us. Up all night in a New England forest during sugaring, it was explained to me that the maple's streaming sweetness courses upward, a sap flow that de-pends not on stasis but fluctuation, of warmth and cold pushing sap up and out a wound in the trunk, boiled for hours, and drunk down like nectar.

Movement is everything, and so with us. We don't need the stable in any sense of the word, nor does the horse. We can no longer demand what we want and get it. The horse tried to teach that to us long ago, but we went on with our undisciplined needs.

We pour foundations without asking for permission and expect the mountain to bow down, the stream to fill, the grassland to stay green. We search catalogues for the generative sprouting seed engineered for fruition. We grasp and reject, we stumble forever inept and desperate for this paradise in which to embed ourselves, yet can't empty and open our minds, or find the interior door through which a mountain can enter.

At best, home is a momentary thing. Under the rugs at the long-ago ranch house were taped-together topographical maps of the entire region. We often rolled the rugs back, not to dance—though we did that, too— but to try to understand exactly where we lived and who our animal and botanical neighbors were. Soon it became clear that no static point on a map, no home address, no parental house, no structure or furnishing could locate us. Only elevation, water course, meadow, mountain, seasonal shift, animal migration could tell us where we were. But not why, nor was that question necessary.

❖

Hearth is time as much as place. The time it takes for three pine logs to burn. It is historical context times birth hour. We are each nonspecific and utterly unique, scurrying for a slot in a city or for a patch of meadow in some untrodden place in an overcrowded world. Yet sometimes we long for home. For a moment by the fire, a cuddle under a down quilt, a kerosene lamp on a dark night, or, when very hungry, a plate of food, or a plea for unconditional love. Don't look back, Dylan reminds us, or was that Theseus?

These days, I wear red jeans and black shirts: red for fury, black for grief. But what color signifies our indisputable integration with the mountain under our feet—or the subway stairs?

In the beginning there was exile. From fetal intimacy to polluted air. From a vade mecum womb to an ambivalent or serially absent mother and father. Family is a cultural construct that can be elusive. Blood-links can vanish or sour. When things get very difficult, which elder will instruct us? What animal or song or dance or place will teach us how to behave?

Once, seriously hungry in northern Greenland, I was shocked by my atavistic behavior. I hoarded a tiny piece of salami—not from others, but from myself—saving it for a day when I was hungrier, then found it had rotted. I dreamed about lavish meals but on return home couldn't eat solids. I swam through constant hallucinations as I trudged along, not quite sure in which mirage I was drowning.

So much of our privileged lives consist of flyovers. We wander, not as the ancient Chinese hermit-poets did, but in jets and commuter planes, a Cessna or caravan, wondering how we will recognize the proper site on which to build the hearth. We lurch from place to place, supplanting alpine vistas with desert, sand dune with cityscape, urban comfort with brutal open oceans, and back again, forgetting to cut through habitual thought so we can see what's actually there.

Flying for hours over virgin forests, rippling grasslands, whitecapped oceans, we can't seem to get close enough. The eye grows hungry. The road grows hungry for our feet. But on arrival at our destination—one of our many "theres"—we find we've already exhausted a world we haven't taken the time to touch.

So much has gone missing: abalone, giraffe, snow goose, reedbuck. I applaud the lawyers who advocate for the rights and "personhood" of a river, mountain, desert, or animal—humans last, please. When talking about "saving the planet," which we have failed to do, people speak only of saving it for their grandchildren, never for the sake of the Earth itself. Why bother to save it for humans who will just destroy it again? We live in a culture of abuse and untruth, a carelessness so profound it has the power to kill us off in a way more sorrowful than any disease.

❁

In my Greenland "home" the conditions in which sea ice can form have disappeared. In west Antarctica, Pine Island Glacier cracks and slides into an ever-warmer sea. At Dibangombe, in Africa, the river is thirsty, the great herds diminished, and the trees are dead. Last week in Montana, seven hundred snow geese, lost in a storm, landed on a toxic mine pool and died.

Takuss, a Greenlander might have said once. It means "see you soon" in a loving way. Maybe not. I still try to grow vegetables, herbs, and fruit. At dawn, I collect dew and sprinkle it on my garden.

New Home: An Excerpt from the Novel *Tazkira*

INTIZAR HUSAIN

Translated from Urdu by Alok Bhalla and Nishat Zaidi

"**B**ete Akhlaq, what wilderness have you dumped us in? Even the sound of the azaan does not reach this godforsaken place." She would pause and begin again, "Arre, I had warned him against moving to this place miles away from nowhere. But your father cast such a spell that I couldn't think. Ae lo, he passed away in peace soon after coming here and left us to deal with this bleak forest. How can one live in a place like this? I haven't even heard the call of an unfortunate street vendor. All one hears from morning till evening is the *caw, caw* of crows. Arre, I'll become a heart patient if we continue to live here."

In a way, Bu Jan was right. She had recently migrated from Chiragh Haveli where there was so much hustle and bustle from morning till night that the betel-nut cracker in her hands never stopped clattering inside the zenana, and the tray of paan made its rounds continuously in the men's quarters outside. But here, the evenings were haunted by ghostly silence. It's not as if the days were full of noisy activity. And how could they have been? There wasn't a house or a shop nearby. Only a few small houses were scattered here and there in the vicinity. From a distance they appeared to be uninhabited. A little away from them there was a broken gate. Every summer at dawn, one could find five or six carts loaded with slabs of ice stopped outside it. In fact, an ice factory was located there. Once the carts left, the road was empty again. During the day, one heard only the chirping and screeching birds that flew in and out of the dense trees in the area. The shadow of crows seemed to cover the entire sky. Except for the small houses, the surroundings were covered with trees that changed color with the change of seasons: dark green leaves turned yellow and brown. In spring, the leaves were so dense that it was difficult to guess how many processions of birds flew in and out of them. In autumn, when the trees shed their leaves they appeared dry and dead. But as soon as spring returned and fresh leaves sprouted, even the driest of branches were clothed again in rich green leaves. Flocks of birds found ways of playing hide-and-seek in the trees and lay foundations for new nests. Even the courtyard of my house had several trees. One of them was a maulsari, whose tender fragrance filled the air in spring. The other was a sprawling peepal tree. These two trees were enough for me, and I didn't make any effort to find out about the others.

In fact, the home I lived in was the annex of an abandoned redbrick building known as Lal Kothi. Who had forcibly occupied it now? I never tried to find out. Occasionally, a heavy-set man in soiled clothes could be seen going in and out of it on a bicycle. He never tried to introduce himself and exchange pleasantries nor did I make the effort. When he did introduce himself, it was only to inform me that the entire building had been allotted to him. Without any further discussion, I accepted my status as a tenant. When he saw the matter so amicably settled without an argument, he, too, made no demands. He happily accepted me as a tenant. Then a few days later, he locked the house, gave me his address, and left for Multan where he had been allotted a wheat mill. As I noted down his address, I learnt that his name was Barkat Ilahi. Every month, punctually, I sent him a money order for my rent.

Initially, I felt disoriented here. These surroundings were as alien to me as they were to Bu Jan. But slowly, along with the trees and birds, the surroundings became a part of my being. Every morning, when I went out for a walk, the isolation of the place seemed to touch the recesses of my heart. Ancient monuments, with their air of antiquity and desolation, make a deep impression on us and their impact can be felt. Here, however, there were no remains of old buildings that could leave their imprint on one's feelings.

The house was built on a large, low-lying plot of land where a few broken, dust-covered steps made from the decorative nanakshahi bricks from the Mughal era were partly visible. One morning, absorbed in my solitary contemplation of the land as it was slowly lit by the rising the sun, a stranger, brushing his teeth with a neem twig, joined me. Morning walks instill a sense of comradeship in men. Strangers begin to exchange pleasantries: comments about the weather first turn into a discussion about politics and world affairs, and then into a more intimate conversation, as if the men had known each other for ages. At first that man and I chatted with each other about this and that; but as we walked on together for a while, I don't know how or why we continued to talk and talk. Then, quite causally, I asked about the desolate, uninhabited ground we were walking through.

He replied, "This is Sita Kund!"

"Sita Kund?"

"Aho ji! Sita Mai used to bathe nearby."

"Sita Mai? Do you mean Sita ji? When did Sita ji ever come here?"

"That's what is said. This city was founded by her son. A mother, after all, lives with her son."

I didn't quite believe the legend but it aroused my curiosity about the place. I quietly resolved to seriously explore the story further. I thought I would do so on Sunday morning when I didn't have to go to work and would be more relaxed. But something happened before Sunday that made me change my mind and lose interest in the place. Barkat Ilahi suddenly returned from Multan and announced: "Now ji, I will live here!"

"Really?"

"Yes ji, an abandoned shop has been allotted to me in Anarkali."

"How about the mill allotted to you in Multan?"

"That too will continue. I've left my employee there."

"Well, it's good that you are back. This house is in urgent need of repairs."

"Yes ji, I will have to do something about this place as well." Looking around at the surroundings, he said, "It's overgrown with trees and bushes. I will clear the area and build shops here. I have learnt that this place is going to be declared a commercial area. These shops will then turn into gold mines."

"But what about these trees?"

"I'll cut them all down."

"What? You will cut down these trees?" Anxious and shocked, I stared at his face in disbelief.

"Yes, why not? Why should the place lie unused, especially when it can fetch good money?"

I was very worried. I suddenly remembered the maulsari and peepal trees to which I had become so attached.

"But this maulsari tree?"

"Yes ji. This maulsari is occupying a lot of space."

I continued to stare at his face. "But this peepal tree is very old."

"Yes ji. It's very old. It too needs to be chopped down. I'll take care of them in a day or two. The entire place has turned into a jungle. It'll have to be cleared."

"So soon?" I was very worried.

"Yes ji! Once I decide, I don't hesitate or delay. But you needn't worry. I'm not going to touch the building for the time being. I'll think about it later. You can continue to live here. I'll not ask you to vacate it."

"No, you won't have to ask." Saying this, I walked away. He kept surveying the trees for a long time.

❖

"Son, have you gone mad? I tell you, we should not leave this place. How long can we move like nomads with our pots and pans from one place to another?" Bu Jan had gradually reconciled herself to the place that she had earlier called a wilderness. But I had lost interest in it.

"No, Bu Jan! We'll not live in this house anymore. This Barkat Ilahi is a man without any grace."

"Bete," Bu Jan sighed. "There is no grace left in the world now. Besides, why should we bother about that wretch? We'll remain huddled in our own corner."

"By the way, I have already rented another house."

"OK. As you wish. I was only concerned about your troubles. I am very old now. Who will do the packing and cart the luggage?"

"Everything will be taken care of. You only have to give instructions. We'll move in the morning."

"Ai hi, you should've taken some time. Such haste is not good."

"Bu Jan, once we have decided to leave, why delay?"

"You seem to be possessed."

Yes, I was possessed. How could I explain to Bu Jan that in the morning men will arrive to cut down the trees and I wanted to leave before that calamity?

I spent the night with difficulty. I kept tossing in bed till late into the night and slept just before the dawn only to wake up again when I heard the rooster call. I stood up as though I had not slept at all. I splashed water on my face, folded my shirtsleeves and pajamas, and began packing. There wasn't much to pack. It was not like the luggage we had in Chiragh Haveli. If one lives in a place for long, one accumulates household goods. We had not yet settled here. We had only a few things for our daily needs. How many times Bu Jan had complained to me, "Bete, I can't sit on my haunches and work. Once I sit down, I am unable to get up. Get me a low stool. And I have asked you again and again to buy a rolling pin! You should have bought it along with the tongs and the blowing-pipe." But I bought neither a stool nor the rolling pin for her. That should give an idea of how much luggage we had. By the time the sun rose, I had finished my packing.

Then I went out to take a breath of fresh air. I decided not to go for my morning walk. I thought I would like to meet my neighbors for one last time; my last day here was also the last day of their lives. We met. I was sad. But they bore no sign of regret. On the contrary, at the touch of morning sunlight, they seemed to be smiling. More than others, the peepal and the maulsari trees stood in their majestic grace, neither exuberant nor gloomy, but silent. After all, there was no wind at that time. I took a deep breath under the shade of maulsari, picked up a few tiny flowers from the ground under its shade, and went back into the house.

Bu Jan had finished saying her morning prayers and was busy making breakfast. I quickly ate my breakfast.

"Ai Beta, did you not sleep at all in the night?"

"Why, Bu Jan, why wouldn't I sleep?"

"Ai Beta, when I woke up in the morning, you were already puttering around."

"Bu Jan, you got up late today. I woke up with the first call of the rooster."

"Yes, maybe I got up late this morning." After a pause, she said, "Son, you have packed everything, but who will carry the luggage? Have you arranged for it or shall we carry this junk on our heads?"

"Bu Jan, there are carts in the ice factory. I have arranged for two of them. Once they finish carting the ice, they will come here. They must be already on their way. We will hire a tonga from the vicinity."

As soon as I finished my breakfast, I went out to look for the carts and make sure that they had found their way. The woodcutters had already arrived with their axes and saws. Barkat Ilahi was giving them instructions.

"See, Barkat Ilahi Sahib, I had made a request yesterday."

"What ji?" He became nervous at my harsh tone.

"I asked you to cut the trees only after we had left."

"Yes ji. But you will leave today. This is what you said yesterday."

"Yes, we are leaving today; in fact, now. But let no tree be axed till we have left."

"Very well, ji." He quickly turned to the woodcutters. "Ai bhai, look, go and have some tea. The work will start only after Akhlaq Sahib leaves this place."

The woodcutters stared at me in surprise. They continued to stare even after I turned away from them and walked toward the gate of the house. When I looked back, I saw Barkat Ilahi whispering something to the woodcutters. I heard only one sentence: "That man is a little crazy."

The carts arrived. So did the tonga. I quickly loaded our luggage on the carts. Then I helped Bu Jan sit on the rear seat of the tonga along with her bag and bundle. I carried a few things in my hand. I clutched the folder containing my father's papers under my arm and sat on the front seat.

How strangely the woodcutters stared at me as the tonga drove away! As soon as we reached the gate of the house, I heard the sound of an axe falling on the tree. Anxious, I turned around to see. The damned fellows had begun with the maulsari tree.

Home Is Elsewhere: Reflections of a Returnee
Boey Kim Cheng

There is a ghostly whisper in the air, an echo that feels braided of sight, sound, and smell, and which becomes more palpable as I walk around to the far end of the glitzy restaurant that is the current incarnation of Clifford Pier, the landing point for early immigrants and visitors to Singapore. Not more than three decades ago the greasy water around it was populated by huddled flotillas of bumboats and Chinese barges that ferried goods and passengers to and from the ships out on the sea roads; the moss- and barnacle-encrusted steps of the landing stage were laved by teal and tea-colored tides that brought in wrack, driftwood, the occasional coconut, and bracing smells of the sea, giving one the sense of expansive breadth, of horizons unlocked to the immense reaches of the Malay Archipelago and rumors of the world beyond. Once, just after turning eighteen, I watched *Death in Venice* at the British Council Theatrette across the road and came to the deserted pier for a smoke; as I inhaled the nicotine and salt-sea air, I experienced a fleeting transcendental moment, being borne aloft on a sampan to the soundtrack of Mahler's adagio and glimpsing before me the moonlit waters of the lagoon, the lido, and the moored gondolas, like the bumboats at anchor on the murky waters, their dark bobbing shapes a semaphore of promise and escape. I felt then that I could love this country, forget my quarrel with it, and stay.

This was the last place in Singapore I visited before emigrating in 1997. I covered the waterfront, to borrow the title of one of Billie Holiday's signature covers, incessantly in the years before I left. My walks through the Change Alley across from the pier, a tarpaulin- and zinc-roofed one-lane bazaar nestled between the Rubber House and the Winchester House, where you could buy anything under the sun, so the shop owners boasted, and through its upmarket neighbor, the Arcade, Moorish with its keyhole-arched windows and its twin onion-domed rooftop pavilions, and around the crumbling shophouses and godowns along the strong-smelling Singapore River, and then through the grand

Doric-columned General Post Office and other colonial edifices around Raffles Place, savoring the poignant odor of decay, would invariably circle back to this point, where the Singapore River decanted into the sea, where you could feel an exhilarating air. It wasn't just the smell of diesel from the chugging sampans, tongkangs, and bumboats, and the riotous mix of faces and bodies floating on the pier, but it was as if the air held a whiff of the essence and key to the city in the meeting of water and sea-wall, the soothing metronomic lapping of tidal water on the stone foundations of the city.

Now the water is tame and drained of character, its tidal cadences stilled as the Singapore River and the harbor off Collyer Quay have been turned into a huge water catchment. Bridging the gap between long elbows of reclaimed land is the Marina Barrage, erected to keep the seawater out. It is a shock to anyone who lived in the country in the '70s and '80s and has been away the last two decades to see this drastic transformation. Back then you could track the bumboats and tongkangs out to the sea roads where freighters and tankers rested on the gently heaving swell, drinking in the dazzling blue vista vague with hints of archipelagic islands; now the horizon is closed off, and the past has been eclipsed by the monumental three-towered Marina Bay Sands hotel capped by the longest rooftop swimming pool in the world and a plague of postmodern structures. Of the historical precinct around the waterfront itself, only a scattered few among the glorious colonial edifices have survived, like the Edwardian General Post Office, now a luxury hotel.

Previously, on return visits, whenever I came back for a walk around Collyer Quay, it was the ghost of the city I once knew that haunted my steps and hovered behind this global corporate stronghold. The Singapore of my childhood and of my father lay like a buried city, like the ancient Alexandria beneath the harbor, a pentimento only the X-ray vision of memory can glimpse. Now, as I arrive as an expatriate, it is something else. It is a strange word, *expatriate*, and I wear it like a mismatched shirt, or something I haven't grown into. I left Singapore a native and return a foreigner. I had to surrender my citizenship when I became Australian, as the Singapore government forbids dual citizenship—taking my place among the two million or more nonnative residents, new arrivals that the government has admitted to boost its falling and aging population. *Ex*, out of; *patria*, fatherland, home. Am I out of my home country or am I back home? My whole idea of Singapore, of home, started undergoing a process of revision and translation the moment I surrendered my Singapore passport. My idea of home has become mixed up in a way I could not have foreseen, in the years of living under a different sky, inhaling eucalypt-scented air, learning the varieties of gum trees, watching their leaves sieve the fierce sun, perceiving the pour of evening light on the Blue Mountains, the light strumming the scorched songlines of the ancient country, light that sometimes seems liquid, sometimes solid, lapidary, but always penetrating, pure, the light that bathes the harbor city in chords of didgeridoo-like chromatics. The light that hits you like homecoming as the plane enters Australian skies, and you realize how homesick you have been for it.

In the first few years of my life as a migrant it was clear to me that home was something I had left behind, and even as I renounced my citizenship and surrendered my Singapore passport, the rediscovered love of my place of birth seized me and filled me with pangs of misgiving and regret. Then, as the children arrived and I began writing about Singapore, reconstructing it brick by vanished brick, I found I could no longer keep the two apart, could no longer isolate that vast antipodean sunburnt country that is my adopted home from my place of birth. The two countries, two islands, really, not dissimilar in shape, have come together in some kind of migrational drift, my memories of Singapore infusing the new experiences as an immigrant, the bleached colors of Australia seeping into the lush equatorial palette, dyeing and altering my perceptions of the past. I started to see bifocally, to feel palimpsestically, the vastness of the driest continent in the world contained in the tiny equatorial frame and the tiny island turning up everywhere in the olive-toned bush, in the outback, in the red interior, and in the city whose heart seems to reside in the gleaming cusps of the Opera House. An in-between land seems to have arisen like a new country from the depths where deep waters of memory, imagination, and longing meet. In my travel memoir, *Between Stations*, I wrote about the liminal state of being a migrant:

> You are an emigrant to those you left behind and immigrant to your new friends. But in between the tags fall off. You lose the certainty of the state you are in, as though you are on a train whose front half rests in one state and whose back carriages lag in another. In between you pass the same stations again and again, stations whose names blur and become interchangeable and you forget if you have a destination.
>
> You get the sense that your whole life is a memory; you even remember things you have not lived through.

For an adult migrant who has spent half his life in his country of birth, the life in the new country can at times feel like an old story that is being revised or rewritten, rather than a new chapter or book waiting to be written. In the first few years of my settling down in Sydney, I had the impression that the life I had left behind in Singapore was still somehow continuing, that some doppelgänger was in my place, living the life I had decamped from, while I was reliving the past in a new life and country. It was supposed to be a clean slate, a fresh start, yet there were many moments that felt like déjà vu, where I was encountering the past anew, remembering the old places in new ones, experiencing the feel of the old and lost home in an elsewhere that I must now call home. I couldn't say the word *home* without stabs of uneasiness and guilt. It had become an alien, difficult concept; it had ceased to be a fixed point of reference. It was hard to feel at home when home had become disembodied, an ineffable idea, elusive, spectral.

❖

For five years after emigrating I did not visit Singapore, but Singapore visited me again and again, in dreams and waking reverie. I found myself not so much writing the present of new life in Australia as rewriting the past. I began to wonder if that is what all adult migrants do, reconstructing in memory and imagination the homeland they have forfeited, immersed in a project of remembrance of things past. Yet it wasn't so much a total recall as fractured, splintered memories, partial and unreliable, ghostly, coming in fits and starts, the most vividly real ones coming unbidden, seizing me by the throat or rising up in me so ineluctably that they must have been waiting for the right word or trigger to release them. One such involuntary memory occurred when I was walking on Pitt Street in Sydney, savoring the sensation of anonymity, browsing in the row of used music and bookstores that had adult shops discreetly sandwiched between them, the sidewalk awash with a dozen or more countries, the medley of faces and voices reflecting how far the city had come since the early '70s when Gough Whitlam's embrace of nondiscriminatory immigration opened the door to Asian migrants. My friend Andrew recalls that before Whitlam's open-door policy there were just a few Australian Chinese restaurants in the city outside of Chinatown, and the fare was invariably tailored to the bland Australian palate: sweet-and-sour pork, corn soup, Mongolian lamb, nothing too spicy. In the late '90s, Asian groceries and restaurants were starting to displace the porn, music, and bookstores on Pitt Street; one could sense the city was readying itself for the Asian century that was dawning. Something in the air on Pitt Street made me pause, tantalizing my senses, easing open the door of memory; perhaps it was the way the shaded sidewalk contrasted sharply with the blinding sunlight on the street, or the musty air of the bookstores, or the mix of faces and voices of the shopkeepers, but for a suspended moment, I was neither here nor there, floating, adrift in space and time, and then it all came flooding back: I was in the covered sidewalk outside the row of shops on Bras Basah Road in Singapore, book hunting in the string of secondhand bookstores that was my place of discovery, where I encountered writers and books that changed my life forever. It was a Proustian moment, unsought, the involuntary memory taking hold of me so entirely that it felt like revelation, an epiphany that somehow telescoped the near and far, the past and present, where I am and where I have come from, into a shuddering self-erasing moment.

One day, while browsing the used DVDs in Lawson's Records on

Pitt Street (its Malaysian owner reminds me of a bookseller on Bras Basah Road), I came upon *Saint Jack*, Peter Bogdanovich's film adaptation of Paul Theroux's eponymous novel. Theroux had left Singapore under controversial circumstances after three years teaching at the National University, and his book confirmed his persona non grata status. Until 2006 the film was banned in Singapore for its depiction of Singapore as the hub of the Asian sex trade. It was filmed entirely on location in Singapore, under false pretenses: Bogdanovich had submitted a different film script to the government, entitled *Jack of Hearts*, as he wouldn't have got its blessing otherwise. I had read the book but hadn't known about the film. The opening is a bold continuous three-hundred-sixty-degree view from a spot not far to the left of Clifford Pier, the camera pivoting to encompass breathtaking shots of the pier, the harbor, the Hong Kong and Shanghai Bank, and the General Post Office. I like to think just outside the right border of the frame, as the camera turns from its seaward perspective, are the tiny figures of my father and me, for we had come upon the shooting in that month of June 1978. It was a week or two before my birthday and my father had surfaced out of nowhere and taken it into his head to buy me a watch. From where we stood we could see the film crew and a few spectators kept at a distance. Neither my father nor I knew what was being filmed, and later that day, after lunch at the now vanished Empress Place Hawker Centre, we chanced on Steve McGarrett (played by actor Jack Lord) and the *Hawaii Five-O* crew filming along Boat Quay. Strangely, *Hawaii Five-O* had come to town at the same time; unlike *Saint Jack*, it received a lot of fanfare and there was no objection to it portraying Singapore as the hub of the Asian drug trade. For years I thought it was *Hawaii Five-O* we saw that morning; watching *Saint Jack* thirty years later in a new life and country the scene came back in a kind of revised vividness, a double take and exposure that brought back my father and the boy I was to the home I had found in Australia.

There were many more such moments of rediscovery and involuntary memory. Visiting a Chinese medicine shop in Sydney's Chinatown, I would suddenly feel my grandmother's presence and could almost hear her ordering herbs in melodious Teochew. Holding my son up for a photograph on the steps of the Opera House I could feel myself held up in my father's strong, calloused hands for a Kodak moment in front of the National Theatre. These are liminal moments of double exposure, when you inhabit an in-between space and feel at home, albeit fleetingly, accommodated to the state of being in two places and two moments at one time. Being an adult migrant means you carry a lot of baggage and are more resistant to the pressures to acculturate and assimilate; it also has its advantages: it is like being given two lives, having access to two narratives. True, the strain of a double life can, at times, be telling, but as a writer it means having two sources of material to draw from. Straddling two places and two lives is part of who you have become, a mode of being, or rather, of becoming, and writing. In my early years as a migrant, my senses were honed, alert to a complex weave of readings of the new environment, and alive to the subtle intimations and promptings from the subterranean past.

These moments of déjà vu and bilocation were moments of conjunction anchored in time as much as in space. I was shuttled between the here and now and the there and then. I was learning to temporize, to move in time, and in doing so, I became aware of writing as movement in time, and writing as manipulation of time. If there is anything of value that a writer learns at all, it is that he has a unique ability to move time along a space continuum. In his essay "Temporizing," the Alexandrian-American writer André Aciman observes that to "temporize" is to "forfeit the present" and "move elsewhere in time . . . from the present to the future, from the past to the present." For the migrant writer especially, the malleability and fluidity of time is a gift, and time travel also means space travel. As he moves back and forth between two places in memory and imagination, the migrant realizes he can reshape space as much as he can revise time. Sometimes it seems the migrant writer has no choice—he has to temporize and extemporize. Between the life he has lost or forfeited, and the life to come, he floats in on a raft made of elsewheres, or inhabits a collage of memories and places that he must somehow turn into a narrative of home. In Invisible Cities, Italo Calvino captures the liminal condition and task awaiting the traveler: "Arriving at each new city, the traveller finds again a past of his he did not know he had: the foreignness of what you no longer are or no longer possess lies in wait for you in foreign, unpossessed places." In Australia, and in the places I had visited on a year-long backpacking trip before settling into my migrant life, I discovered again and again the Singapore that I had not known I loved.

When I started *Between Stations*, I had wanted to recreate my year-long trip that had begun with Calcutta and ended up in Morocco, but inexorably Singapore took center stage, and after my father's death, the key to the work became clear: the restoration of the Singapore of my father and of my childhood. Even as news arrived of the disappearance of places and people that I loved, I began my salvage project. Singapore came to me in ghostly visitations, in whiffs and touches, the intoxicating smell of the Change Alley, the aura of the old colonial edifices around Raffles Place, the chugging of bumboats and the puffs of diesel fumes and the rainbow slicks of the salt tides slapping against Clifford Pier. One memory triggered another, one essay leading to the next, as street by street and building by building the architecture of memory came to life. There were gaps and blanks, but imagination came to memory's aid when required in the process of narrative mapping. In my essays I assembled an imaginary homeland, to use Salman Rushdie's words, a home that is lost, or one that perhaps never existed. Behind the cities covered in *Between Stations*—Calcutta, Alexandria, Xian, and Sydney—hovered an invisible city, to use Calvino's words: Singapore. But it wasn't the Singapore that had driven me into quitting it—the authoritarian government and its repressive policies, the relentless demolition of the past and the frenetic pace of change and living—it was a Singapore glimpsed through a kaleidoscopic screen of other places, especially Berowra, a bush suburb in the heart of the Ku-rin-gai National Park north of Sydney, where we had found a home.

From my favorite lookout, on a large sandstone shelf overlooking Berowra Creek, the bush fans out to the northern and western horizons in uninterrupted gray-green waves. Only the slightly elevated contours of the Blue Mountains arrest its march westward to the vast spaces of the interior, where early explorers dreamed of an inland sea. Down below, around the creek, you can find shell middens, faint traces of rock paintings and petroglyphs that lead back into the mists of unrecorded time. Sometimes in the wind among the eucalypt leaves, through the blue wrens' flutterings and the currawongs' liquid notes, and the ragged cries of cockatoos wheeling across the evening sky, you can hear voices of the long-vanished Guringai and the Dharug tribes in the area, reverberating on the placid, sun-dappled channel of viridian water. You can feel the call of the songlines, a vast and intricate network of routes linking the vital places of an Aboriginal tribe's dreaming, a lyric directory of tracks coded in the words of songs recited as much orally as with the feet on walkabouts. But the songlines of another country beckoned to me as I sat on my sandstone seat, my shadow printed on the still-warm rock: the routes of memory laid in my childhood on long walks with my father around Raffles Place, along Collyer Quay, the waterfront, and the Singapore River.

It was part nostalgia—maybe it was mostly nostalgia, I am not ashamed to admit. In researching my master's thesis on travel writing a lifetime ago, I came across the etymology of the word *nostalgia*. It comes from the Greek *nostos*, homecoming, and *algos*, pain, first coined by the Dutch physician Johannes Hofer in the seventeenth century to describe a medical syndrome among soldiers fighting or students studying abroad: "The sad mood originating from the desire for return to one's native land." The word was an abstract concept then, but by the time I was writing *Between Stations* it had invaded my entire being. My postmigration work constituted a kind of nostography—writing about the return home. It wasn't that I discovered what or where home was as the book took shape—far from it. The essays were like a kind of homecoming practice but there was no epiphanous arrival; rather, what emerged was the realization that home was nowhere: it was lost the moment I decided to leave. The Singapore I had painstakingly resurrected in my work had no correspondence in reality. *Between Stations* elegized a vanished Singapore and the part of me that had disappeared with it. Further, it had become increasingly difficult to see Singapore apart from Australia. For me, home is always elsewhere, hovering in the liminal zone between two places, in the no-man's-land and in-between spaces that I have to map over and over each time I want to sort out my thoughts about home or who I am. Thus displacement becomes home, and I become nostalgic for the moments when the writing catches the fleeting idea of home and the words become the "resting-places for the imagination . . . like shadows which a man moving onwards cannot catch," to use Darwin's words.

The migrant learns to live and move in these in-between spaces. The medieval theologian Hugh of Saint Victor says: "The person who finds his homeland sweet is a tender beginner; he to whom every soil is as his native one is already strong; but he is perfect to whom the entire world is as a foreign place." In his 1937 classic, *The Importance of Living*, Chinese writer Lin Yutang adds: "A good traveller is one who does not know where he is going to, and a perfect traveller does not know where he came from." The true cosmopolite is at home anywhere; and the transnational in the global age enjoys multiple affiliations and attachments. But there will always be a longing to be grounded in an idea of home. As T. S. Eliot says: "The end of all our exploring / Will be to arrive where we started / And know the place for the first time." In his essay "Dream of a Glorious Return," Salman Rushdie speaks of the place that India occupies in his work. In all his novels, he confesses, the imaginary return to his homeland is the underpinning theme. He adds that the emigrant writer "can never really leave," since the home country determines "the shape of the way you think and feel and dream." Rushdie concludes: "Exile is the dream of a glorious return." This is echoed in Milan Kundera's novel *Ignorance*, where the only constant in the émigré characters' fluid and uncertain lives is the dream of returning to Prague; they are governed by "the return, the return, the great magic of the return."

Like Rushdie and Kundera's characters, I have wakened to this call of return, to a yearning for beginnings, a sense of home that is bound up with tradition, roots, and origins, all of which might never have existed in the first place but which now form a polestar that for better or worse has redrawn the cartography of my reading and writing. The key of return has come to dominate my work, a homecoming, or rather homegoing, tendency that is a ghost chord clamoring to be sung, but which remains ineffable.

When we finally made a trip to Singapore five years after I had moved to Australia, my Australian friends said, "You must be excited about going home." My mind balked at the idea: Was I going home or merely visiting?

I felt like an imposter, an interloper traveling on false papers. It wasn't exactly the return of the native. I had changed; Singapore had changed. We had both become foreign to ourselves. There were the inevitable letdowns; the pace of change hadn't relented, and places were still disappearing at an alarming rate—the National Library on Stamford Road, the National Theatre, all the old shophouses around Bencoolen and Brash Basah. I felt on that visit and subsequent trips very much like a tourist in my own country. Yet there were moments when I glimpsed my double and slipped into the life I might have had, as if I hadn't left.

Now, I am in Singapore as an Australian expatriate, and once again the idea of home has to be renegotiated. Emigration and expatriation compel acts, or rather processes, of reevaluation; they make you adopt a bifocal lens, look at the here and now, and also look back, but with a revisionist lens. The word *revise* comes from the Latin *revisere*, to visit again. In the years I have been an emigrant my perception of Singapore and what home is underwent a sea-change; it was no longer the country I wanted to escape but one I was learning to come home to. In these last few months, since I began settling into my three-year work contract, I have sensed the ground again shifting, if ever so slightly, and the coordinates seem no longer valid, the lay of the land no longer matching the readings of the map. It is time to bring out the looking glass of imagination and memory again, and train it this time on the distant upside-down place under the antipodean skies. Here, the dusk is brief, quick, imperceptible almost, and the harbor lights come on eagerly, and the entire marina is lit up opulently, the water no longer dark, seductive, but wearing a giddy luminescence. Under this dazzling show, under the opaque veil of the equatorial night, I can glimpse the quiet glow of the last light on the Blue Mountains, the star-studded expanse of the southern sky, and in the silence I hear the silent call of the dreaming country around Berowra, the ancient land stretching out in bush-covered scarps and ridges to where the sky begins, and the scores of pathways inscribed in immense plains of red earth, mirroring the songlines of constellations over it.

The lens of migrant memory can be bifocal, can be stereoscopic, too; like the rotating three-hundred-sixty-degree opening shot of *Saint Jack*, it can pan across one scene, one landscape, the Singapore that I knew and lost, lingering on the busy harbor and the elegant art-deco shape of Clifford Pier, and then pivot to Berowra, that far country where I have written my own story, which seems abandoned, unfinished. I can see my double back on his Berowra sandstone lookout, silhouetted in the slanting, fading light, the sky above him fired up for a last glorious burst of crimson song. I can see him retracing his steps along the fire trail, putting on speed as the dark chill descends, back along the last street in Berowra, and walk up the steps to the little yellow house on a rise, and hesitating as he raises his hand to the door, wondering if there is someone home to let him in.

The Rent Not Paid

KAVERY NAMBISAN

After three and a half decades of being a surgeon, last year I quit. I wanted to try my luck as a general practitioner; to find out if I had the mettle to survive on my own, listening to patients, talking to them and treating their simple ailments. My surgical career in far-flung places helped me stock my mental cupboard with untold wealth. Along the way I understood the worth of my own intuitive faculties.

We were like two migratory birds, my husband and I. My love for the rural life and Vijay's decision to leave mainstream journalism and shape his own creative destiny opened our lives to unpredictable adventures. Ultimately it brought us here, to my own rural countryside. Halligattu, where we now live, is a seven-hour drive west from the city of Bangalore into the heart of Kodagu district in Karnataka, in the foothills of the Western Ghats. It is an hour from my mother's home where she gave birth to me, assisted by my grandmother and the cook, and slightly closer to the village of my paternal ancestors, the Cheppudira clan of Kodavas.

The Kodavas are a small community of ancestor worshippers. Along with several other tribes, we have lived in this magically beautiful valley of Kodagu for no one knows how long. Our written history is as recent as the eighteenth-century and so much of what is ancient is presumed, imagined. What we do know is that we have lived by farming and hunting for several hundred years. Most of Kodagu was thickly forested and its fertile soil ideal for growing rice, fruit, pepper, cardamom, and coffee. It attracted traders, mendicants, runaway armies, and invaders. Some, like the Haleri kings (seventeenth to nineteenth centuries) and the British who came soon after, stayed on and ruled, for a total of three hundred years. The kings brought the ritualized Hindu religion, the temples, priests, and trade; the British who deposed the last of the Haleri kings improved the administration, built schools, and introduced the cultivation of coffee. They also bequeathed us a sliver of "Englishness" that we are reluctant to let go of. We accrued wealth, many material benefits, and some education. Our fortunes and our futures changed forever.

The coffee plantations and the rice fields required workers. In the beginning, our sister tribals—the Yeravas, Kurubas, Kudiyas, and Paniyas—were happy to earn a very modest livelihood from such work, the payment for which was a weekly measure of unhusked rice and a few annas in copper. Then came migrants from the neighboring districts. They are the Moplahs from Kerala, the Tamils, Kannadigas, and people from the northeastern states thousands of miles away. They work hard, demand more, get more. Their children go to school, to college, and move up, never to take up the plough or scythe. They set up flour mills, provision stores, repair shops, taxi services, cyber cafés. The transformation of this hill district has been rapid in the last twenty years. Two-thirds of the population of Kodagu is made up of "outsiders." The life that was once rich in tradition, ritual, and pastoral plenitude is fading. Today Kodagu attracts weekenders from the cities. Those of us who have always belonged are trying to adjust, but it is not easy.

When I was young, the village school was a half hour's barefoot trudge away. I studied under an oil lamp until age sixteen, when electric bulbs first lit our home. After medical college and surgical training in England, I came back to India and was immediately attracted to rural work, some of which has been in my own district, Kodagu. Work has become part habit and part need. A year ago, having wound up my full-time surgical career, I rented a room for a clinic in Ponnampet, a town of modest proportions five kilometers from our home. I furnished the room with a table, chairs, an examination couch, and a few essential tools. I set up trade. That my clinic is between two barber shops is an appropriate reminder of my surgical ancestry, the first association of surgeons, in England, having evolved from the barbers' guild. My clipper-wielding colleagues come to me with their medical problems, refer their clients to me, and at times keep guard when I need to use the only toilet in the building complex (the door latch doesn't work). In exchange, I wheedle my husband Vijay into having his hair shorn by one and then the other. Our professional friendship pleases me to no end. I am as anxious for their trades to thrive as I am for mine. We have not borrowed tools from each other, though. Not yet.

The medicines I use are few and inexpensive. But while I am frugal in the use of therapeutic chemicals, I am lavish with advice about food, exercise, and cleanliness. Most patients listen with polite helplessness, or sly amusement. The regulars sometimes leave their personal belongings in the waiting area—a cubicle with some chairs and a side table stacked with old magazines. They shop, visit the bank, the post office, bakery, or one of the four liquor shops before coming back to collect their things. On a busy day, the waiting room of my clinic contains umbrellas, bags of fruit, and on rare occasions a child or two, quietly tearing bits off the magazines on the side table or indulging in brief bursts of rowdiness until a parent or grandparent comes to claim them. The other day a woman paused to show me a "blouse-piece" she had purchased. Would it match her mango-green sari?

I decided to see patients at home, too, in the evenings, for the benefit of those who live near our home in the village of Halligattu. We partitioned off a portion of the veranda, and I stocked up on the essentials—tablets, salves, injections, bandages, and splints. I have no fixed hours. Rural cordiality ensures that patients are willing to wait while I finish bathing, boiling the milk, heating chapattis, or finishing a call. Some evenings I return from my walk to find Vijay with half a dozen patients in our living room. An old woman coughing, a baby crying, a boy retching, and my dear husband offering glasses of water, toys, reassuring words. The curious among them will get a conducted tour of the house, only to go away visibly disappointed by the profusion of books and paper that occupy every room. The privileged class don't frequent my clinic very much. Perhaps they are put off by the "equalizer" effect of my shabby-looking clinic. "You should discourage these laborers," says a friend. "They spread all sorts of diseases. And how can you trust them? They will observe everything, then come back and rob." Such fear is regardless of the fact that there has been no such incident in the village. He also accuses me of encouraging workers to send their children to school. "If they study and land better jobs, where will we find workers during the coffee-picking season?"

Patients who seek my advice at my home clinic are the daily wage earners—colorful, chatty, curious. They are neatly turned out unless they have rushed here straight from work. The fish seller stops by late in the evening. He has had no time to go home for a bath before coming to the clinic and is apologetic about the fishy smells that linger on him and later in the room. One woman whom I treat for her arthritic pain regularly requests me to "hide" a few hundred rupees for her, safe from her husband. I think the man knows, or do I imagine the dirty looks I get from him? Excitement is always 'round the corner. I see patients with "heart and sugar" problems, with epileptic seizures, dog bites, and injuries that follow drunken brawls.

One early afternoon there came the grumble of an agitated motor-bike approaching our house. It signaled an emergency of some sort. The bike bumped to a halt in our front yard, inches away from our semisacred tulsi plant so lovingly housed in by bricks. Rajan, who was riding the bike, sprang away as the bike fell. Mani the pillion-rider jumped, too, but fell sprawling next to the spinning wheels, entangled in which was an incredibly long, yellowish-brown snake, heaving and whipping at the metal spokes that imprisoned it. Rajan had a bite on his shin and Mani was in shock, which changed to relief when he realized that the snake was not a cobra, krait, or viper. "It is a rat snake," he said, backing away nevertheless. Mani is a carpenter, in constant demand for his work. Rajan, a self-taught plumber, can be counted on to set right any pipeline dilemma. They had picked up the unfortunate passenger when negotiating a stretch of coffee plantation in order to take a shorter route into town. The bite of a rat snake causes a severe chemical reaction. Rajan would need treatment for a month or two perhaps, if the bite got infected, but he would be OK. For the snake, it was the last journey.

Snake, wasp, and scorpion bites used to be very common in Kodagu. Now the plantation workers have footwear and better clothing for protection and therefore they are not so common. The Kodavas, like tribals everywhere, tend to stay close to nature. They depend heavily on the animal and plant world for sustenance. The meat seller once wrapped purchases in a plantain leaf and tied it with a string stripped from its fibrous rib. Leaves of turmeric and plantain were used to wrap food or tacked together into shallow bowls in which just-plucked blooms were kept fresh by flower sellers. Until a few decades ago the locals could boast of robust health largely due to a good diet, physical labor, and clean surroundings.

The good diet comprised wild boar, bison, fowl, rabbit meat, and fresh greens and mushrooms, with rice used in a variety of steamed preparations. Modernity brought many conveniences; but motor vehicles led to sedentary habits and less physical activity, television, and packaged foods. The change in the pattern of disease is very much a part of changed lifestyles. While earlier I treated work-related injuries, wasp and snake and scorpion stings, worm infestations, and the like, the classical triad of high blood pressure, heart disease, and diabetes are the ruling afflictions of today.

The village of Halligattu is home to about five hundred people. Our neighbors are from different local communities—Moplahs, Yeravas, Kurubas, Kodavas, and several Kannada-speaking people of the district. The coffee plantations that surround our home are lavishly wooded with a profusion of birds and creatures that scamper and crawl. Adjoining our bedroom upstairs is a balcony wide enough to hold two chairs, with a banister on which you can place a book, a drink, and an ashtray. Vijay spends a lot of his time in this most cherished part of the house, reading, doing crossword puzzles, smoking, writing poetry. I join him late in the evenings. We talk about this and that. We look at the trees patterned blackly against a silver sky and watch the bats and the occasional owl swoop like trapeze artists. We listen to the throb of life in the embrace of darkness.

Our life is rich in rural comforts and poor in some others. We must go without electricity for days, letters must be collected from the post office in town, the roads are cratered and pocked with stones, and when the rains get heavy we are cut off from the town due to fallen trees or damaged electric poles. Inside the house the floors seep moisture and the tiled roof leaks in places. A colorful parade of buckets and trays is marched strategically around the rooms. Imprisoned by leaden skies, we live out the weeks in a drama of mopping, drying, wringing out. Three shows a day, or five, or six when the rains refuse to take a break. Similar scenes are enacted in most homes.

Like the good girl that (I think) I am, I compartmentalize my days. Leisure toward the end of the day, every day. An evening walk, some television, balcony time, and reading. On my walk I meet Yashoda, the village tailor-cum-entrepreneur, schoolgirls on their way home, women carrying subsidized rice in sacks half their weight, or one of the landed gentry, such as our neighbor and coffee planter, Willie, in his lumbering, once-white classic Contessa. I sidestep little kids practicing on adult bicycles, gossip briefly with the women at the water tap filling their pitchers, or stop by at Yusuf's. Yusuf's is the local sanctuary for a small glass of tea, a friendly bidi, banter, or a murmured togetherness. Tribal women, evening tipplers on their way home, kids eyeing candies in glass bottles, a retired army captain in urgent need of a smoke, Vijay, and others like to sit in the neat little porch fronting the shop that snugly stands between the homes of Yusuf's two sons. I think he and his wife have living privileges in both. Yusuf shares a warm yet formal friendship with me. We sometimes exchange small gifts like a few bananas, coffee powder, toffees, a glass of tea. On my way back home I stop at Chaya and Maimoona's home to collect the still-warm milk of their cow that has the sweetness I love.

A few times every week I see Mara, his unmistakable loping steps recognizable from afar. He is a wisp of a man, bare of feet, in trousers that can hold two of him tied with a string around his waist. His shirt is ripped over one shoulder. Mara is always on the lookout for some bird, fruit, dried wood, or an empty bottle that may come in handy. He challenges my professional knowledge by explaining the medicinal values of the plants that he tries to sell me with engaging sincerity. The other day he came home with a bunch of greens in his hand. "For your sugar-patients, Avva." Like most of the tribals, he addresses me as Avva, mother, or Akka, sister, and I far prefer these to the recently fashionable Aunty. I look at the small, crescent-shaped, crinkle-bordered leaves. "Rat-ear leaf," he explains. "To be chewed raw or cooked."

I have learned remedies from Mara and others like him who nurture the age-old wisdom about health. The older generation of tribals is familiar with herbal medicines that can be used in stomach infections, fevers, jaundice, and skin ailments. And there is the popularly used "medicine leaf" with which the locals make a signature dish every year in the month of Kakkada (mid-July to mid-August). For a mere fortnight, this ordinary-looking hedge plant renders the goodness of eighteen different ingredients that rejuvenate and boost immunity. We boil the leaves in water until it turns a rich maroon, and with this liquid we make a steamed rice flavored with cardamom and grated coconut. It is slightly bitter and eaten with ghee and honey. We loved it, even as children, not just because of its unique color and taste but the fact that it makes the urine a purple-red. Boys made a sport of it and competed with their vivid mictuary arcs.

There are many tribals, like Mara, who are other than Kodava, in our area. Their houses are on a narrow path next to the school. It is called Seetha Colony. Most of Seetha's residents are Yeravas and Betta-Kurubas (the so-called hill people), and like many of the poorer tribes of this district, their future is grim, mainly because they lack aspiration, in the modern sense of the term. Moreover, their absolute preference for the outdoors and the wild has meant that they have largely side-stepped education and then been ignored by it. The richer landowners find it convenient to use them for manual labor and so the cycle of poverty continues.

Kali, a Yerava woman, lives in a thatched, mud-walled home in Seetha Colony along with her own daughter and seven grandchildren. Her sisters Kethi and Chomi live next door. Kali has worked in our home for six months, three days a week. The flowered green fragment of an underskirt wrapped like a scarf around her frizzy hair frames a small face that was once pretty. Her brown eyes lie deep in their sockets; her lips are forever reddened with the juice of areca nut and betel. She works slowly and meticulously—sweeping floors, washing clothes, cutting vegetables, and cleaning the fish we buy at the weekly market. Kali does not approve of needless chatter, and even if I try it, she will rebuff me with a grunt. When she is paid—she insists on being paid every day—she gives me a ragamuffin grin, grabs the note, and is off. It is rare for her to become voluble, but when she does she talks about family, grandchildren, and her two daughters and a son who have all died. At least once or twice a month she skips work, without notice. Sometimes she bunks an entire week.

It is frustrating, though when I confront her she comes up with a reason. She has much weighing on her—one or the other of her grandchildren needed books, a distant relative has died, there was a wedding to go to. Sadly, Kali is also a regular tippler and she saves up for a binge every now and then. The reason, she said, was that she had lost two daughters to "illness" and the son to an accident. The grandchildren must be cared for and her grief must be submerged in country arrack. Four of her grandchildren we know. In the early days of our moving to this village, they came in twos and threes to our house and rang the brass bell that Vijay has hung on our porch with a length of green string. It is more reliable than an electric call bell. Two of the girls win prizes in school every year. Three of the older boys dropped out of school in the sixth standard. No amount of beating, berating, or pleading can get them to go. Now they work in the fields and in the evenings loiter, aiming their catapults at sparrows. Kali knows that going to school is part of the process of improving one's earning power. She does not know why. The eldest of her grandsons has taken to drinking. Not with the disciplined compulsion of his grandmother but in furious binges that leave him senseless. Each time, Kali nurses him back to health and it means skipping work for days together.

Thirty-year-old Yashoda makes up for the shyness and taciturnity of other young women of the village. She pedals away on her sewing machine and turns out clothes for many of the local children and women. I, too, am beholden, for she not only sews new clothes but mends the old. Yashoda prepares and sells powdered spices and heads a small subcenter of a microfinancing cooperative for women. She has motivated them to save and invest in small profit-making ventures. It has transformed shy, disheveled women into neatly-turned-out young ladies who have discovered self-reliance and dignity. Their monthly meetings are held in the small front yard of Yashoda's house. I hear their laughing voices as I go by, and their leader's assertive answers to their questions. Yashoda herself adopted a child twenty years ago. He is now in college. She has dreams of sending him abroad. Her love for him borders on the excessive.

Family is very much a part of my own identity. Halligattu is just fifteen kilometers from the childhood sanctuary of the home where I grew up. For me, it is still the most restful place to be. It brings back memories, real and imagined, my own and those of my ancestors who lived there for over a century and a half. Here my father's mother gave birth to her thirteen children; here during India's struggle for freedom from the British my father typed revolutionary pamphlets for circulation. The police came with a search warrant but found no evidence, the typewriter being safely hidden in the embers of the fireplace. Subsequently he was arrested when hoisting a national flag in the village and spent three years in prison.

We Kodavas believe completely in our rights. Kodagu is our land. It belongs to us, and to the smaller sister tribes that have always lived here. We tolerated the "outsider" as a boss or as a menial worker. For centuries the straight-backed, big-shouldered Kodavas lived as though (gun in hand, or spear or sword) we had nothing to fear. Besides other wild beasts, tigers were killed during hunting expeditions and the victorious hunter was "married" to the dead tiger in a real ceremony, with the groom seated next to the spread-eagled carcass of the beast. A man who had killed a tiger was allowed to grow the *galle meese*, the heavy, curling mustache that blends with the sideburns. Many families including mine have photographs of fathers, uncles, or some near relative being wedded to a tiger. Fortunately for the hunter, this did not prevent his marrying a female of his own species.

Throughout history, Kodavas retained a certain exclusivity and importance in Kodagu, largely because we owned much of the land, which might be why other tribes were denied many rights. The Haleri kings and then the British found it convenient to focus their attention on the Kodavas and ignore the rest. We landed government jobs. We learned that growing coffee would yield good returns and converted vast areas of paddy into coffee plantations. The British were suitably impressed. As we moved up the economic and social ladders we looked upward but never down. It was better to keep on climbing. That is the general drift of humankind.

In the last few decades we have had to accept the fact that others, too, have similar aspirations as ours. They, too, can climb and reach what was once beyond their reach. They can buy property and settle in Kodagu where they were once migrant workers, in search of a livelihood. We resent this invasion of our dominance; we resist it with grumblings, protests, and petitions to the authorities. Our little district is only a miniature of the whole—where it was once people *for* people, it is now people *versus* people. Every race perceives the other as a threat, and we are no different, pulling, pushing, driving out, wiping off, all in order to retain what we believe is our identity and our right to power.

I look down and see my claws.

Ashamed, I resist this drift. I resist with all my being this selfish driving out of others. Much as I love our isolation, I want to be connected. Not through the vaporous zones of invisible friendships but through heard voices, visible faces, human touch, and that friendliest gesture in the world, eye contact—all the more precious for those of us who do not have smartphones and such. If there is one thing I dearly want in life, it is to be able to sit talking to another person (one person, two, or three, but preferably one) over tea, coffee, or nothing. Talking. Not talking.

The primitive desire to nestle for warmth and love is persistent, untiring. The home nurtures personal dignity. Yet there are many whose only home is the inside of their skulls. I have the privilege and choice to remain here, or move elsewhere. Not many have the advantage. Some have much less, no place to call their own. I grieve for the things I have not done, the rent I have not paid to earth for its generosity. I cannot think of any other place I would rather be than this, a village in my beloved Kodagu. I have the security of a home, closeness to nature, the trust and love of my people. But a question gnaws at my happiness: If all of this is mine, why is it so? My good fortune troubles me as much as it fulfills. Why should my husband and I have complete authority over a piece of land while millions in my own country are homeless?

What belongs? Nothing really. We grabbed this land with the tinsel hoarded through the years while people like Kali, like Yashoda, Yusuf, and Mara live in hardship. I remember the day we moved into our new home when our families and friends came bearing gifts that would make our home more comfortable and beautiful. Later that evening, sitting in our new balcony for the first time, we were pleased, very pleased. Now I look back and wonder why we were not at all worried for the people who walked the streets of the city through the night because they lacked the tanner that would help them rest their buckling knees.

What It Will Bear

Frank Stewart

I settled in the Hawaiian Islands in 1966, married a local girl named Lisa, and began raising a family. A few years before our daughter, Emma, was born, Lisa and I bought five acres of old pastureland on the lower slopes of Mauna Kea, a broad, snow-capped volcano that filled the horizon. We built an off-grid farmhouse, and soon after purchased two young goats. Lisa was pregnant at the time, and while we liked the idea of organic milk and homemade cheese, we never thought we'd make a living from the goats: we had mainly wanted the pastureland and open spaces and never intended to be full-time farmers. As for goats, we'd learned to appreciate them because of our neighbor, Dean, who was a real home-steader and kept several dozen long-eared Nubians on his farm.

Two years after we bought the land, one of our does was ready to deliver her first kids. Like twitchy grandparents, we fretted over how Buckwheat would ever manage on her own. We cleaned out the barn, rebuilt the manger and stanchion, and partitioned off a birthing room. Should we sleep there, with lanterns and a veterinary kit, in case she needed help in the middle of the night?

Goats almost always bear twins, and as it happened, Buckwheat de-livered two black-and-white babes at 9:30 on a sunny Saturday morning. By the time we got to the barn, the kids were nodding and murmuring around Buckwheat's hooves in the wet straw. Twenty minutes later, they were on their feet, staggering right and left, wagging their tails, and learn-ing their way around their mother. In a week, the kids were too high-spirited to be kept in the birthing room. Out in the paddock, they bounced and kicked up their hooves from one end to the other.

I remember standing inside the fence one afternoon when Emma was eighteen months old. She could already tell that the kids were crea-tures not much different from herself, only more independent and willful. She waded through the toddler-high grass and shrieked in ecstasy when they came bouncing by her, ears flapping, legs flying in all directions. She was impressed. Glancing over, I saw her becoming distracted by some dark-chocolate, marble-sized balls she'd noticed on the ground. From a distance, Lisa and I watched her pop a couple in her mouth. In a flash, Lisa was beside her, popping them back out.

A week later, we put the kids into the larger pasture so they could feed and roam in the waist-high grass. Goats are smart, especially about finding the food they like; they're serious about browsing and don't do much sightseeing. On occasion, though, before they returned to the barn at dusk to bed down, I would see them pause and gaze about with a dreamy look in their eyes, as if assessing how big the world was, how much of it was theirs, and how far they could ramble. Could they see Dean's farm up the hill, where the male goats stayed? Did they register the chattering leaves in the tall eucalyptus of the Kalopa Forest across the mountain gulley? And Mauna Kea, her white summit and motherly flanks, blending into the sky?

❖

The next spring, Buckwheat's sister, Sugar, was pregnant with her own twins. Because Buckwheat's delivery had been so easy, we didn't worry about Sugar. But then she delivered prematurely at midnight and caught us off guard. We didn't realize it until the following morning when we found her standing in the birthing room, clueless and confused, unable to figure out the puzzle of the two wet lumps whimpering at her feet. Nursing these unknowns was out of the question. Sugar shivered her flanks, looked away, and murmured. Nothing we did could make her mother the twins. That same day, the female newborn died.

Without Sugar's care, the surviving buckling, Homer, needed bottle-feeding for several weeks day and night. Emma helped by holding the bottle for him when he would drop onto his front knees in front of her, vigorously wag his tail, suck noisily, and prod at the rubber nipple. Emma squealed. The milk ran down Homer's chin and became a sticky, sweet beard.

Day by day, with constant attention, Homer grew stronger. Whenever Emma came into the paddock, Homer recognized her and they'd play together. But despite her happiness, our keeping a male kid wasn't possible. When bucklings grow up, they smell worse than you can imagine. When they rut, they spray their urine over their face, beard, legs, and chest—and on anything nearby. The smell is airborne, so just getting close to a buck makes you smell like one. They also grow too large and heavy to handle if you need to move around or trim their hooves. In the presence of does, or even female humans, they become overexcited and aggressive. Anyway, if you need baby goats, it's easy enough to take a doe to a stud buck.

Twelve weeks after he was born, it was time to sell Homer. Lisa placed an ad in the newspaper and found a buyer. She loaded Homer and Emma into the cab of our truck and drove into Hilo town, forty miles down the coast. On the way, Lisa explained Homer's relocation to Emma.

Over the following days, Emma asked many times where Homer had gone. "To live on another farm," Lisa would say, "where he has lots of new goat friends, lots of good grass, and a bigger paddock."

Emma would pause. "He misses his mommy?"

"Probably a little. But goats aren't like people. They grow up faster, and Homer is very happy where he is."

Emma would let the explanation cook for a while. Soon, we bought her a toy sheep, which she named Homer. She quizzed him regularly, asking about his new home and whether he was lonely. We watched her spoon out medicine for the toy Homer's diarrhea, check him for lice, and nurse him with a tiny bottle. Gradually, Homer was becoming a spirit in Emma's mythological world. Today, he's probably more present in my dreams than in hers. When I hear or read his name, it kindles subtle yet palpable things ordinary language can't bear.

These days, thinking about being on our farm stops me from thinking about whatever else I'm doing. In her notebooks, Simone Weil talks about something she refers to as "pausing," a state free of the brain's tyrannical busyness. She gives the example of the hero Arjuna, in the *Mahabharata*, pausing on the plains of Kurukshetra, reluctant to go into battle against the Kauravas. Standing beside him, the god Krishna halts cosmic time in order to explain, by means of an extended song, why Arjuna is obligated to fight and slay thousands of people. Arjuna's birth was fated and the very cosmos, Krishna says, has led him to this dreadful responsibility.

In Genesis, Yahweh pauses after six days to think about what he's done, decide if his work is good enough to keep, and if, considering everything, it will all be worth it. Several times in the *Iliad*, Achilles pauses, but the most important instance is on the evening when Priam comes into his tent, not long before they both die, to ask for the return of his son's corpse. The two men weep silently over their separate losses, suffering, and foreshadowed fates. They fall into a reverie. Then Achilles, the raging killer, stands up, if only briefly, into a moral human being.

Having returned home, slaughtered the suitors, and hanged the dozen servant women who betrayed his hearth, Odysseus still hasn't done enough killing. In Samuel Butler's translation, when the men of Ithaca attack Odysseus at his father's house, Athena "raised her voice aloud, and made everyone pause. . . . Pale fear seized everyone." The men run for their lives. Odysseus, though, has to be told twice; but when he, too, pauses, the killing is over and reconciliation begins. Here, and elsewhere, the meaning of home and hearth is present, not in a location, but in a moment of cleansing, a pause, an axis within an important story in order to consider where we have come from, and the possibility of inner and outer coherence.

Recently, heavy rains on our upland farm have broken a long drought. It's the end of summer: the wild fruits are mostly overripe; the strawberry guavas—sweet-skinned purple marbles—have mostly fallen. But in the forest across the gully, there's a steep, grassy hill that can be reached by walking through our neighbor's field and climbing over the barbed-wire fence. Near the top of the hill, there are loquat trees that ordinarily ripen late.

One afternoon when the weather started to clear, Lisa and I set out across the field to search. After several days without letup, the rain had saturated the tall grass and heavy branches. Clouds seemed to be rolling over the ground like wet fog. Pushing our way through tough guinea grass, sedge, and patches of old cane, we were soon as wet as if we'd been wading through a river. We struggled up the slope, flapping for balance like a couple of soggy moths angling toward a refuge of orange lights.

The wild Hawai'i loquat trees bear fruit the size of a small plum, shaped like a fat tear, with firm yellow skin that darkens to gold as it ripens. Inside is a juicy pulp with a delicious, tart sweetness hard to describe. At the center of the fruit are several shiny brown seeds, smooth as polished beads. We pulled at branches burdened with fruit. And as we stuffed the pockets of our rain jackets, all at once the downpour swept over us in a torrent. The staccato pounding of the rain in the eucalyptus trees clattered like a rapid drumbeat. The rain and wind rain rose up like the roar of storm surf. By the time we emerged from under the loquats and headed downhill, we were soaked and sodden. Running wouldn't help. We tramped toward home, parting the waist-high grass, our pockets bulging with the wild yellow loquats. Up ahead, the goats inside their dry barns peered out at us, quiet and glad to be where they were.

A Tea Ceremony for Public Lands

TERRY TEMPEST WILLIAMS AND SARAH HEDDEN

Preparation <> One Encounter, One Chance

There is no beginning and no end to the preparation for a tea ceremony. For a student of tea, her life embodies and reflects her readiness, and yet each gathering presents her with an opportunity to be fully alive at this time, on this day, in the arc of the season. In Japan, there is an expression: "ichigo ichie." Roughly translated, it means "one encounter, one chance." As she harvests water and lays coals for the fire, she orients her whole focus toward the evanescence and particularity of this one meeting.

Castle Valley is a small desert hamlet in southeastern Utah near the banks of the Colorado River to the north; the LaSal Mountains to the south; Porcupine Rim west and Adobe Mesa catching first light in the east. It is a community that values starlit nights and solitude, a town of self-described recluses, renegades, and ruffians in the respectable form of teachers, architects, gardeners, environmentalists, militia men, peaceniks, wine-makers, goat-herders, artists, writers, photographers, and retired oilmen, potash workers, and entrepreneurs. What binds us together is the beauty of this red rock landscape and a stillness so vast that we count on the wing beats of ravens to remind us we have not become deaf to the noises of the outside world.

We are surrounded by hundreds of thousands of acres of public lands, lands that belong to *We the People* in this country we call America. These lands are a varied palette of color and geography from sagebrush seas ubiquitous to the West; to petrified sand dunes now monuments of stone; to buttes and mesas, hoodoos and spires; to arches and windows blown open by wind, water, and time. This is an erosional landscape where geology reveals the open history of Earth.

Sarah Hedden and I are neighbors. We have been friends since she was a child. She was born in Castle Valley, the second daughter to Eleanor and Bill Hedden, back-to-the-landers who sought a simpler life after graduating from Harvard. Her sister is an artist named Chloe. Sarah is a sophisticate in a rural setting.

I moved here with my husband, Brooke, in 1998. We left Salt Lake City because it felt crowded. Our need for wildness pulled us south. We are writers and have made our lives about watching shadows and light. In the desert, some call it a pastime. For those of us living in Castle Valley, it is our morning and evening occupation.

As Westerners, we take our public lands seriously. We know they are our birthright as American citizens. They are the lands we graze, mine, drill, frack, log, wander in and recreate on. They are also the lands we recognize as our national forests, seashores, wetlands, national parks and wildlife refuges. Breathing spaces, I call them, in a society increasingly holding its breath. Six hundred and forty million acres. Our public lands are under threat by the fossil fuel industry's last gasp in this era of climate change. They are also being loved to death by what the writer and desert rat Edward Abbey called "industrial tourism." The undermining of our public commons is at a feverish pitch as there is a growing national movement to sell our public lands into private hands, to the highest bidder.

❖

Bowl Tea <> Meditation

November 8, 2016: Donald Trump wins the presidential election. He will become the 45th president of the United States of America, defeating Hillary Clinton who won the popular vote by over 3 million people.

❖

Opening <> Presence

To open the ceremony, the host strikes the singing bowl three times. The first tone summons body, the second, mind, the third, spirit. She then bows to her guests.

Sarah Hedden is an architect of sacred space. She is preparing a Tea Ceremony in Castle Valley, Utah, inspired by the teachings of Wu De, a tea monk ordained in the Soto Zen tradition, who studied gongfu tea under Master Lin Ping Xiang. She is dressed in a long black robe, simple and sleek, and casts an elegant form against the white wall of the Tea Room as she engages with the ritualized gestures of tea-making at the low wooden table made by her father. Schooled at Berkeley's School of Architecture, she left the traditional confines of her profession and returned to the red rock desert.

We gathered together inside the Hedden home, eight neighbors in need of solace.

We were mindful of the preparations required and being made for the tea ceremony.

❖

Purification <> Consecration

Even though the tea ware is "clean," the host must purify each vessel in front of her guests as a show of respect and to consecrate their time together. For the duration of this ceremony, all are equal. With the non-dominant hand, she pours hot water from the kettle into each of the tea bowls. Taking each bowl with the dominant hand, she decants the water into the wastewater vessel while spinning the bowl at a 45° angle. Moving counterclockwise, she purifies her own bowl last.

We felt dirty, which we were, even as we bathed ourselves in the red water of the Colorado River as a form of purification that morning after the election. The whole presidential outcome felt like a betrayal. Some of us saw it coming. Some of us didn't. What we didn't understand was the rancor among us, the invisibility of those around us, even members of our own family whom we had never bothered to ask how they were feeling in a country increasingly hostile and foreign to them. In a world more global than local, more fast-paced than focused, many of our fellow Americans had gotten lost. Now, they felt seen. Their candidate outside the political system had won. We felt we had failed our own nation, not by voting against Donald Trump, but by watching others voting against themselves. That is how desperate the situation felt in the United States of America. We were awake and it was painful.

Steeping <> Respect

Quieting the heart with her breath, the host picks up the kettle. Tea is prepared from this place of stillness and nowhere else. She showers the teapot with hot water to warm the vessel before adding the tea leaves and "rinsing." This first encounter between leaves and water is an invocation, inviting the spirit of tea to be present for the ceremony. In this way, the host shows the tea her utmost respect.

We respect each other. We respect this moment of abrupt change. We respect the slow, conscious pace of ritual, of deep tradition that settles our souls in place, where we can find our own architecture of meaning even as everything around us feels like it is in a state of erosion. Falling rocks cascading down the mesa signal that the outer landscape is mirroring our inner landscape. Present tense. Sarah brings out the container of tea and opens it: an aged pu-erh from the 1960s. We respect the tea as we pass it around the table and smell the earth.

Serving <> Fluency

Through the ceremony, the host balances the qualities of precision and fluency. Each movement is performed with her full attention, yet completed in one breath without hesitation. As each bowl is filled, a line is drawn, linking the vessels together as part of the whole.

Awaiting our tea, each of us reflected on these lands that have determined who we have become. This was our intention. I cannot know where others around this tea table traveled. Our eyes were focused down, the first time my eyes had rested in days. But what came into my focus was Bears Ears, two buttes adjacent to each other that from afar resemble their namesake. A full moon rose in my memory; we had been in Dark Canyon for seven days. I was leading a group of people; in truth, they were leading me. My father was one of those on the trip. Strange things happened. We witnessed a lightning bolt strike a juniper; the charred bark is charged bark to the Diné, worthy of being kept inside medicine bundles. We continued walking down the wash with burnt bark in our pockets until tiny frogs took hold on our legs. We wondered why, until the smell of damp leaves and a thunderous roar reached us. We scrambled up the hillside for safety, energized by our fear of being whisked away, only minutes later to watch a flash flood hurling cottonwood trees uprooted and boulders the size of cars down the canyon. Nature's fury left us shaken inside our own small selves, alongside the blessing of survival. My father spoke the word, "lucky." After sunset, a rare rainbow at night followed. Not long ago, he told this story to his great-grandsons, with the caveat, "Maybe one day you, too, can go there."

These lands, these sacred lands were now part of the Bear Ears National Monument. They were at risk of being rescinded or reduced by the nation's new president. The reverence this place holds for some is what others, in revenge, seek to destroy. They call it a federal land grab. Jonah Yellowman, a Navajo spiritual leader, says, "Bears Ears is special. . . very spiritual. . . It's a protector of this land through prayers and songs. Why do you want to undo your shield? That would be a mistake like opening a door for something bad to enter."

Preparing tea is a way for me to locate my patience.

❖

Infusing <> Reverence

The same tea can be infused many times. The host and guests show their reverence and dedication to the tea by filling and emptying their bowls repeatedly until the tea steeps clear. Often, the most potent bowls of tea are the least "saturated."

Sarah pours the pu-erh into the bowls with the sound of water falling from great heights, creating a small pool in our earthen cups, and gracefully hands each of us our tea, which we lovingly receive. We drink in a meditation shared that honors the paradox found in wilderness where one feels alone yet part of the living community that surrounds us. Birdsong and the humming of insects initiates a calm heart, just as the flame of the candle before us soothes our souls. I see in the bowl of varied hues the ocean tides, high tide, low tide, and I try to steady my hands between sips to reach some kind of equilibrium where no waves create the slightest disturbance. I am disturbed by our present situation—that these public lands held in public trust will be sold to the rich ones, the corporate and careless who desire them for their own taking with an eye for profit over beauty. I see the razed lands, the roads, the rigs, the frack lines and flares, the burning fractured desert—and between sips my mind is contemplating violence. I drink the last tide pool of tea—close my eyes and swallow my rage. When I open my eyes, Sarah meets me with hers, dark and penetrating. She leans toward me to receive my empty bowl. Our heads bow, acknowledging the exchange. I wonder if she sees my fire?

People tell me there are trade-offs involved in getting what we want. I see these as compromises and that is an action I try to avoid. I am holding my ground, we are holding our ground with reverence which is public and private like this tea ceremony.

We sip four more bowls of tea, each time the quality of the tea is refining itself as the Earth refines herself, we are complete in our silences.

❀

Connecting <> Openness

Each time the tea is served, the host brings the bowl to her heart and offers the tea with an open and unobstructed gaze. In this way, both host and guest give and receive benediction.

We are met in ritual and in community.

❀

Completion < > Harmony

Even though the practice is never-ending, the host must bring the ceremony to a close. Rinsing the bowls, she serves each guest a last mouthful of clear water. She then strikes the singing bowl three times and bows.

The tea ceremony is over. Sarah invites us to speak. In the aftermath of the seismic shift of American politics and all its ramifications for land, wildlife, borders, clean air, clean water, and all that is at stake with a warming planet, we tell stories. We tell stories that remind us we will resist and insist that our communities be built upon the faith we have in each other, as it has always been—and most importantly, in the faith we have in these lands that have shaped us. We anticipate, we plan, we caress our dreams, even as we fight for a civilized society in the midst of a violent overthrow of democracy and decency. We acknowledge and recommit ourselves to a different kind of power, the enduring power of Earth.

Our public lands are where daily acts of respect must be practiced with the precision and attentive gestures of a Tea Ceremony, where what the Right Hand does and what the Left Hand does are as mindful as an unceasing prayer rising upward like the slow swirling smoke from a fire circle burning in the desert.

❋

On December 28, 2016: President Barack Obama established Bears Ears National Monument in the southeastern corner of Utah, protecting 1.35 million acres of public lands. It was a handshake across history between the Hopi, Navajo, Ute, Mountain Ute, and Zuni Nations and the United States government honoring their ancestral homelands. A collaborative land management program will be forged between the Tribes and federal agencies where traditional knowledge will be respected alongside western science.

On April 26, 2017: President Donald J. Trump signed an Executive Order calling for the Department of Interior to review the validity and size of all national monuments established between 1996 and 2016 under the Antiquities Act of 1906. twenty-seven national monuments are targeted in ten states, comprising over one billion acres of protected public lands, including marine monuments in the Pacific and Atlantic Oceans.

On December 4, 2017: President Donald J. Trump signed a proclamation radically reducing Bears Ears National Monument by 85% and cutting Grand Staircase-Escalante National Monument with a 50% reduction. On February 2, 2018, 2 million acres, once protected, will be open and vulnerable to oil and gas development, uranium, and coal mining. Over 100,000 prehistoric artifacts are also unprotected. Lawsuits have been filed by the Bears Ears Intertribal Coalition and national conservation organizations. The Antiquities Act of 1906 will be tested in the courts on the legality of President Trump's actions and will have broad implications for the future of our public lands and national parks and monuments.

A Staircase with a View

Ameena Hussein

I was born and lived much of my life in Sri Lanka's capital, Colombo, but have always yearned for a home in the countryside. Twelve years ago, my husband and I bought a plot of land on a hillock overlooking a lagoon. It was scrub jungle in an area where few would venture because of its proximity to the northern border, about fifty kilometers away. The border was where fighting was taking place, and therefore the land came at a price we could afford. We had to pass through three major army checkpoints and umpteen smaller ones on our journey from the capital to the land. My husband built me an eccentric house and planted trees. Then the war ended but still no one new came to the area. Except for most of the checkpoints vanishing away, life was much the same for the people who lived there. Like many of them, we have no electricity, and our family and city friends wonder how we can live there for weeks on end. But we do.

Two years after buying the land and building the house, I was diagnosed with cancer. My visits to the countryside had to cease. I was now on a crippling cycle of home, hospital, home. My hospital room was much like a toilet. It was small, cheerless, and tiled white from floor to ceiling. The air conditioning was cranked up so high that I slept with a blanket and wore flannel pajamas and socks. A Rexine sofa was crammed into a corner where my husband slept at night and where my friends and family sat on hospital duty, bringing food I could not eat. The chemotherapy took eight hours to be administered. As I lay on my hospital bed watching the colored liquid drip into my shrinking veins, I would go on a journey, leaving the hospital, my doctors, nurses, husband, family, and friends behind.

I traveled to my land. I noted every landmark we would pass—the little roadside stalls where we bought fresh vegetables and fruit; the bridge over the wide river where pilgrims and picnickers bathed in shallow waters; the rest stop overlooking a bustling fishing harbor with chugging boats of violent hues; the farm where we bought small pots of buffalo curds and kithul treacle; the first sight of the calm blue waters of the lagoon; the bearded and bespectacled ice merchant with his short, checked sarong, skull cap, and broad smile, who would chat to us about his five children while we bought blocks of ice to stock the crude icebox we had fashioned out of cement and Rigifoam; the shimmering salt pans with conical piles of salt heaped on the side, as valuable as white gold to the locals. I passed a succession of coconut estates, cashew estates, the little round brick church that signaled the turnoff to our country road, unpaved and rutted. I passed the village carpenter, who always stopped us to talk philosophy, and the small grocery shop stocked with emergency essentials, then turned the curve onto a sandy path that allowed only one vehicle to pass at a time and where I always hoped we wouldn't run into a tractor.

Once we saw a dancing peacock in the middle of the path and we killed the engine to watch it dance for a few minutes before it shrieked and rushed away. Another time a jackal fled in fright at seeing the advancing vehicle, galloping down the path, swerving violently into the bush to disappear into the thick jungle. And so my imagined journey would be peopled with all the creatures of the land. The peacock, jackal, sea eagles, rock squirrels, kingfishers, monkeys, and on and on. A little white iron gate led into the land, revealing a twisting sand path that wound itself around the property. The path was lined with coconut trees and went past the little brick house for the resident worker and another little thatched mud hut for the hand tractor, eventually ending at our tall recycled house made out of everything our friends and family threw away, or gifted, or sold—designed by my husband who has no architectural or building training. Descending from the vehicle, I would climb the rock steps, but just as I entered the cool space with hardly any walls and a view of the lagoon from almost every side, by this point of the imagined journey I would find myself rudely back in the hospital bed feeling the cocktail of medicine working on me, making me feel awful, uncomfortable, nauseated, hot and cold, itchy, and sensitive.

Twisting and turning on the bed trying to make myself comfortable, being soothed by loving hands, soft voices trying to console me, I would leave them yet again. I willed my mind to focus—the house, the house—I would force myself to climb the stairs of the house. They were steep wooden steps with no balustrades and a sheer drop to the ground on both sides. The landing on top gave a view of the back of the property, acres and acres of jungle land, one land giving onto the next onto the next to create a sea of treetops. I would enter the vast bedroom, each floor plank creaking with my steps, and open the white French doors that lead onto an even larger wooden deck. A lone deck chair is placed in the middle. I settle myself in and look out onto the magnificence of the view—water, greenery, horizon, sky, sun, moon, stars. Everywhere I looked there was beauty, there was love, there was healing, there was spirit.

Through seven months of chemotherapy, this was my ritual. Thankfully, I recovered. But my journey never left me. The landscape has changed vastly, but even now, ten years later, when I go to the land, every landmark that exists or has disappeared is seared into my memory. I look at the house again. It, too, has changed, now dwarfed by tall trees, defined by doors, windows, balustrades, and walls that have come up. But it will always remain in my heart as it once was: a tall building with only a roof and a steep staircase that led onto a wooden deck that gave me a view that became my hearth.

ART

Genesis: An Excerpt

Sebastião Salgado

This work is . . . a visual ode to the majesty and fragility of Earth. But it is also a warning, I hope, of all we risk losing. . . . In *Genesis*, I followed a romantic dream to find and share a pristine world that all too often is beyond our eyes and reach. My goal was not to go where man had never set foot, although untamed nature is usually to be found in pretty inaccessible places. I simply wanted to show nature at its best wherever I found it. And I found it in boundless spaces of immense biodiversity which, amazingly, cover almost half of the Earth's surface: in giant, largely untouched deserts; in the frozen lands of the Antarctic and the north of the planet; in vast expanses of tropical and temperate forest; and in mountain ranges of awe-inspiring splendor. Discovering this unspoiled world has been the most rewarding experience of my life. . . .

My search for ancient communities proved more complex. There are still "uncontacted" tribes in the jungles of the Amazon and New Guinea, but of the remote peoples I visited, only the Zo'e Indians in the Amazon and the Stone Korowai in West Papua have barely been touched by the outside world. Many others maintain strong identities and have kept the age-old shapes of their wooden homes, their languages, religious rituals, hunting methods, and diets. But they no longer live in total isolation. Visits by missionaries and even by groups of ecotourists are bringing the frontier of our consumer society ever closer to them.

My aim was to portray these peoples as close as possible to their ancestral way of life. Some might wear secondhand clothes distributed by evangelical groups, but I wanted to show the ceremonial attire and tribal customs of which they are most proud and which in a few decades may survive only in photographs. Sooner or later, the modern world will touch them—or they will go looking for it. I wanted to capture a vanishing world, a part of humanity that is on the verge of disappearing, yet in many ways still lives in harmony with nature.

The subjects of our research—landscapes, animals, and people—often overlapped. . . . The result is a mosaic presented by nature itself. It is this that *Genesis* celebrates.

Colours

Tony Birch

Before I was sent to the local school for education, my grandfather was my only teacher. He would take me out to the paddock behind the government house we were given on the Reserve and tell me to look up at the night sky while he took a pouch of tobacco from his pocket. Pop wouldn't speak another word until he'd finished his cigarette, a habit he enjoyed years after the advertisements on the TV started warning us that people who smoked would lose their legs, eyes, and tongue and die a painful death.

When smoking time was over Pop would point a pair of nicotine-stained fingers at the stars and tell me that the day would come when they would be there to help me. He'd then wave a hand in the air, smile at me, and raise his eyebrows like we were sharing a secret. But the secret was his alone, seeing as I didn't have a clue what Pop was talking about. Even though alcohol was banned on the Reserve, Pop drank a lot of grog back then; *too bloody much*, my mum used to say. *Cooked himself.*

This fella, he told me one time, raising a bottle of wine in the air, *I love him, but he don't love me*. Mum was working on the chicken line and Pop was supposed to keep an eye on me. He didn't mind that I took off on my own for the day. Down to the supermarket mostly, where I'd lift ice cream and biscuits. He'd sometimes forget to feed me. And he hardly ate at all himself. The grog was his only tucker. He also loved a fight back then, against anyone who might be up for it. He'd tell all-comers to *fuck off* and up with the fists he'd go. He'd fought in the boxing tents when he was young. Pretty good, too, they reckon. But once he hit the drink hard, he was ruined. He'd mouth off in a pub or in the street, get into a blue, and end up belted 'round the street like an old dog. The coppers went after him plenty of times, locked him up and gave him a smack as well. He was always telling me, *ya see the gunji coming, run like hell*. And I would. Anytime they drove down our street, coming to the house for him, I'd run to the dry riverbed and hide until they left, sometimes with Pop in the back of the van, kicking at the doors, letting them know where they could go. He'd come home the next day with blood under his nose, maybe a cut on the head, and tell me that the *fucken gunji done this*. Maybe they did, I reckon. But then Pop could easily get into a fight on the way home. Like they say, my Pop could *find himself a fight in an empty house*.

The Welfare were gonna put a stop to me seeing him, and then my mum, she died. She had a bad heart from the day she was born and was always catching her breath between smoking plenty of cigarettes, just like her father did. She was walking down the road after work from the chicken factory with one of her sisters, my auntie Beryl. Mum said to her, out of nowhere, *we had good times when we were kids, didn't we, Bee?* She fell down in front of Auntie and was dead. At the funeral Pop kneeled on the ground and grabbed two fists of dirt and shoveled them into his mouth, almost choking himself. Some thought he was crazy and tried to stop him, until his older brother, Ronnie, stepped up, put his hands in the air, and said *let him be with himself*. And they did.

Pop lay down and cried into the earth. He told the ground he was ashamed of all the drinking he'd done and he was to blame for his youngest daughter dropping dead in the street. Ronnie kneeled next to Pop and told him he wasn't to blame at all. The drinking was his own doing, for sure, but not mum's bad heart. The doctor at the co-op had said her heart had been *broken in childhood* and no matter what anyone had done she'd have died anyway, sooner before later. Didn't matter to Pop. He took his daughter's death as an *omen*—that's what he called it. He gave up the grog from the day of her funeral.

He got himself into a different sort of trouble from that day on. He marched around town and told everyone, blackfellas and whitefellas both, that the grog was an evil, and they had to stop drinking if they were to become *decent*. Some of them drinkers, old mates of Pop, they got sick of his preaching, threw empty beer cans at him, and told him to *fuck off home* as soon as they saw him walking along the footpath toward them. A couple of famous drinkers, Salt and Pepper, who sat out front of the post office on the bottle most days, threw a half bottle of wine at him one time. The altercation did nothing to stop Pop spreading the word every chance he got.

He became spiritual too. Most thought it was the craziness from the drinking he'd done and the knocks on the head he'd taken. They paid no more attention to the religion talk than they did to his sermons about alcohol. He'd been on the church mission as a kid, and out with the old fellas in the bush before and after the mission days. His spiritual talk was a jumble of blackfella and the Bible. He didn't make sense to most people, me included. But he could tell a good story in there with the religion and I liked to hear that from him. Once he'd quit the drink I loved him even more and looked forward to sitting with him after school. He'd make us a cup of tea and watch TV until my auntie Beryl came and collected me once she'd finished work at the factory.

We kept our love for each other going like that until he had a stroke. It stopped him from moving on one side of his body. He couldn't walk proper and he found it hard getting his words out. Auntie Beryl tried looking after him, but couldn't keep up with the cooking and feeding and washing him as well as going to work. So they put him in a home with the other old people, out beside the irrigation road that runs out of town. Blackfellas, yellowfellas, and whitefellas, men and women. I moved up to the high school at the same time Pop went into the home, and after school each day I would head out to sit and talk with him. I'd never seen a mixed mob like it. And they got on together like family, singing songs and playing cards, and the old boys telling dirty jokes. I'd walk the mile to the home after school and sit with Pop for a time, then walk the mile and a bit more to Auntie Beryl's for my tea.

Pop liked to take me by the hand, using the other hand to prop himself up with his walking stick, and lead me out to the garden. He'd talk slow and jumble some of his words, but I could make out that he said *It's a good night*, pointing his stick into the sky and talking about *constellations*. I'd listen carefully. He told me that blackfellas all over the country had their own names for the stars and their own stories. One night he whispered a *special story* to me, slow and sweet. I can't tell it to you here because it's his story. Doesn't matter who you are, blackfella or whitefella, Elder or kid. Only Pop can tell it.

He finished the story and put his open hand on my chest. Pop told me I had a strong heart and I was to remember the story he'd told, and that it would be important to me to remember the shape of the *constellation*, which star went where in the dance of the story. *Right there's your map*, he said, *there in the sky*. I ran all the way home that night, the stars above looking out for me, following me down the road, through the bush track I took for a shortcut home, all the way to Auntie Beryl's front door. I hopped into bed that night and looked out of the window and up at the sky. The stars were there, watching me, the story whispering its way into my ear.

The next weekend I was sitting with Pop in the dayroom and told him I was certain the stars were keeping an eye out for me just like he'd said they would. He smiled wider than he had back when he was enjoying a big day on the grog. We worked together that day, making the Aboriginal flag—black, yellow, red—from colored paper. Others in the room were making their own flags. Families all together. When we'd finished, the carpet was covered with scraps of colored paper. I collected them with the idea of taking them home to make a picture. Pop closed his eyes a couple of times while we were sitting. He'd worn himself out and wanted to go to bed. I helped him climb into his cot, tucked him in, said good night, and kissed him on the cheek like I always did when it was time to leave.

Afterward I skipped down the middle of the road, feeling happy with myself and looking up at the stars. I was close to my auntie's place when I saw the gunjis speed by me in a highway car, kicking up dust, two coppers in the front seat and one in the back. I heard the car brake, looked around, and saw the police car doing a U-turn. I started to run, like Pop had taught me, about to head into the bush and lose them. But I was too slow. The car pulled into the side of the road and blocked my path. The driver got out and slammed the door. It was Camel. An ugly old copper everyone hated. He'd been kicking blackfellas around for longer than anyone knew. *What shit are you running from?* he asked, hitching his pants up. I kept my eyes off him, looking down at the dirt until he poked me in the chest, real hard, and barked in my ear that I was a *half-caste cunt*. The other copper from the front seat, he got out of the car too. A big fella I hadn't seen around the town. He was drunk.

You been drinking? Camel said to me. I shook my head. *Liar*, he said. *You all drink, your mob. Can't stay off it, don't matter what age you are.* He turned to the young copper. *You know their fuckin' women breastfeed them grog.* He grabbed me by the throat with a claw, pressed hard, and shook me. *I reckon we need to take him in,* the young copper said. *He needs a lesson.* Camel stopped shaking me, smiled, and patted me on the cheek. *Yeah, why not?* He put his arm over my shoulder. *Back to the lockup for some fun.* They threw me in the back of the car with the third copper. He was sleeping against the back of the seat with his mouth open and a bottle of grog in his hand. He come to and looked across the seat at me like I was a mystery.

Camel looked in the rear mirror and called out to the copper, *This is our little mate. Give the boy a drink, Murph, and warm him up.* Once the copper worked out what Camel was on about he grabbed me by the jaw with one hand and tried pouring the grog down my throat with the other. It went into my mouth and I tried spitting it out so it wouldn't choke me. Most of the grog went over my front, the rest in the copper's face. He got angry and punched me in the mouth. I could taste blood, mixed with the grog. I started to cry and Camel called him off and they let me be until we were back at the lockup. They walked me through the office, one copper under each arm, Camel out front like he was leading a lynching. Another copper, a lady sitting behind a desk, saw the blood on my face and the grog stains on my T-shirt. She stood up and was about to say something when Camel gave her a *shut it* look. She turned away and sat down. Camel grabbed hold of the bunch of keys swinging from his belt and opened a cell door. One fella was in there, one of Pop's old drinking mates, Corky, lying on the cement floor in his vomit. *No good,* Camel said to the young copper trailing him. He opened another door. The cell was empty. He threw me inside. *Tidy yourself up,* Camel yelled. *We're coming back for a play.*

The cell had no windows, a rubber mattress on the floor, and a toilet in the corner. I walked over to take a piss but the toilet was blocked. I read the messages scribbled on the walls, some written in shit, about who'd been in the cell before me and which copper was a NO GOOD DOG. I could hear the old fella moaning in the next cell and started thinking that when they came back to my cell the coppers would be out to beat me. Or kill me. I remembered then that Pop had once said to me that there would be no place worse to die than in a police cell. *If that happened,* he'd said, *everything, my body, my heart, would be taken.*

Pop came to me then, inside me, and again put his hand over my heart. He whispered in my ear that he had one more story to tell me. And he did, reminding me that I had the many pieces of colored paper with me. The black, yellow, and red. I took them out of my pocket, one at a time, and chewed on each piece for a bit, rolled them into small balls, and stuck the colored dots on the wall in a proper order. My map of the sky. It wasn't long before I'd made my own constellation, with Pop's help. Chewing on more scraps of paper, soon enough I'd created a night sky full of stars, each one with its own story. Camel came walking along the hallway, marching toward the cell, his keys ringing like a broken school bell. I could hear the young copper behind him, screaming something I couldn't understand. I pressed my body to the wall, where *my* stars were dancing with one another, where *my* story was waiting for me. When the coppers opened the cell door and looked inside I was gone. They turned the mattress over. The young copper was silly enough to put his head in the toilet bowl searching for me. Camel stood in the middle of the cell, scratched his head, and said *fuck me, he's vanished.*

Hearth
CHRISTOPHER MERRILL

In certain dialects in northern England and in Scottish dialects *hearth* still rhymes with *earth*.

An obsolete meaning of the word is *hearing*, which in my mind connects heart to hearth, since it is in the nature of the imagination to find correspondences between one thing and another.

For example, the only usable fireplace in our house on Prospect Street was in the renovated kitchen, the masonry in the older rooms having fallen into disrepair before we moved in, so we spent much of the winter in the kitchen with our young daughter.

The Dutch oven installed by the last owners was for show, and yet some days I swore I could taste the soft pretzels delivered weekly to my Pennsylvania Dutch grandparents' house.

After his last patient left in the evening, my grandfather, a country doctor and water dowser, would climb the steps from his basement office to sit with me in the kitchen, slathering mustard over the pretzels he washed down with a beer.

His witch-hazel divining rod in my hands revealed nothing until he placed his hands over mine, and then it dipped toward the ground, his muscles tensing, as though he could not control the force issuing through his body.

Here was my first, and most enduring, lesson in the art of courting poetic inspiration.

This I recalled while clearing brush behind our house the autumn before we moved away.

Intending to plant enough vegetables to feed my family, I cut down weed trees, shrubs, poison ivy, and sumac, and raked them into a pile at the top of the hill.

It took weeks of pleading and a forecast of rain to secure permission from the fire department to burn the brush, which smoldered for a drizzly day and a half.

Our neighbors, an elderly couple descended from Woodstock's original settlers, did not speak to us for three years, until the spring we put the house on the market.

Thought you folks liked it here, the woman said to my wife, who wanted her to explain their silence.

Nor could I defend my decision to move halfway across the country to take another job.

As for the cleared land: the buyers preferred a sloping lawn to the work of sowing and reaping.

Corn, tomatoes, lettuce, squash, onions, garlic, kohlrabi, strawberries, potatoes—all grow in my imaginary garden watched over by a real—American—toad.

❖

Last night I dreamed of the spicy sausages my mother served with pancakes for Sunday dinner, which we ate in the den, with *Lassie* whimpering on TV, prompting our English springer spaniel to bark and bark.

Why did I not think to ask my mother for her recipes before she started repeating the same question over and over?

The first known use of the word *dementia* occurred in 1806, as a synonym for idiotism, which best describes my reaction to my mother's decline before her diagnosis was confirmed.

A doctor coined the term not long after Wordsworth completed *The Prelude, or Growth of a Poet's Mind*, which would not be published until after his death in 1850.

Envisioned as the prologue to *The Recluse*, an unfinished epic philosophical poem on the theme of secular redemption, *The Prelude* was his true masterpiece.

"Don't you, like me, forget your way into the future?" the poet asked our class, after my tedious presentation on Wordsworth's childhood theft of a bird trapped in another man's snare.

Of which I recall nothing save the music of his blank verse, which still shapes my hearing.

But now from somewhere rises the memory that his joy at the start of the French Revolution turned to despair when England went to war against France and he was separated forever from the woman he loved and the child she had borne him.

Also how the Reign of Terror left him permanently skeptical of the power of reason.

If past is prologue, then it is reasonable to assume that the series of concussions I have suffered over the years, on the soccer pitch and in car accidents, will afflict my memory.

What to remember? How my mother listed an antique desk and hutch, the grandfather clock, two end tables, and the gun collection, including a Revolutionary War–era flintlock, as items for me to secure at the meeting my grandmother called to divide up her possessions.

Because my parents could not attend the meeting, I was supposed to keep my alcoholic uncle from taking advantage of his younger sister, depriving her of what was rightfully hers.

In this I was only partially successful, which I regret, though not enough to have apologized to my aunt, who outlived her brother by decades.

Forty years later, when my sisters and I performed the same rite at Easter, my mother kept ordering my father to go buy Post-it notes so that they could keep track of what would go to whom.

As for what I remember of our house in Iowa? That we had no hearth around which to gather as a family, and so we drifted farther apart.

❖

The widowers, divorced men, and bachelors walking dogs in the Peninsula, a planned community built before the river flooded the only road in and out, nod to one another at daybreak.

I was bereft even before my older daughter left to study in Strasbourg, her mother and sister having decamped to a suburb north of Chicago in search of a better life.

Hearthward was the adverb that should have modified everything I said and did from the first days of our marriage.

Toward, or in the direction of, the hearth, as in: What can I do to help?

From early on my moral compass was set heavenward, for I was drawn to the writings and example of the Desert Fathers, who fled the city to live in caves beyond the Nile River.

Devoting their lives to the praise of God, becoming wise in the ways of the Holy Spirit.

Why did I ignore the central precept of their faith until it was too late?

And if I have the gift of prophesy, Paul wrote to the Corinthians, *and know all mysteries and all knowledge; and if I have all faith, so as to remove mountains, but do not have love, I am nothing.*

I can say now with certainty that I am nothing, unable even to trace the outlines of the mountains rising in the distance, much less predict what will become of us.

When the river spilled over the banks and carried away our neighbors' houses, we were grateful to be living on high ground.

And though I strained the muscles in my back, filling sandbags to pile around the water treatment plant, the library, and the house of an art professor, I did not believe I would be absolved.

Eventually the water subsided, the debris lodged against the damaged bridges floated downriver, the National Guard removed the sandbags and stored them for the next flood.

The family we took in hung their wet clothes along the fence in our back-yard, devising plans to return to their home in Mosquito Flats.

It is true that I wrote them off as victims of a delusion, failing to grasp how their love of home and hearth bound them ever tighter together.

Time to heed the wisdom of this sentence rendered into English by Thomas Merton: *It was said of Abbot Agatho that for three years he carried a stone in his mouth until he learned to be silent.*

❖

As with many of my poems, "Hearth" took shape from an image—of a fireplace, in this instance, in a nineteenth-century farmhouse in New England, where my wife and I began to raise a family. It was, in retrospect, a crucial time in our lives, when we made decisions, for good or ill, that would inform our relationship, the lives of our children, and the very nature of our walk in the sun. For this tripartite meditation I chose to write in versets, lines adapted from the Psalms and employed to great effect by such different poets as Walt Whitman, Saint-John Perse, and Czesław Miłosz, and I tried to obey the dictates of the language filtered through my imagination, probing material that was by turns personal, historical, and spiritual, hoping to give an honest account of my time here below, painfully aware of the multitudinous ways in which we may deceive ourselves. In this I was guided by something that Miłosz wrote toward the end of his life:"I am not, and I do not want to be, a possessor of the truth." That sounds about right to me.

The Ink of Cemeteries

Mihaela Moscaliuc

"The place where Toni the clockmaker tends the graves, that's home." When, in 1997, I came across this sentence in Herta Müller's *The Land of Green Plums*, I took it to be an ordinary sentence, a sentence that delivered a common truth. I had arrived in America the year before to pursue a graduate degree and didn't know, at the time, that each return to my homeland and family in Romania would be, from then on, temporary. What I also didn't know was that not all cemeteries were wombs around which families regrouped every Sunday, as we did, armed with picnic baskets and local papers, so we might start the new week right.

Over the years, memories and desires that originally shaped my relation to my first home have disintegrated, reconstituted, or morphed, while my hometown's cemetery has assumed centrality, its significance both clearer and harder to translate. It is here, to this cemetery perched on a hill and guarded by a fourteenth-century fortress in Suceava, northern Romania, that I return most often for emotional sustenance, old tales, gossip, a taste of strangers' recipes, the smell of hand-rolled wax candles and calla lilies, the tin cup that dips into the fissured bucket of the well that's quenched the thirst of every mourner, every beggar, every knuckle of cracked earth. This is where mushrooms churn the town's dead to feed the living. They thrive in the shadow of the pines that rim the cemetery. This is where, as a child, I'd look for ink mushrooms that sprout among graves so I might stomp on them and watch the dark fluid seep in. For a long time I believed that a letter from the dead would eventually reach me.

This cemetery is also where, in 1999, I took the American man who would become my husband to ask for my hand. My paternal grandmother died at sixty, only months before I found out I would go to America. She had been insisting, all through my adolescence, that I not rush into starting a family as she did, but wait instead for some prince to come along, or, as she put it, an American at least. Her vision of America had been shaped by *Dallas*, the only western TV series broadcast on national television and whose intended purpose, to fuel anticapitalist sentiment, managed to accomplish just the opposite. With the right twist of fortune, my grandmother believed, I would be an Ewing. Here I was, three years later, seeking her blessing. Under a trellis of preserved roses blushing above her headstone, my deaf and mute grandfather rendered our words in sign language, accentuating each iteration of love (as arms crossed against his chest and fists drummed rhythmically) with raw, liquid sounds. His translation, much longer than our original, must have morphed into his own love narrative.

Since moving to the United States in 1996, I have called my maternal grandmother, Bica (an affectionate contraction of *bunica*, grandmother), almost every Sunday morning. One Sunday, about thirteen years ago, I mistimed my call, so the conversation was three-way: the two of us and Esmeralda, the protagonist of a soap opera she watched religiously. It wasn't exactly easy to discern when she was addressing me and when Esmeralda, whose betrayal she hoped to prevent by yelling vigorously at the screen. A quick turn in her disjointed narrative was followed by "So Dumitru's home, did I tell you already?" She hadn't.

Dumitru, the next to youngest of her six siblings, was a carpenter. After he lost his three-year-old son, Liviu, to meningitis and, ten years later, his sixteen-year-old son, Marian, to prostate cancer, Dumitru built a miniature castle, five feet high, by their gravesite. Through the tower's magnifying-glass window you could peep into their lives. Black-and-white photographs spun on a spool propelled by a copper knob affixed to the outside wall. Dumitru's wife, Marioara, died a few years later, of heartache, or what people called "an implosion." Dumitru disassembled the tower of the miniature castle and brought the film to my dad, the town's photographer, so he could redo the montage to include his wife. They were all photos from before—before she refused to speak or leave the house, before her cheeks disappeared behind the eye bags bulging with grief or anger, we did not know.

I don't remember ever complaining about the routine of our Sunday visits, the three miles up the hill fighting nettles in summertime and trudging through snow in winter. Not only that, but whenever the cemetery slipped into a conversation at school or in the interminable lines for rationed food, I rushed to add, in a non sequitur, that my uncle was the master builder of the locally famous miniature castle. If I had some particular interest in impressing my listener, I also volunteered, proudly, that I was in one of the photos, the blond toddler perched on a chair to help a smiling Marian blow out his fifteen birthday candles. My cheeks were so pumped with air, my face so close to the flames, I was concerned no one would recognize me.

When we no longer needed to be lifted up to reach the oval window of the castle, at ten or eleven, we stopped being treated like children. "Tall as the tower, old enough to make your bed and fold your clothes," parents would badger us. But the castle did not lose its allure. While relatives chatted on the graveside bench, my brother and I continued to use whatever *One Thousand and One Nights* or Jules Verne plot and characters had captured our fancy to weave intrigues and plan our cousins' escape from the earth's stomach through the tower.

In the years that followed his wife's death, Dumitru kept busy. Half the town had some shelf or cabinet built by him, paid for with drinks and a cooked meal. He returned to his apartment only to sleep. In the mid-90s, he announced he was leaving for the mountains to build a house for the woman he was getting close to loving. After the communist totalitarian regime was overturned in December 1989, many started the tangled process of reclaiming land that had been confiscated for the "common good of the people," and she had repossessed a patch in a village in the Carpathians, in the area of Sălaj. We never heard from him again. There were rumors he built something out of wood he had felled himself, rumors the house was a replica of the graveside castle, rumors he bought a tractor, rumors she kicked him out and he slept on the bench in the town below the mountain, rumors that while asleep he had been mauled by a bear but survived.

It feels good to have more than rumors, to know that he's returned.

I prod Bica for details. What follows comes in fragments, delivered matter-of-factly over the transatlantic line. *Esmeralda* is nearing the end, so things are getting pretty intense. The week before, my grandmother and Aneta, her younger sister, hired a man with a reliable car (that is, a car running on undiluted gas and that, the driver promised, wouldn't need to be jumped every twenty miles) and made the ten-hour drive to the Sălaj mountain village. They reached the cemetery after midnight. I thought you said he's home, I interrupt. *Yes, he's here*, she adds before Esmeralda sweeps her attention again. When the thread reconnects, she adds, *But we went because there was a rumor that he'd died three months ago, half a year, maybe longer.* Aneta had phoned a clerk in a nearby Carpathian town, someone she hadn't seen in thirty-some years, but who still owed her a favor. An hour later he called to corroborate the story, and that afternoon the two sisters were on their way to the mountains. *We didn't spend the night. Didn't even go to see the house he'd built. Right to the cemetery.*

Ayayayas, followed by deep moans, cross the Atlantic in what I recognize as funeral wailing, and I wish I could be there to console her. The casual voice resumes almost immediately, though, and I hear the sappy tune of the running credits blasting in the background. My Bica loves her cliffhangers. At the cemetery, they bribe the old grave-watcher with bottles of homemade brandy so he would point them to the grave, then pay two brawlers they collect at a pub nearby to dig up Dumitru. *She buried him in cheap pine, and so poorly made we pried it open in a blink, like it was nothing. A hyena, that woman. May flesh melt on her like a candle.* I couldn't understand why they needed to see the body. Did they suspect foul play? No, he just needed to come home.

The man sets his bottle down in front of his shoes and says that a man who's mourned a lot when he dies becomes a tree, and a man who isn't mourned at all becomes a stone. But what if somebody dies in one place, says the woman, and the people doing the mourning are somewhere else—then it doesn't do any good, the person still becomes a stone.

They wrapped him in some blankets and fit him snugly in the trunk. Busy with crying, laughing, curse-sputtering, and reinternment plans, they did not feel the hours go by, though they had to jump the battery twice. The stench turned sweeter as they reached the dawn and sweeter still as they reached the hometown cemetery. Back with his children and wife, he will start all over, as if he'd never been buried anywhere else, as if death has just caught up with him. And they, the four sisters still alive, will start their work: the third-day commemoration, the ninth day, fortieth day, three months, six months, one year, and every year after for seven years, at which time they'll exhume and clean his bones. *The past doesn't pass away so quickly here. You could be dead for a long time.*

It's July 2016, and I am back at the cemetery on the hill with my son, husband, and Bica. We pass through the gate buttressed with lethargic strays and bearded women whose ancient looks speak of destitution rather than old age. We pay no heed. As we amble down the main path to the first destination of our rounds, the length of my grandmother's right arm rests on my left, her elbow snug in the crook of mine. Air and light corset her body and constrict her breathing. Her intolerance to open space has increased over the years, so these days she ventures out of the one-room flat only to bury or visit with her dead. Life is what happens between cemetery visits. When she's not with clients whose fortunes she reads in coffee dregs and old-fashioned playing cards, she plans the *pomana* (alms in the form of food, drinks, ware, handkerchiefs, and towels) for the next remembrance day. In my culture such days are many, and though they are generally connected to Christian beliefs I'm mostly ignorant of, they harken back to pagan traditions. Pagan, Christian, what does that matter. A dance on the grave is a dance on the grave.

We spoil the dead the way we did not or could not spoil them in life. What wouldn't my mother's twin brother, Ticu, have given for the bottle of rum tucked inside his suit's breast pocket before the lid was sealed shut. He was the most recent to enter the cemetery gates and never leave, in November 2015. He died in Bica's bed, a straw on the precipice of his mouth, a last sip of unrefined alcohol before he reached for her hand and pressed it against his lips. My mother had just stepped out to buy him new shoes. He had waited for her to leave. Later that afternoon, she washed his body while still warm, clipped his nails, dressed him, rouged the cheeks that, she and my grandmother swear, had never looked smoother. Minutes after death, all the huge pimples and sores covering his face had disappeared; the body has absorbed them so as to restore his dignity.

"I would have recognized Ticu's grave anywhere," my son says as we make our last stop. *How so?* "Look at the vases with straw flowers. Pringles. Who puts flowers in Pringles tubes? I bet grandma brought them from the States." He turns to me. "Mom, your people are just so weird." He recalls how last time he was in this cemetery, mimicking Bica, he picked a handful of the forget-me-nots that adorned, opulently, one grave, and placed them on a neglected one. Bica smoothed his father's disapproving look: *The dead don't mind. They love sharing.*

As we hobble toward the gates, Grandmother pulls some small banknotes from her bra and hands them to my son to give to the begging women. Her arm has returned to rest on mine. *It's so good to have you home,* she smiles, dentureless, lips sunk inward. The small abyss of her mouth fills with burning air. She slips a coin into my hand and clasps my hand into a fist. *You should keep one of these there, in America. Never be unready.* She's never been unready. She changes her mind about the farewell outfit at least once a month. The fads set by the local paper complicate, time and again, the decision making. Black is the only constant, but shapes, cuts, length, materials remain negotiable. The shoes are the main variable and a headache in a town with such few options. Her feet keep swelling. No matter what, shoes must be new, fit to handle a long journey.

One beggar lifts my son's palm to her lips. She holds it tight. She presses hard. My son pulls back, gently. He curls his fingers in my palm. They are stained with mushroom ink and wild strawberries. He does not ask.

The coin for my mouth fits only my mouth.

The Great Big Rickety World My Father Saved Me From

Debra Magpie Earling

Most folks are probably familiar with Atlas, his shoulders bowed beneath the monstrous weight of the living earth, carrying all of our beauty and all of our wiggling troubles. Poor Atlas, robed in a sphere of stars, destined to hold up the sky for eternity while the universe spins around his misery, a dark and dismal job without thanks.

My father's middle name was Atlas, and he was mighty, so strong he hoisted washers and dryers and refrigerators up the concrete porch steps and into our house without help, and as easily as if he were lifting a featherweight. Some cussing, but no sweat. But I couldn't or wouldn't see the true strength of my father for most of his life, and for most of my own life, really. I was too busy being uncomfortable around him.

My father could talk a leg off a stranger, and did, at the gas station, in the campground, at the grocery store, on the street, at the swimming pool, in restaurants, in coffee shops, and in any line, in any town where we would be waiting for anything, and yet at home my father possessed a quiet, grumbly countenance that left me sad and bewildered. He wasn't a daddy or a father-daughter man. He never asked me how my day went or what I wanted to do with my life and rarely what I thought of anything. I cannot think of a single time he wrote me a letter, although sometimes his scrawl would appear at the bottom of a Christmas card my mother had sent. *Dad*, plain and simple. He was not a sullen man; my mother called it "undemonstrative." My father wasn't a hugger and would rarely say "I love you," but he was anything but *undemonstrative*. He demonstrated his feelings through hard work, anger, and undeniable generosity. Throughout my childhood and into my teenage years, he was short fused to an explosive temper. An undeniable rage. Laugh too hard at the dinner table or push your knees into his seat back while he was driving—and lickety-split—you'd get his blister-weltering belt or a monstrous cuff to the head. He wasn't someone you could sit down and visit with, not usually, anyway. You did things with him: shoot cans, ice skate, work on cars—*Get out here and help!*—weed the garden. But when my best friend's family needed heating fuel my father paid for a tankful without hesitation. Anyone who entered our home was offered something to eat. If anyone needed help my father opened his wallet and his home without question or reprisal.

The only time I got my father to talk was when I brought up his old days in the ring. He was known as the Golden Boy of Rose Lake, Idaho. He'd boxed in the Spokane Coliseum and had a boxer robe and old photos of his boxer days to prove it. My mother pulled his boxing robe from the back of the closet. I remember the rough, moth-bitten black wool, his title in yellowing whipstitch felt letters across the back. Most of all, I remember how my father fell silent, his face lit by wonderment.

If you happened to get my father going, he'd fire off rounds of stories that always ended with the same punchline in which some lippy unsuspecting charmer would get smacked in the kisser. You couldn't squirm away from Dad once his stories began. Make no mistake. Virgil could round a haymaker on any fool not smart enough to recognize he was primed to get pounded, and he could also talk up a bluster with such intensity you couldn't escape. You were in for a rollick but not a good time.

By count, my father must have cracked the heads of a thousand knuckleheads and busted another thousand in the chops. I'd always hoped that one of his stories might contain, not a different outcome necessarily, but a snigger of epiphany or empathy, a jab of miscalculation that would have exposed my father's sly world as human, too, an indication that everyone, including my father, got a comeuppance.

Not a chance.

In hundreds of renditions of Dad doling out just desserts to swaggering suckers, the outcome was always the same. Men hit the ground or banged against cars or flew up in the air with astonished cock-eyed wonder. They smacked unwittingly into hog troughs, careened into fences, and landed on other unfortunate cocky bastards. Usually a single moonglow punch would render them down for the count. There was also the random dumb cluck who would make the mistake of getting back up and, like a rolly-rocky Bozo punch bag, be rendered *cuckoo cuckoo cuckoo* by my father's endlessly clobbering fists. If my father would have pulled out a comb and ribbed his hair, it would have suited his narrative. His ham-blush face, his eyes sharp, almost glittering.

I was mortified when my father would pounce on unsuspecting visitors, any friend or stranger who stopped by. If you were a Jehovah's Witness, you were in for a sorry afternoon of big talk and glory days. I tried to shuffle people quickly from the room when they came to visit. If I made the mistake of going to the bathroom, my father would seize the opportunity to chat about his boxer days, cocking back his arm to illustrate how he'd punched some jerk's lights out. Then there was no easy exit. My guest and I would be in for a long night of fight stories until I pulled my friends from my father's colossal grip. I apologized profusely once we got out the door. I feared they'd think my dad was lying, or worse, that they'd feel sorry for me. My father's ferocious stories revealed a crazy pridefulness that even as a teenager I recognized spelled a deeper layer of violence. And at the surface, I knew his stories sounded like fabrications. I mean, *criminently*, as my dad liked to say, how could you knock out every single opponent, even if he was a numbskull? But I'd never known my father to lie. He may puff-chestedly brag but he was a man of his word. He possessed a bald-faced honesty that was humbling.

When I was nineteen years old and working in the tribal court system, I'd come home with stories about abused children who'd been removed from their parents' custody. My father listened ashen-faced and shaken. He admitted he'd been wrong about many, many things, sorrowful things, and that he never should have hit us. He realized we could have been removed from the home because of his violence, and that we rightly should have been. He listened solemnly while I recounted the past, the belt welts that had turned to bruises, the many times he had struck my brother and me for simply laughing, or the time when he held my sister down and shaved her eyebrows because she'd plucked them. When my mother stepped between them, she got a black eye for her efforts. My sister hid in the woods just beyond our house for weeks afterward, washed her clothes in the horse trough, crouched in the bushes, and slept in the neighbor's barn. My mother didn't kowtow to my father. She expressed her anger through shouting matches and slapping. Both of their angers disintegrated into long nights of dreadful and stomach-quaking arguments.

"Dad," I said, "we were afraid of you."

He accepted my story without additions or yeah buts. He shouldered the responsibility for his actions and never shifted blame. He understood he wasn't the father or husband he should have been. His mea culpa was genuine; his apology was in practice, not words. He desired to become a better man, and he did.

It's difficult to juxtapose the almost childlike man my father was when I was growing up, his insane anger, his lashing out against the soft-spoken and gentle man he strived to be, and eventually became. He lost height, but grew in moral stature as he aged, shedding the detritus of his past by always endeavoring to do better.

Last year, my brother reminded me of a story I'd put out of my mind. When Dad was no more than seven years old, barefoot and stacking wood for his step-grandfather, he stepped on a nail that pierced his foot clean through. Old man Huelsiep called Dad to the chopping block and lifted the flat of his axe, and without flinching smacked the nail back out of my father's foot. "Get back to work," was all he said to my crying father. Though Dad would never have used that incident as a reason to forgive his own brutality, my brother and I recognized he'd experienced a cruelty that was difficult for him to overcome. Other monstrous stories resurfaced, how the old man had repeatedly raped my father's sister Vernice, banging her bleeding head against coat hooks, knocking her to the shit floor of the chicken coop, ravaging her again and again on the kitchen floor while her biscuits burned, while her soup bubbled, while her canning jars boiled dry and hissed on the cookstove, until one bright fall morning at the age of sixteen, she'd walked up the road and run away with a Canadian. For my father and his siblings, there were unforgiveable degrees of violence, and then there was the violence of survival.

I've often wondered if my father accommodated my mother's family because he longed to provide the home he'd so desperately desired as a child, or maybe because his own family had disowned him after he married my mother. I've tried to draw conclusions, to understand the contrast of love and violence.

Vernice once told me that we weren't considered part of the family because we were Indian, as if the statement wasn't hurtful, as if such a thing could never be cruel. Romantic notions of unconditional love that I associated with my Indian mother couched in my father's white heart. He welcomed all her family into our home, and faced the toll. Murders, alcoholism, and death, car accidents and death, stabbings and death, children and death, beatings and death, and death, death, death. My father took in my mother's sister's daughter, who became my sister Cheryl, and lamented that he had not taken in Cheryl's brother as well, after he was struck in the head by a baseball bat wielded by a nutcase relative in a fit of rage and drunkenness. Harold, always a sweet dark-eyed boy, would remain seven years old forever, even when he was stabbed and pummeled to death by two hoodlums when he was fifty.

At one time or another, my father took care of every single one of my mother's family, including Harold. Her grandmother, her sisters, her nieces and nephews, even one or two of my mother's old boyfriends disguised as my aunt's companions.

Our house sagged under the weight of sullen-faced alcoholics, baby-dolled prostitutes, ghosts of dead Indian relatives, and a parade of my mother's mean and entertaining siblings who brought with them their own weird and disagreeable companions. Quibbling broke out in our house, if not out-and-out fights. Drunk shirttail relatives stole per capita checks and threatened to get my mother fired. One kooky cousin bragged he was going to put rattlers in our mailbox. When I was sixteen, my jealous aunt slammed a glass into my mother's face and left a puckery scar forever. Wild stuff. And yet my dad took them all in and gave them a second chance (even my aunt, years later); he fed and clothed them, calmed them, and stood beside my mother at all the funerals and wakes. During this time, my parents continued to have fights, scary all-night rages, while my brother and I trembled behind our bedroom doors. My father was both doorman and bouncer to the misfortunes that careened toward us.

It wasn't until my own life took a terrible turn at the age of seventeen and the man I'd married threatened to take me down the same path my father had taken us that our world transformed.

I was taking classes at the community college and I had a few short minutes to change and get to work. I was pulling back my hair when my husband stumbled into the apartment, drunk and stroppy. He was supposed to be at work hours before but had hit the bars instead. I was as acquiescent as a beaten pup as he zigzagged into the kitchen. I believed in my own childish and dopey way that I could save my marriage, and my husband. I pretended I was happy to see him but kept my distance, a girl bedazzled and bedraggled by love.

Barry was wobbly-walking with a jug of milk when he lost his grip. Milk sloshed across the floor, glug-glugged out of the mouth. I tiptoed toward the door, walking backward with my head down. If I could make it out of the house, I'd be OK. I was ready to push open the door when he grabbed me and tossed me toward the mess he'd made. I lay still in the milk puddle hoping that there wouldn't be a siege this time, that this humiliation was the end of it. When I finally got back up, he rag-dolled me, double-fisted my coat, and pressed me to the wall. He was incoherent and spitting, his face iron-hot as he knocked his head against mine, cussing me, blaming me for the spilt milk, for everything.

My father had taught me how to throw a haymaker, one ferocious punch that could catch someone by surprise and get a person out of a bind. I took a deep breath and maneuvered my way to the side of Barry, leveraging the whole of my weight. I rounded my arm slowly back and threw myself forward, but my best shot wasn't good enough. He returned a fist pop to my face. I got a purple, swelling eye. A split lip. A dancing swarm of stars. When Barry went to the bathroom, I made my escape. I drove home to my parents.

The moment stands out in all my recollections of youth—the startled moment of plain and simple recognition—not a memory, a forever living moment. My father's burning blue eyes. His back bowed against my mother's screams. "Leave him," my mother shouted so loudly I covered my ears.

"She can't leave him, Ma," my father said, "because she loves him."

My mother was incredulous. She pointed at me.

My father's watershed moment was my puffy face, my bleeding lip. He cast a desperate sadness, as if he finally grasped that love couldn't redeem the husband who beat me nor forgive the violence he had wreaked. The conundrum. To save himself from violence, his own life was predicated on violence. Violence had to end.

After that night, my father stopped fighting with my mother. Oh, the bickering glittered on like fizz but the shouting stopped, the bullying and trouble stopped. It occurred to me, much later, that the moment marked the end of our era of family violence. I do not recall another wrenching moment that passed between my parents after that night.

Eventually I came to my senses as well. I couldn't afford my husband's rising debts, his escalating abuse, so I divorced him when I turned twenty-one, and he never forgave me. Barry took his life the year before I graduated from college. I took it hard, moped around, wrote into the early morning hours electrified by guilt. I visited home more often. My father regretted he'd let me get married in the first place.

When I landed a full scholarship at Cornell University, life seemed dreamy and big. But during my second year of school, I made a dumb mistake. My dorm roommate had experienced a breakdown and was convinced her professor was trying to sabotage her. Her stories grew more and more outlandish and conspiratorially alarming. I wanted out.

I imagined myself at a writerly desk in one of the grand old houses around Ithaca, looking out onto sweeping meadows or peering into the lush green woods for new inspiration. I was tired of graduate student housing, the tiny room where I heaped my books and clothes on my side of the room.

June, the housekeeper in my dorm, recommended her brother's house. "He's got a beautiful three-story home. Just what you want. You can have the whole upstairs for dirt cheap. Store your stuff there over the summer," she told me, "so you won't have to haul it all the way back to Spokane. My brother's a great guy, and not home all that often. You'd practically have the whole place to yourself." I liked June, trusted her, but I felt hard-pressed. She told me that I wasn't like the other dorm residents. "You're not a snob," she told me. "You can certainly tell you was raised right." I felt implicated. Few students spoke to her and when they did they were rude and dismissive. I didn't want to be like them. I was ashamed of their behavior. My mother was a housekeeper. I didn't like the idea of living with a stranger, let alone a man, but June reassured me. "A super-nice guy!" she said, as she helped me haul my books and belongings to the car.

He met me at the door and before he invited me inside he offered to carry my boxes in. I don't think I'd said a word when he opened up the hatchback and began hoisting up a stack of my boxes.

"That won't be necessary," I said.

"No sweat," he said. "My name's Vince. June said you needed to store a few things." He headed for the house and I followed, skunked, unable to extract myself without insult.

Vince wasn't what I expected. I thought he'd be a jolly sort, maybe older, too old to chase me. This guy was a middle-aged man with grease-combed hair. He was wiry and moved fast. He urged me upstairs to show me the place he was renting. I followed like an idiot, clutching my keys in my knuckles. Was this the man my father had warned me about—*If a strange man scares you, kick him in the balls and run like mad*—when no one spoke of rape or murder or the terrible things that happened to women and girls? I'd been warned by my father, by Vernice's hushed stories of old man Huelsiep.

Pink billowy curtains hissed in the wide-open room and floated up and around me. Dead moths dusted the floor. I looked out the windows in every direction and saw that I was clearly in trouble. Except for the big red barn, stubbled corn fields surrounded us. The nearest house was a mile or more away. What had looked so charming and inviting as I'd driven up suddenly looked sinister and inescapable. No one would hear me.

"Whadaya think?" he said. "Suit you?"

"Yes," I lied. I'd already surrendered my boxes. Bargaining with myself. If I could get out of here I'd never come back. I was relieved when he turned and clattered back down the stairs. I was ready to make a run for it but he stood in front of the door.

"Sit down. Have a cup of coffee," he said.

"No," I said, "really, got to go."

"What's your hurry?" Vince said. I felt snared. I struggled to come up with a good excuse to grab my things and leave. He poured me a cup and gestured for me to sit.

I sat down reluctantly, ready to sprint, my posture straight-back alert. Vince slowly lowered a heaping spoonful of sugar into his coffee and made a tinkling noise as he stirred and stirred. He lit a cigarette and took a long drag.

"My wife left me about six months ago," he said. He squinted at me through a haze of smoke. "She lives up the road a ways."

"That's too bad," I said. I looked at my watch.

He snorted and cupped his cigarette in his palm before he tapped it in the ashtray. He had an odd, unhealthy cast to his face, a pukey greenish gray that matched his hair.

"Left me for my field hand," he said as he thumbed his brow. His eyes were as oily as his pores.

"You see that corn chopper, back there?" He swiped his hand toward the window. "That big thing by the barn doors. See that there?" He sniffed as if he were proud. "That's a stationary corn chopper."

I followed his glance, ready to make my exit.

"You feed the corn into the bottom there," he said, and took a long draw on his cigarette, then pulled the cherry off.

"When that sucker jams . . ." He squished the cigarette into the ashtray and held the pull of smoke. "Let me tell you, you don't want to kick it, cause if that sucker catches . . ." He drew out every line. Pausing too long after each statement. He was revealing a secret and I was transfixed with the horror of what he was telling me, not quite believing what I was hearing. "I found him near upside down. He must have kicked it hard because it pulled him right up into the blades."

"You mean," I began saying, "your wife's boyfriend . . ." not finishing *was killed right there?* He nodded. Creepy-smug and smiling. He raked his nicotine fingers through his hair and I felt a shiver lick my spine.

I don't know what I said then. I focused on extracting myself from the room, extricating myself from his presence. I nodded my head in deference to him. Acquiescent. Seeking mercy. I got to my car as quickly as I could. I planned to leave my boxes and never return.

My father wasn't thrilled to drive clear across the country but it wasn't my mother who convinced him to go. Over the summer he came around to the idea that he had to rescue me from this jerk. I sensed the wheels turning in his head. How big was the town of Ithaca? Were there other towns nearby? What other knuckleheaded trouble could I get myself into? I was too old to be in this predicament, and yet he was aware he'd dropped the ball earlier in my life. He wasn't about to shirk his parental duty this time.

Two years after my ex-husband's death, this college living situation was solvable, a mistake he could fix. I wished I'd kept my big mouth shut; I didn't want my stuff back. It could rot in that upstairs farmhouse. Vince was that creepy. But my dad had made up his mind. He'd drive back with me and take the train home. It was settled. He was going to Ithaca to find a safe apartment and retrieve my things.

We left on a hot, sticky evening as the sun boiled down into the distant hills behind us, and things were all jazzy and fight-stories galore until we crossed the eastern border of South Dakota. My father became noticeably quiet and folded his hands in his lap. The sun glared in our side mirrors and the west disappeared like a cowboy riding off into the dusty sunset.

My father seemed dazed and dumbfounded by the vast Midwest and the increasingly busy highways, the miles and miles of interstate that took us farther and farther from home, the rising empty factories that lobbed the horizon, the endless stop-and-go islands with their unsmiling grimsters and long-haul truckers doped on coffee. He insisted on paying for everything and would give me a half-kidding glum look when I opened my purse. "Put your money, away," he said. "You're going to need it."

I felt like a child again, only this time I was safe, without worries. My father was taking care of me. He would handle it. And I got the feeling he wanted to.

This wasn't the fragrant mountains of northern Idaho. This wasn't the dreamscape of Montana. The flatland made my father lonesome. I thought I could feel his sadness, or maybe I was feeling my own lonesomeness. Having my father with me made me realize how far away from home I'd traveled. I tried to imagine the world through my father's eyes and felt both annoyed and dejected. He wasn't impressed or mildly interested in the journey. He'd never been farther east than Billings, Montana, and once we left the boundaries of his territory he would neither spell me nor guide me by map.

I took a wrong turn in deep fog and detoured through Erie, Pennsylvania, where we found lodging at two in the morning in a dodgy motel. My father snapped off the lights as soon as we crossed the threshold and told me to sleep in my clothes without pulling back the sheets.

The room had an odd smell of mildew and factory waste and when I complained, Dad told me it was just a stopover and to shut up and go to sleep. In the dim, gluey morning, I discovered the fresco behind my father's bed was actually mold—a black octopus mass of it. He chuckled at my pickiness. It was just a place to sleep. For crying out loud, we didn't have to live there. I was glad I didn't have to stay there alone.

✦

I was anxious for my father to see Cornell. After years of crappy decisions, from dropping out of high school to my sad/bad marriage, after years of ugly depression and making my family miserable because my ex-husband had leapt from a bridge to his death, I thought I had made it. I was going to an Ivy League school on a full fellowship. Silly thoughts, after my father footed the whole tab for our cross-country journey, from the greasy biscuits and gravy to the motel rooms.

The first thing we did when we hit New York state was make a beeline to retrieve my belongings. I was nervous and jumpy but my father dismissed my fears. "It'll be OK," he said. "Let's get your stuff and then go get some lunch."

When we arrived at the farmhouse my father took note of our surroundings. "It's way the heck out here," he said.

Vince pushed open the screen door and sauntered toward us with a slick smile on his face.

My father was just exiting the car when Vince leaned on his door and tried to keep it wedged open. "Hello," he said to my father; then he bent down and squinted at me. "Have a good summer?" he asked. "You're looking good."

"Lock the doors," my father told me, and backed the man off as he got out of the car. I felt a lilt of glee. I kept the window cracked so I could hear.

"Where's my daughter's things?" my father asked.

"In her room, upstairs," Vince said, as if I had lived there awhile and we were familiar with each other. "I've cleaned some stuff out so now she can have room on the second floor too."

My father snuffled a laugh. "That won't be happening," he said. "You say her stuff is upstairs?"

Vince nodded, sheepishly.

My six-foot-two father towered over him. Even in his sixties, my father was no one to mess with. Dad turned to me. "Stay in the car," he ordered, like I was a four-year-old. I was thrilled. Two minutes later my father was back with a stack of boxes in his arms. He opened the hatchback with his keys and placed the boxes efficiently and quickly inside. "Is this it?" Dad asked me, and I nodded.

Vince had followed my dad outside and was still attempting to bargain with him. "If it's the rent, I'll lower it," I overheard him say. My dad dismissed him. Vince looked wounded, oddly surprised. Before my dad got back in the car he turned to Vince and gave him a hundred dollars "for the storage."

"Dumb jerk," my father said, under his breath.

And then, so easily, we drove away. This time my father had rescued me.

We sat on the grand balcony of Willard Straight Hall looking out over the mad fall foliage, and my father shook his head and looked at me in genuine puzzlement. "Why you wanna come here?" he asked. At the time, I didn't understand that my father wasn't questioning my accomplishments, he was questioning my desire to remove myself from the sphere of family. Why would I want to be so far away from everything familiar? No one in my family lived more than an hour's drive from Spokane.

Loyalty and love were difficult concepts for me to grasp then because my deepest feelings were still confounded and obscured by old trouble. Any move toward clarity or simplicity angered me. I could not see Dad's question as part of a bigger whole that wasn't meant to put me down. I saw the world through layers of bullshit and complications. I was too dumb to get my father's gist.

Why you wanna leave your family and go to a school so far away from us, so far away from me?

I wished I would have answered simply. I'll be home soon. I'll never leave you. I love you.

When the people I was close to were dead and gone, when my phone stopped ringing, and my life stopped for long enough that I could look beyond myself, it was my father, who had annoyed me fiercely at times, who came into view. And maybe it wasn't the first time, but it was the profound time, when all the pieces fit and I saw the whole of my father.

In the most brutal times, when suicide or murder or car accidents occurred, my father was unwavering. Things didn't fall apart. There were funeral arrangements to be made and funeral clothes to be selected, food to be bought, people to be tended to, as well as gathered up. At all the sad get-togethers and wakes, my father was calm and unfailing. He was a pallbearer, a babysitter, a dependable nondrinker and nonsmoker. In the midst of chaos and drama he was a reminder of the living. You still had to buy groceries, make dinner, read the newspaper, and go to work. He hadn't always done his best by us, but my father's tranquility in times of trouble had been a gift.

Perhaps my father became attentive to the needs of others because he had not been tended to. Perhaps his anger and compassion began with his own beginnings. At the age of seven he'd lost his mother to child-birth, and that same summer, while wading in the shallows, he'd looked up to see his father cannonball from the dock's end. A thunderous splash. Rose Lake lipped over his father, then swallowed him up. Bubbles fizzed the surface—a boil pot aftermath—and waves rippled toward him, then lapped the shore.

My father squinted into the haze of shattered water and waited. Light peaked the sky, stacking heat. A flock of geese exploded on the other side of Rose Lake, and for a moment he was distracted as they passed overhead. Downy feathers seesawed downward before catching a ragged updraft and flittering up again. Water shivered in circles and wrinkled around the pilings.

Walter popped up from the deep spluttering like a pranking teenager, calling for help.

No one took his call seriously. Was it a joke?

Seven-year-old Virgil thought his father was kidding, too—that his silly rolling eyes were a hoax, an antic of some sort. The trees overhead rushed with wind and the moment cindered. My dad noticed an awkward hilarity in his father's actions, the first flickering alarm of the day's sudden and terrible reversal. He fixated on his father's frantic hands slapping finally downward as life frayed outward and up as if the last puff of his father's breath unleashed the first scatter of rattling leaves.

The hazy water stilled, reflecting the wiggling dock, my father standing in the shallows, and then only the clarity of the ghostly sky overhead, driven with clouds. Others paid glancing attention until waves and sound reverberated to shore, lancing the blister of their ordinary evening. The silvery blade of the spinning day became a buzz saw unbolted, and life zippered away.

As my father neared the end of his life grief shimmered up from his earliest experiences as if they had been hard-etched on heavy steel plates and then promptly buried. He dug the memories up shovelful by shovelful, searched yearbooks and old photos, traced his mother's face, then his father's, shuffled through local history books looking at the same photos over and over again, poring over his past. My brother Benny, from his first wife, too soon dead, and just before him. He looked longingly at the faces of my mother's dead relatives. All of his immediate family dead too. His grandmother long gone. His twin sisters dead now twenty years. His brother gone, too, in the nursing home where his own mean in-laws had left him. And the long-ago dead, the hateful step-grandfather he had scooped up from the field where the son of a bitch had died, his mean spirit gone now, gone and over, and nothing but his dead weight to carry a mile home and finally bury after seventy years of carrying him.

❖

When I think of hearth I think of my father even with all his strife. My father who fought to tame his own anger—though he wasn't always successful—so that he could at last protect us. My father who'd shrugged under the weight of my mother's burdens, and all her family, and voluntarily hoisted them up. And for a length of time—and beyond what was humanly possible—my father struggled to balance a world not of his making. He held up my mother's heartache and had the courage to admit the heartache he had caused.

When I think of hearth, I think of my father holding up the great big rickety world, rocketing back his muscly arm against the darkness that threatens to engulf me.

Even in the Loneliness of the Canyon

Geffrey Davis

I've been an angler all my self-conscious life and so find fishing a sooth-ing constant among the otherwise unstable paths leading back into childhood. An early sense of home was defined and displaced according to my father's low-functioning addiction to crack cocaine. My mother re-cently calculated—her face tense with the difficult calculus of loss—that we had lived in fourteen different houses in ten different towns before more or less settling in Tacoma when I was ten.

Our family never migrated completely from the South Puget Sound, but in each new location that we tried to resurrect belonging, my father would build debts or burn bonds until our best option was to move again. Sometimes the shifts in landscape were drastic, which might be why I always flinch a little when asked if I grew up as a city kid or farm boy—I have sensory-stirring memories from both environments, but neither feels quite right.

Names are another thing I got good at leaving behind. I have few grade school teachers or friends from the past whom I can match accu-rately with specific grades or ages. Although I still struggle with learning the names of the new people I meet, I see that old forgetfulness as a kind of survival now: how it helped to shorten the chain of lost hearths my father had forced us to drag around the Pacific Northwest. It took two decades of categorical hurt before my mother could quiet her love low and long enough to give him a final ultimatum, which he failed.

I never get used to the sensation of seeing a flock of birds first as some dark constellation flying underwater: the shadow of them swims through my downward-focused read of a river, and for a moment I am flooded with misunderstanding. I love this miracle of confusion, and I always hesitate before looking up into the sky for confirmation. But, now a father, I need more than a river to feed my difficult belief in something familiar perched impossibly on the window of change.

❖

By the time I was a teenager, my father could get clean only long enough to win back my mother's trust in giving him new keys to the changed locks on our doors, but never fully enough to give him a chance to relocate us again—which meant never meaningful enough for me to feel comfortable in claiming my father back.

Streams, however, became sanctuaries for our complicated communion. I can remember standing in shared water—whether coastal channel or Columbia tributary—and pulsing with the security of my connection to a man who otherwise seemed forever poised for exit or perish. Only while combing for schools of spawning fish that held in tight patterns against the current's push back toward the vastness of the Pacific, only there did I accept with any certainty that if I looked over my upstream or downstream shoulder I would find my father, fixed—which is to say, his dark silhouette anchored hip deep against a vibrancy of old-growth pines that lined the river, at home inside his own concerted casting into the silvery alchemy of contact.

In the midday effort to soften the sun's open-ended questions about a body's comfort, I decide to join some friends at the local swimming hole. I am late to arrive and ask, How is it? When they reply from the opposite bank, already adjusted to being inside the sharp comfort of the river's cold mouth, I can hear an honesty warming the assurance in their voices: The water's fine, they are saying, which I need to reach my ears because rivers have been scaring me lately. I can't afford to forfeit the most important ritual of my life. I dive in and receive my new breath. After paddling out to be with them, we spend the next hour creating a diversity of laughter while daring the beauty of our bodies to find new ways of entering the water without danger. Then we carry part of the river back in our hair.

❖

Psychodrama, bioenergetics, eye movement desensitization, and reprocessing—numerous psychotherapies have been designed to alleviate distress associated with traumatic memories. Such treatment works with the assumption that the mind, not unlike the body, can recover from psychological trauma. When cut, the body attempts to close the physical wound. If a foreign object or repeated injury irritates the physical wound, it will fester into pain. If the blockage can be removed, however, the body's natural movement toward healing will resume.

To approach this recovery occurring in the mind may be the scariest and most necessary beginning.

The river offers me risk to understand the trauma of my blood: no bank safe from excess, no choice other than submission to the stubborn forces that form and reform its complex circuitry. It lives and draws from more sources than we can perceive, which gives the river such reach. Our sense of suddenness in a flood is evidence that we have dammed or forgotten that reality. We know this according to our history of redirecting rivers and building structures that we love on the old banks that bide the perfect conditions to remind us of the boundlessness of water. When we curse the flood, we add another prayer for forgetting that first sacrifice. How many floods make a blessing?

❖

The summer after I finished high school marked what would become the longest and most decided silence I've ever placed between my father and me. One morning, a week before I was to leave for college, an argument broke out between my parents. I was sleeping in and could hear the frustration in their voices loading and reloading below the floorboards. When my sister came up to my room, I made space beside me. She climbed into the bed, and I tried convincing her to find escape in more sleep, until she replied through tears of confusion:"No, Dad hit her—he just hit Mom." I didn't hide my breaking point, punching several holes in the wall on my way down toward the newest wound of him. My final image of *father* for the next six years would be that morning's rage-blurred shape of him running out our back door, my mother demanding me to stop destroying the house.

After so many disappointments and such erosion of the notion of *home* that it seemed more a miracle than an idea with him around, I couldn't conjure another reason for staying in touch. I couldn't consider one more meeting with that body that wasn't mere violence. My mother wouldn't divorce my father until my sophomore year of college, but I could tell she, too, was nearing the completion of her own quilt of tragedy in which to bury her love for him. By the spring term of my freshman year, there was already a noticeable diminishment to the questions I could tell he was feeding me through my mother over the phone. If I could sense him getting the courage to take the line, I hung up.

I've been known to linger on a section of stream that's baffling me: crosscurrent drags, small-window casts, undersurface eddies. Long after the water's been disturbed by my blundered approach and all fish have fled or hid, I'll work and work until I get the look I need for a first chance. If no loved one waits upstream or no dear friend doubles back to break the lock of my concentration, I will stay as long as it takes to feel closer to getting it right the next time.

❖

My father tried at least twice to keep a long-haul trucking job. He began his second failed attempt after I had started college, so I planned my visits home to avoid any chance of overlap with his breaks from the road. My mother was quietly honoring my excommunication and, within months of its genesis, had altogether stopped bringing my father up in conversation. My younger siblings, however, still had faith in the nuclear church of home and told me of the tears my name brought, pleading for reconciliation. I honored their dreams with my reserve, only breaking the fourth wall of hope once.

It was Christmas and my father had orchestrated a surprise visit to ford the bitterness between us. As he stood outside, waiting for some warm reunion to emerge, it must have been my siblings' shocked account of the scene inside that got him to realize the bad idea and retreat, my fiancée trying and failing to stop me from cursing and pacing a rage as honest as extinction into the cold cathedral of the house.

When I think back to that day, I have an odd sense of pride in my success at holding on to the thinnest cord of control I've ever asked to pull me back from my own lost temper—because it could have been much worse. I could have opened that door.

Heave.

❖

As so often is the case, it took the blunt edge of irony to soften me enough to break back into contact with my father. I was going through my own divorce and the heaviest drinking of my life, and one morning I spent two long hours on my hands and knees searching a shitty apartment for my only pair of glasses. I had awoken earlier on the floor and was too drunk the night prior to remember when or where I had taken them off, and they had since blurred and blended into the brown shag carpet.

By the time the first hour of unsuccessful searching had passed, my semiblind cigarette breaks on the front porch stopped being enough to keep my emotional state from swaying hysterically: absurd humor to livid frustration to cosmic shame. When I finally found the glasses (tucked under the couch, an arm's length away from where I had passed out in the dark), I sat on my loft steps and cried into an emptiness that still reverberated with this bizarre rendering of my mental life. Adding more pressure to the wound, it occurred to me that I had reached (if not passed) the age my father was when I was born. I wiped my eyes, reached for the phone, and dialed my brother: "I'm ready to find Dad."

The first few weeks of real rain reveal more than the relief of trout that have spent the dry months stressed by low and warm conditions. I like to stand from a bridge on high water and watch how the muddied river starts touching the old banks and new growth that were beyond its reach all summer. Then, when the river drops back to clarity, the long, troughed bottom becomes a vantage of where and why this river might continue to press its belonging into the earth.

❖

My father had committed himself into another drug rehabilitation program—this one hidden away in the forested foothills of rural western Washington, and only a short drive from a section of the Cowlitz River that I'd never explored. Before making the trip, my brother and I got permission from the rehab's director to check my father out for an afternoon of fishing.

At the river's side, we took longer than usual to rig our rods, and our casts seemed to happen in a graceful slow motion that joy can sometimes create. The entire time my father kept stopping to look me over until I returned eye contact, then he'd smile and shake his head, whispering to himself—more, it seemed, out of wonder than fact—"My son." It's my only memory of him speaking of anything other than fishing while standing on the banks of a river.

It wasn't spawning season, so no real numbers of salmon were running upstream, but to say that nobody caught anything that day couldn't be further from the truth.

While I almost always start with a nymph pattern (my instincts and experience pulling my imagination toward what's unfolding invisibly under the surface), fly-fishing has broadened my habits of attention and my willingness to transition tactics. I often fail, however, with stopping at slow water, drawn by the promise of a riffle around the bend. This despite my knowing how, every once in a great while, if I let one small rise give me permission to sit beside a pool and wait, I'm rewarded with the chance of witnessing a river-rare fullness to feeding—I've seen insect hatches that startled me, the sky and water so full of questions and answers to desire.

❖

The first time I lived beyond the epic gaze of the Rocky Mountains was in my early twenties, when I moved to central Pennsylvania for grad school. Instead of flying, I drove the 2,643 miles—each one an opportunity to question the reality of being outside the reach of my most beloved rivers: the Satsop, the Newaukum, the Cowlitz. By luck, I arrived in Happy Valley and found myself surrounded by Class A trout water. And so began my full conversion from spin-fishing to fly-fishing (although, while visiting my mother in Washington, I still pick up my spinning rod—and probably will for the rest of my able life—twice each year during steelhead season).

Nearly a decade later, when I was considering professional options for setting down new family roots, the only metric I added to the list of deal breakers was a reasonable range from the nearest cold running water. In fact, whenever I travel for work, if I will be there for any length of time, the first things I research are local streams; if there is trout water within hitchhiking distance, I adjust what I plan to wear in order to make room in my luggage for a fly rod and waders.

I think what I'm trying to say here is that a river has been the most played song on the soundtrack of my life. Without it, I would lack the noise I need to reset the sonic backdrop of everyday havoc in my head. Without it, because I don't know if poetry is enough, I may not be here today.

✳

When I was growing up, my father's addiction was not exactly banished by the river's edge. Despite my mother's protests, he occasionally brought along the addict friends he accumulated from his string of rehab stays.

I once met a large, heavily bearded man who watched me from the bank for half an hour as I struggled with a grotesque skein of monofilament seizing my reel. When I looked his way in impatient agony, he told me he wasn't allowed to touch fishing gear anymore. Before I could crack a grin, and with a sobering candor that I had caught in my own father's voice, he added: "I'm a recovering fishing addict." I had never considered the possibility, and the tribe in my throat trembled.

The man remained in a quiet calm behind me during the second half of the hour it took me to finally clear and retie my line. The whole while I thought about my mother experimenting with similar sanctions, but always on the number of dollars my father could carry in his pocket or how much gas we could put in the car's tank before the threat of his next relapse became a promise.

But if my father craved a thing, he also abused time for it. When that thing was fishing, he would neglect necessities like food and water rather than be pulled back toward the everyday teeth of the world. And during the peak of a salmon run, work and family could suffer. In the middle of the night or early the next morning, we'd shuffle with exhaustion through the front door, smelling of evergreens and, if we were lucky, of fish—neither of which would unfold my mother's worried arms.

To this day I, too, will ignore hunger and hours if I reach my full stride while fishing or writing. So in a sense, from the beginning, my art of angling (and of poetry) and the well-being I experience while wading into stream or page have been entangled—and perhaps even leavened—according to the elements leveling home all these years.

A river will hold its one long sigh until the throat goes dry—sometimes that takes centuries. I want to carry this fact home as peace, to feel drenched with that much healthy sound.

❖

I still depend on the immediacy I gain while on the banks of a river: past and future thinned into the more manageable margins between which I am responsible only for reading the water and the moment before me. The time I spend like this works to refuel a belief that my being in the world is vital.

It's been a decade now since I last fished with my father. Against prediction, he still rises through the uncertainty of his latest absence, and each time he does, I recognize less and less of him inside his own voice over the phone; I hear a life flattening into one dry season of desire. The drugs continue to cleave. And I feel close to losing my line to him for good. I fear what my rivers will mean to me then.

A group of mergansers drifts downstream, just off the far shore. Their formation resembles a letter C—the mouth of which they have aimed and move closer toward the bank. It's not until they dive in unison that I understand the hunt: they've corralled a school of panicked baitfish into shallow water. When each duck surfaces with something small and brilliant flashing silver against the dark decision of its beak, I can't see or hear anything but hunger thriving along this moving body.

Dream Shelter

Angie Cruz

"I should say: the house shelters day-dreaming, the house protects
the dreamer, the house allows one to dream in peace."
—GASTON BACHELARD, *The Poetics of Space*

For over ten years I lived in two realities. The reality of my marriage,
motherhood, and teaching at a university in Pittsburgh, all of which
are legibly responsible behavior, and my other reality, one often referred
to as irresponsible, where I piled on debt to sustain my New York City
apartment in Washington Heights.

In the year 2000 I secured an apartment in Washington Heights
with my name on the lease. Back then I thought I would never marry, or
have children, or move from New York. It was a place where my neighbors called me *querida, amor, corazón, mi'ja*. The same ones who judged
me for the men and women who entered and exited my apartment at all
hours of the night because they didn't look like family or weren't from the
hood. Where the reggaeton blasted downstairs, making my floors vibrate
under my feet, and the children across the way shrilled songs from the
film *Grease*. Where anyone who needed a place to stay had a key. I often
left the front door, guarded with an old-school bat, unlocked, for writers
passing through to New York. It was where folks pissed in the elevators
and littered the stairs with the guts of cigars, candy wrappers, and beer
bottles. The roof door was padlocked and the lobby had a security camera
that streamed on my TV. While I worked late nights at my computer,
I binge-watched those lobby doors, anticipating who would enter, who
would exit, completely absorbed by it.

Having a space of my own, in the heart of a neighborhood that
has served as my muse for all of my writing career, gave me footing
with my immediate family who lived within blocks. Before I moved
to Pittsburgh that apartment afforded me the ability to write in the
utmost alive way, spontaneously, desperately, urgently, erotically. I was
able to access the knowledge and inheritance of my body, the darkness,

the horrific, the spiritual. In that apartment I was fertile. Everything was possible.

My seven-hundred-fifty-square-foot apartment faced the back alley. Hardwood floors. One bedroom. Eat-in kitchen. Ceramic mosaic tiles in the bathroom. Light filled, prewar, high ceilings. Elevator in building and laundry in basement. Next to the A train's 175th Street station. I could get to midtown in twenty minutes. To the West Village in twenty-five. Dominican food up the street, open twenty-four hours. It was on the "safe" side of Broadway. Minimally furnished, just essentials: a platform bed, a makeshift desk, an Aeron chair, a retro laminate breakfast table snugged into the kitchen.

This apartment was where I fucked the Verizon guy who came to install my phone, and the contractor who blew my fuse while working upstairs. Where I made my straight friends cum with my hand, with my mouth, when they told me they were sad and feared they would never find love. Where I met with fellow writers and activists to plan readings, protests, to write, to cook, to dance. Oh, how we danced, up until all hours and scratched the floors and emptied the bottles of tequila, rum, wine. Where the laughter shook the walls. The wooden floors creaked. The ghost sounds of marbles rolling on the floor. Where mice squeaked. Where plays were written, and scholarly books, and novels, and stories, and poems. Where the phone rang off the hook and the answering machine was filled with messages from my grandmother who lived eight blocks away: The food is ready, she said. Come get it? And my mother: Can you? Will you? I love you. And my lovers: I can't wait to see you. Forgive me. Fuck you. And of course friends: Let's meet. I miss you. You bitch. Always the bill collectors: This is a reminder . . . And my drunk father: Why don't you love me?

Even when I first took an academic job in Texas and then moved to Pittsburgh, I always said I lived in New York. This apartment in Washington Heights was the home I planned to return to if I could ever get a teaching job in New York City. That was until the bright yellow eviction notices were plastered on my door.

The milk boiled over. The rice burned.

After twelve years of inhabiting an impossible forever I lost *it*. I lost

New York. I lost Washington Heights. The walls that housed my intimacies contracted and expanded with my desire, with my fear, vaporizing, reshaping the world as monster, as adventure. My apartment with the eviction notice on the door was both my cell but also—what if, friends consoled me—also my freedom? Immigrants move. Suck it up. It's New York. It loves no one. Get over it. Home is where your people are. *Really?*

When I was evicted there was no funeral. No "I'm sorry for your loss." I was fully displaced, defeated. Lost. Full of loss. What is a space or place but an imagined set of stories, refabricated over and over with time to corroborate our existence. Yes, I could no longer enter that apartment, but the worst of it was that I lost *it*, the "un/inhabitable space" that lived only in my imagination. Without it I had to accept that Pittsburgh was my only reality. Motherhood, marriage, and teaching filled my days with obligations, deadlines, and responsibilities. All being the antidote to inspiration and the erotic. What about my muse and my writing? How did I allow a love affair with my husband, born in the south of France at an artist residency, to turn into a marriage consumed with the quotidian? For three years I searched for a place that quelled the loss to no avail.

But then I found an echo of *it* in Wedding, Berlin. Much like Washington Heights it was a part of the city that's not in any of the tourist's books. It's right on the periphery, edging with Mitte and the more trendy Prenzlauer Berg. Wedding is Washington Heights in the '90s. But Turkish, African. Slowly being gentrified by German artists. Not Dominican. But yet, the men sit outside of Turkish cafes playing cards and smoking from hookahs. It could've been dominoes; they could've been drinking Presidente. They leer at me like Dominican men often do and wear tight shirts and no socks and have manicured hairstyles. Salons everywhere. Fruit piles, makeshift tables crowded with families. Who wants to be inside a stuffy apartment on a summer day? No one. Children tug on their mothers' dresses, lag behind, tired from doing numerous errands. Mothers chastise them, slap them against their heads. Tough love. Stores crowded with headless mannequins with brightly colored clothes. Music blaring from inside apartments. Broken bottles tucked into building corners. Large bubble-letter graffiti. What year is it again? This is not New York. This is not the Heights. This is Wedding, but also the Heights

I remember, full of music, police sirens and children wailing. Stop and frisk. In Wedding I saw cops slow down their ride, stop some man, not once or twice but three times in ten days. Everyone watched. We held our breath. They were looking for a man with a knife, a machete, an axe, a bomb, for a man that may strike at a doctor's office, on a train, in a train station, at a concert, a parade, at a church.

Maybe it's because I'm not a threat in Berlin. I'm a tourist after all. Wedding terrorized me and for this also it felt homelike. When the smell of *platanos* frying on some stove wafted in my direction from someone's open kitchen window, my heart exploded. It was also a place where for the first time in a long while I remembered the potential of my marriage. I spent my days working on a new novel, while my husband installed art in his studio. My son was with the grandparents in Italy. When we met in the evening for dinner we were charged from making art all day, free from the everyday life stress. It felt like a luxury. A short refuge from the real. But it raises the question: For me, is the feeling of being erotic, creative, alive charged by a person or a place? Both?

And then just weeks later, while traveling alone, I also found *it* in Catania, Italy, at the mouth of the fish market where weathered fishermen unabashedly hollered, the fish glittered, a treasure chest of neonati, silverfish, swordfish, shark, clams, oysters, bluefish. This much, that much, taste this, try that, the smell of fresh herbs, stagnant water, ripe peaches, tomatoes, bananas, cantaloupes. A deluge. The eyes ogle. The older matrons shove. I hide my camera, take photos from my hip, capture purple stilettos caught in the lava-made bricks that blanket all the streets. A pile of roasted onions, a child's hand yanked by a mother. I don't walk the market, I flow with it, dodge the motorcycles and the quick-footed young men with crates over their heads. Gestures of fuck off. Why are you looking at me? Hands in the air, fingers coming together, flipping me off.

I ask for a peach. The vendor with hair like a sail and tartar-filled teeth hands me a rotten-looking one, advertising kilometer zero: fruit with minimal carbon footprint. He kisses his fingertips and says *buonissimo.* The very best.

Don't you have one that's more beautiful, I ask.

Americana?

Why didn't he just slap me? I'm Dominican. I'm from New York. I am American, yes, but fuck. Am I acting like the ugly American?

Ugly Americans are loud, never satisfied, like to return things. They take up more space than they need, order cappuccino in the afternoon, wear flip-flops in the city, always smiling and showing off their big white straight shiny teeth.

He laughs at me and hands over a nicer-looking one but gives me the ugly peach for free.

You'll learn something, he says and winks.

In secret I bite into the ugly peach. It is fleshy, sweet, just right.

Catania felt like home. It was a whiff of the Washington Heights I missed and longed for. Maybe it was the ugly-looking, perfect-tasting peach, or the cold, sweet almond granitas I ate daily. Maybe it was the active volcano Etna, the tallest volcano in all of Europe, that cast its shadow over the city, or the way Etna showed off its eruptions while I swam in the Mediterranean. That sea, warm and thick, like baby's bath water. Maybe it's because Santa Agatha is the patron saint of Catania. When the king wanted to sleep with Agatha she refused and he chopped off her breasts. She was rolled in tar and buried under the church. Now to reach her you must unlock seven gates, all underwater. Maybe it's the architecture, the buildings made with black lava stone. Not a white and bright city like Palermo, like Rome, like Siracusa. Catania was often slammed, even by its residents as not the prettiest city—so dark, so gloomy, they say. But I found this architectonic anomaly comforting. A black-negative city. The black being the substance.

Many people I met reminded me how Etna is heavily monitored as if to reassure me that there is no immediate danger. They knew this from watching countless volcano documentaries aired on TV. I thrived in this tension of not knowing, this imminent danger. In Catania I was swept into a school of women who'd known one another all their lives. They swept me into their clan, asked if I wanted to join them to the beach with the shales, or do I prefer the pebbles. What about soft sand? Did I want to go to the museum—antique or contemporary? Or try the Calabrain restaurant in the dangerous part of town where the delinquents killed cops but the food was cheap and authentic. Not like the tourist traps near my hotel. Let's visit the vineyard, let's go for a walk. Let's have an *aperitivo*. Your choice. You're our guest! Now our family.

It was the first time in a long while that I visited or lived in a place where the people claimed me as family.

The Sicilian aunt invited me to lunch and said, Are you able to appreciate Catania, could you see its beauty? Her question made me want to be the kind of person who could appreciate Catania and see its beauty. I said yes to the summer heat, the fried street food stuffed with cheese, and hams, and ragùs inside of large risotto balls. For ten days I curled up and inhabited Catania, a nook on the earth that captured my imagination, the intimacy and intensity I had yet to feel outside of the walls of my old apartment in Washington Heights. In Catania I wanted to make. I wanted to live. I wanted to laugh. To fuck. To make babies. I wanted to write. I wanted to kiss. I wanted to connect. To talk. To sleep. To dance. To sing. My body vibrating, my soul hungry, my heart open. Like the volcano, charged, threatening, fertile, I pulsed in this city from the soles of my feet to the ends of my hair.

In art therapy for children, when a child draws a house one can get a clue of their "deepest dream shelter" where they have found their happiness. It is rooted, with a foundation, and usually if you ask them what's inside they will name warm fuzzy things they care about, all protected inside. I've tried to draw my house in Pittsburgh. It houses all of my possessions. It's also the home of my husband and nine-year-old son. A Victorian house built in 1888. Once a house for the elderly, the house of a trucker, the house of an attorney general. Now it is ours. Every wall has been painted over. Windows have been replaced. Floors have been stripped and redone. And yet, there is no active volcano casting its shadow. There is no bountiful fish market, no beach nearby, no police sirens, or Spanish music or dancing; there are no schools of women whose daily work is to take care of one another, feed one another. No blood family. My mother, my siblings, my cousins, my family say they will visit, but they never do because it's too far away. People will argue that Pittsburgh has everything one needs, but it's not the same. The weather gets cold, the sky so gray. It's segregated. The urban layout intentionally divisive. People seem to walk in this city as if they're invisible, or maybe it's because in this city I feel invisible, a transient figure much like university students who are still in the search for their forever home.

Before I was evicted from my apartment in Washington Heights my plan was to live part-time in New York and commute to Pittsburgh to teach. But then we bought a house. My son made friends in our Pittsburgh neighborhood. He found activities he's invested in like judo and violin. So my every-two-week visits to Washington Heights became every three weeks, sometimes four. Unwillingly Pittsburgh occupied me. The distance between me and New York swelled, my Spanish broke, the music faded, the familial smells ghosted me, and yet my desire for Washington Heights could not be quelled.

Every time I walk past my old building I feel this phantom sensation, my severed apartment, my home, taken from me because I was flagged as an out-of-state resident. I was caught because I registered to vote in Pennsylvania, because I registered my car and took a job in Pittsburgh. I had to let it go because having a job with benefits was also part of growing up. Because it was good for my family.

When asked, "Do you like Pittsburgh, does it feel like home," I think, will I ever be able to appreciate Pittsburgh, to see its beauty?

Oh, to be inside of my old building. A feverish void. I no longer have the key to enter my apartment, dressed in avocado walls, its bright red apple-colored closets, the sunflower kitchen, the lavender bedroom. Its pulse sucked my breath. I heaved from my crotch. My roots, my orientation, snatched. What now? Where can I go to daydream?

Refuge

William Kittredge

In August of 1936 I turned four years old. My father, Oscar Kittredge, had hauled his family to the brand new house he'd built for us in Warner Valley, on an old homestead site surrounded by Lombardy poplars and gnarled apple trees. From the screened-in veranda that held off swarming mosquitoes we confronted willow-lined sloughs out below us in the Thompson Field and far-side-of-the-valley swamps where Oscar was pushing forward with extensive reclamations.

The massive stone fireplace in our house and those fields below us constituted emotional locations in what was to be my childhood homeland. Out on our lawn in the luminous early morning, barefoot in blue pajamas, I gazed up at V-shaped, undulating flights of waterbirds—darting blue- and green-winged teal and green-headed mallard drakes and redheads and canvasbacks and thousands of Canadian honkers, phalarope, and avocet, and gulls from the distant Pacific—flotillas of migrating birds, their wings sighing in the stillness, soaring, lifting, and clamoring. Oscar told me they were heading for nesting grounds in the Arctic tundra or in river-mouth estuaries beyond the boreal forests, wherever such forests were. My urge to mix storytelling and nature was underway.

❖

In her 2016 book, *Human Advantage: A New Understanding of How Our Brains Became Remarkable*, Suzana Herculano-Houzel, a Brazilian neuroscientist, writes that long-ago humans found that meats and vegetative materials that had been incinerated by wildfires were both edible and nourishing. They had found cooking, a way to predigest foods. Millennia rolled by as they fed cooked food to insatiably hungry brains.

The human brain, she says, accounts for about two percent of our body weight but requires twenty-five percent of our energy if it is going to function. If we ate only raw foods to meet that demand, we'd be constantly searching for food and eating—like gorillas in their jungles.

Thus, cooking led to profound changes in the relationship between humans and their habitats and may have helped us evolve into the "intelligent" species. Families and clans settled around fire pits where cooking took place. Such locations were often thought of as sacred homelands, like Warner Valley, where I lived as a child, was for me.

❖

Annick Smith and I, in the 1980s, roamed the two-lane highways across the southwest deserts, visiting religious sites like Second Mesa and traipsing through the trading post at Hubbell while lusting for Navajo rugs we'd never be able to afford. After hiking into Canyon de Chelly, we studied the White House, an adobe preconquest village built on a steep terrace below towering sandstone walls. We wondered how mothers raised children up there. How had they kept them from falling off? And why had they been living up there?

A dozen years later, at Roque Saint-Christophe in central France, a few kilometers from the sixteen-thousand-year-old painted bulls in the cavern at Lascaux, Annick and I got in from the rain and entered the largest rock shelter in Europe. Families and clans had lived in there, tucked under that stone ceiling for thousands of years. At the deepest rear we stood by fire pits, cooking hearths, used by humans through that same unending sequence of seasons.

The inhabitants of such a shelter could not be attacked from the rear, obviously, and the forward edge looked off a perpendicular cliff to a meadow that reached the Vézère River. They could see trouble coming before it got to them—as had the inhabitants of the White House in Canyon de Chelly. Everywhere, we are busy establishing sheltered homelands, locating human dwellings in ways known as "prospect and refuge." It's as common today—worldwide in suburban enclave after enclave—as it was with our preliterate ancestors.

My father believed in diesel-powered equipment and twenty-four-inch electric pumps and redwood head gates, bulldozers, and draglines. But on a Sunday morning he'd sleep in and fry mush for us to spread with butter and Vermont maple syrup. Then, his work became too successful. His oats and barley, as World War II progressed, were hugely profitable. Eventually, success was not enough.

Oscar bought wooden crates of 12-gauge shotgun shells and Scotch whisky. He befriended out-of-state bankers and regional politicians. Autumn in Warner became hunting season. Self-important, big-bellied men (including a light opera movie star) showed up at our dinner table. My father's pals, I decided, were bullying shitheads. I began suffering from "problems with authority." During adolescence, my connection to my homeland eroded seriously.

✦

It would be a while before I found an adult to trust. During my sophomore year at Oregon State College, majoring in general agriculture, a useless course of study, at least for me, seeking diversion, I signed up for Introduction to American Literature. Herbert Childs, the teacher, turned out to be a type I'd never before encountered, a liberal. Herb Childs took us through Emerson and Thoreau and *Moby Dick* and Emily Dickinson and *Huck Finn*, and then Walt Whitman, and his preface to *Leaves of Grass*: "This is what you shall do, love the earth and sun and the animals. Despise riches. Stand up for the stupid and crazy. . . ." I had never imagined such a message. It opened doors into yet another homeland. I was developing a renewed sense of how to proceed with life.

In my next class with Herbert Childs we read a prose translation of Plato's *Republic* and Sophocles' *Antigone* and civil disobedience and Milton: "Give me the liberty to know, to utter, and to argue freely according to conscience, above all liberties." We examined the ways lying brings down societies, and leafed through photos of naked women and men in chains, emaciated bodies stacked like wood in Nazi camps. We finished with Thoreau, and more civil disobedience.

Herb Childs encouraged my boyish inclination to withstand authorities, inviting me to his office and asking me if I could explain my disdain for Oscar's friends—governors and senators and the like. I told of those men shooting at daybreak and then breaking out flasks of Scotch and how they would not deal with the mallards and Canadian honkers they'd killed. Oscar hung the inert birds in the crab apple tree behind our house. After those carcasses froze, they were taken to Lakeview where women picked them and sent them along to out-of-luck locals. Herbert Childs gave me a sense that I was free to express my indignation. I began flirting with the political ideas that would shape my future, and imagining that I, myself, might turn out to be someone who said what he meant.

❖

The fall of 1967, as my family was selling our properties, I was separated from the wife and the children I'd betrayed. Holed up in a two-room cabin by the icebound Williamson River, one of the ranches my family owned, I'd go out each morning to a snowy field and feed baled hay to dry cows.

My father showed up driving a new yellow Mercedes, traveling with Francis Reynolds, his second wife. Francis stayed in the Mercedes, vapor pluming from the tailpipe as Oscar came in and asked if I had anything to drink. Of course I did, Jack Daniel's. I poured shots and he got down to business. "What are you going to do with yourself?"

This was a reasonable question. I told him I was going off to try the life I'd imagined. Having wanted to be a writer since college, now at age thirty-five, my marriage ruined, sitting on the promise of money in the bank, I was going to make my move.

Come January I'd be gone to Eugene and graduate school. Even though Oscar had jumped through plenty of his own hoops, I was afraid he'd think I'd lost my mind. But he surprised me. "I've done things I hated all my life," he said. "I sure as hell wouldn't recommend that."

After another drink he went down the road with Francis and the yellow Mercedes. There it was. Whatever I'd planned was OK with Oscar. Everybody else thought I was crazy.

❖

A decade later I was teaching at the University of Montana. On spring break, my friend and fellow professor Richard Hugo, the poet, led a gang of escapees on a trip to La Push on the Quileute Indian Reservation. We emerged from the rain forests to confront the roaring, incessant Pacific, a coastline fronted on rocky promontories. Snowy peaks of the Olympic National Park loomed behind us. Hugo maintained that the air at sea level was richer than in the highlands of Montana (more oxygen). Lulled by waves breaking nearby he vanished into a motel room with six-packs of Olympia beer and slept while the rest of us investigated paradise.

Down on my knees, I studied tide pools while wind from the southwest brought the stink of the Pacific, and I looked up to steely orange slants of rain beyond offshore sea stacks crowned with fringes of evergreen. Heart-stopping intricacy convinced me that my days were not pointless. The significance of all this intensified during solitary walks amid the enormous trees and thickets of vines hung with tangled mosses along the Hoh River. Ospreys fed and I admired their clarity of intention; this revelation was weedy with life. Oscar's river-stone fireplace, and my childhood view of the Thompson Field, and this seacoast: Why did they feel so similar to me?

❖

Another decade later, traveling in British Columbia with Annick, visiting with Northwestern Indian artists in the seaside town of Prince Rupert, we drove upstream along the Skeena River. The snowy mountains were releasing a huge early summer runoff. Evening came as we wandered into Kitwancool, a tiny logging town on one side of a narrow road. On the downhill side we parked and studied intricately fenced burial sites and huge carved cedar house poles. The All Frogs pole and the Hole in the Sky pole loomed in the twilight.

A large mother frog rests atop the All Frogs pole, her offspring descending, going to populate the earth. But the Hole in the Sky pole, what did it signify? An entryway that had been carved through its heart once served as the door to an extensive communal house enclosed by cedar planks. Families lived around fire pits—traditional hearths of their own. Children were born, great-grandparents died. The entire communal household inside that great house was thought of as a version of heaven; it was understood to be a realm for the living but also for the spirit of anyone who ever lived there if they were remembered by anyone—hearths as heavens. I'd found a name for my memoir, *Hole in the Sky*.

❖

The notion of hearths as homelands has helped me consolidate the emotions that had swept over me in Warner, a child in rapture beneath soaring, calling, and undulating waterbirds. We spend lifetimes locating homelands and naming dreams.

The Hole in the Sky pole led me to celebrate the usefulness of communal lives, families and clans and individuals dedicated to taking care of mothers and fathers and infants and the aged and cherishing those who exist only in our memories.

It's my belief that we should recognize that the intricate world, terrains where humans have thrived, cannot be replicated. Continuing toward ruination is craziness. We should care for and cherish our physical and psychic commons. Encouraging devotion to the homelands we inhabit is necessary, and our responsibility. It may be our chance at paradise.

The Temple of the Word: Lyric Poetry and the Conservation of the Self and the World

Mark Tredinnick

1.

When God wanted finally to cut Job a break, He gave him a natural history lesson, and He gave it to him in poetry.

Times like Job's come to most of us, often in midlife: grief and depression, an unravelling of self, a sort of exile from one's self and one's world. They've befallen me these past few years, and that's the territory many of my recent poems explore—a long unhearthing, a fracturing of my self it has been hard to get to the end of.

The book of Job, according to Tennyson the most beautiful work of poetry in all of Western literature, is a consideration in sustained metaphor of a theological question: "Why do the righteous suffer?" I don't put myself in Job's righteous shoes. What triggered my crisis—if it did not begin way back at my birth and before—was the end of a marriage, for which I was to blame, and the shattering of a family, which I have labored hard to mend. Though Job wails, "Wherefore do the wicked live, become old, yea, are mighty in power . . . their houses . . . safe from fear?" the truth is all of us get to suffer, some of us profoundly, the meek and the mighty; and the worst of suffering like Job's is what happens afterward in one's mind.

The suffering that is the unmaking of the self is bedded in psychological predisposition, and manifests as a neurochemical disruption in the brain, which we are only at the start of understanding; it is an encounter, unavoidable for some of us, with the shadow-side of consciousness, a darkness that living wide awake one will always come to in the end. It may be set off by trauma, however caused, whoever is to blame, by cruelty or betrayal or loss or illness, by the alienation of one's children, by any of the many kinds of misfortune that are in the nature of things. These digital days, it may be induced by the Internet, by the incoherence of the world and one's identity in it, the pixilation of reality that is a particular aspect of contemporary existence.

Despair like Job's may be understood, whatever causes it, as a falling out of wonder with the world, out of awe, a catastrophic failure of conviction about one's own miraculous part in the larger scheme of things. Life loses shape and refuses form; the hearth that held you lets you slip. One is unhoused from one's days and tortured by one's nights. One is beyond one's own or anyone's reach. My version of Job's lot has felt like profound disenchantment with myself and my work. Even the world of birds and ridgetops and rivers and trees lost its magic. Each morning I wake and my life is something less than a theoretical proposition. My unhearthing is a spiritual distemper; it is a loss of one's grip on the meaning of a life, a nihilism to which, perhaps, those of us most dedicated to the making of meaning are most vulnerable. And it falls especially hard on those who never learned how to care for themselves, who never, early, learned to *feel* what they said they knew—that the nature of the universe is love, and that some of that love is meant for oneself, a birthright, and secure.

The worst of the anguish is not the loss of one's actual hearth, one's people and their love, though that is bad enough; the worst of it is how one comes unhearthed in one's head. The worst of it for Job is not that he's persecuted, but that he persecutes himself; among all his losses the chief is his loss of belief in his own worth. And so depression goes.

The shattering of a self. Loss of life's lyric. A self and a world evacuated of all meaning for a time. A long time, sometimes. Where there was joy, there is panic.

Job loses his hearth, and he loses heart. He is "broken in pieces"; he loses his means and his way, his fortune and his family's affection; "my breath is strange to my wife," and "yea, young children despised me; I arose, and they spoke against me." As Job puts it, perhaps not realizing what he says: "All my inward friends abhorred me." Job, in his travails, lost the capacity to be a friend to himself, to father and console himself, to remember what he belonged to, the family of his affections, and how to delight in it. He forgot how to be grateful for the gift of his own life.

Job finds his way out of woe by chance. By grace. God relents. The unhearthing ends, and he is home again and rich in days. But not before he gets the lecture in natural history and natural justice. Job becomes good when the world (in the words of God) reminds Job of the arrogance of his self-pity and humbles him back home—puts him back inside the wonder of things. God, the embodiment of the mind of the world, wants Job, wants each of us, even in our despair or perhaps as a way out of our despair, to wonder again. At the beauty of all Creation. Job is asked to remember his own life, blighted for a time, as part of all that God hath wrought. He wants Job to make his life now worthy of his suffering, as the Buddha put it in another faith system.

> Hearken unto this, O Job:
> stand still, and consider the wondrous works of God.
> Dost thou know when God disposed them,
> And caused the light of his cloud to shine?
> Dost thou know the balancings of the clouds . . .
> when he quieteth the earth by the south wind?

God asks Job: "Hast thou commanded the morning since thy days?" He asks him, unrelenting: "Knowest thou the time when the wild goats of the rock bring forth?" and "Hast thou given the horse strength? Hast thou clothed his neck with thunder? Canst thou make him afraid of the grasshopper? . . . Doth the hawk fly by thy wisdom, and stretch her wings toward the south?" Beautiful and petulant.

Then God calls Job to action, back into the world. He reminds Job that he, like all of us, has in him the power and the duty to save himself, and to save some others in the process: "Gird up thy loins like a man. . . . Deck thyself now with majesty and excellence, and array thyself with glory and beauty." One of God's creatures and therefore holy;.a human being and therefore compelled to act with conscience: "Look on every one that is proud, and abase him . . . and tread down the wicked in their place. . . . Then I will confess unto thee that thy own right hand can save thee."

God's concluding remarks bring to mind Seamus Heaney's in his Nobel Prize acceptance speech. Poetry, said Heaney, "satisfies the contradictory needs which consciousness experiences at times of extreme crisis, the need on the one hand for a truth-telling that will be hard and retributive, and on the other hand the need not to harden the mind to a point where it denies its own yearnings for sweetness and trust." Poetry's work: to hold the world to account and at the same time to hold everything dear, including oneself. Love's work, too; and the work the unhearthed self must find a way to do, though he finds it almost impossible to get out of bed some mornings and get on with it, with anything.

2.

Most people, as William Styron writes in his luminous reflection on his own affliction, *Darkness Visible*, come through depression in the end. The return of wonder is a sign one has bottomed out, like Dante at the end of his downward pilgrimage through hell. The beloved shows, and the heavens throw light again. Just how and when the capacity for wonder returns is another of the mysteries God would have Job respect. Science still knows little about depression, how it comes, and why it lifts. One thing I know, and the book of Job seems to say, is that there's more than grace involved in its passing: there's time, a lot of it, and there's work, and it may be the hardest you'll ever get to do.

Here's the work: still your mind; find home again among all that you belong to. Healing has to do with making in your daily life and in your habits of mind a new and coherent shape and asking yourself to believe in it and live it out. Healing is making your life a poem again, in which all that you belong to is implied, all grief and all joy, birdsong and books. Healing is a hearth you fashion to replace the one you lost.

A hearth once lost is hard to find again, and harder yet to hold. The loneliness that comes with being dispossessed of yourself, the exile from all that loved you once, is a condition that in its nature refuses the very work that would make it well. It takes Job forty-two chapters to make his peace with the god in him. To stop fighting the river. It's taken me long enough, too.

3.

Hearth contains "earth" and "heart" and "hear" and "art," as many others, I'm
sure, have noted. To return to health (of mind and body) is to become
whole again: *health*, a word so close in form to "hearth," is etymologically
related to "whole." In returning to health of heart and head, one comes together again; all your several and severed pieces find home, and the home,
yourself, finds a world to hold still in, to serve and save and celebrate.

To be truly at home in yourself is to feel you belong to something more
than yourself. As David Hinton puts it in *Hunger Mountain*: "Things are
themselves only as they belong to something more than themselves: I to we,
we to earth, earth to planets and stars." In *Hunger Mountain*, Hinton walks
the mountain near his home in Vermont, giving thought as he walks to the
poetry he has translated so limpidly from the Chinese. "Wisdom for [the
ancient Chinese poets]," writes Hinton, "meant belonging deeply to that
cosmology of restless hunger" that is the landscape and all of us within it.

It is precisely that sense of belonging that is lost in depression. How
do you conjure belonging back? The hearth where the outer world meets
the inner, where all the selves you are, inside and out, is remade, I think,
mostly by faith and hope. One of my recent poems, "Back When," puts it
this way:

> Love's work now
> Is five parts hanging in there, and four parts
> hanging on. Waiting

> Out the fracture. Sweeping up the mess.
> *Backfilling every rift*, meantime,
> *with awe*. Keeping faith in silence.

Somehow, you hold open a space for your whole self, not your old
one, but one more at ease with the way things are, with the sorrow of
things, to return—a space like a garden in which a renewed belonging
takes root and leafs out. And perhaps the work of holding open that
space—refusing the doubts that close your mind against it, the despair

and self-pity that are the prevailing weather—is itself a hearth, a poem, a place of welcome waiting for you to be ready to feel it.

And one day, as for Job, the future does return, and you find yourself in it, with "world enough and time." For the belonging never really ceased—no matter how one was defamed, abused, disparaged, or exiled, no matter how deep the grief ran, and how long the despair played, that disappears the truth. As my unhearthing persists, I experience moments of ease, a few hours here and there, sometimes half a day. And mostly those moments of coherence and something close to joy are brought on by reading or writing poems, by acts of friendship, and by walking out into the world.

4.

Self is a verb; through our lives, we selve.

In his pioneering psychological writings, William James proposed that the self is never whole. For one thing, one is the knower and the known. For another, one is a being among many: family, community, peers, society, lives past and present, stories, times, moments, all beings. All we belong to is who we are. We compose ourselves, James meant, and we do it in a daily conversation with all that is not merely oneself. We are not merely subjects (victims, heroes); our selves are intersubjective. In particular, James emphasized, the self is a state that includes the world around. One negotiates who one is in conversation with where one is and how one adapts. Job's world comes to an end when he loses sight of the world, when what afflicted him became all he was.

Self is a hearth you make and keep making, like a fire. Selving is the work of *re-membering* all that you are. The hearth of yourself is not all your own work, either, but the work of that constellation of belongings you share, which after a time insist on your presence among them again. Your self is an accompanied place, a meeting house.

When you lose touch with the world around and dwell too much in your head, you lose your mind, you lose your self. "When," as I put it in my poem "Frog Nocturne," "all along you were out there, everywhere."

5.

Coming back into the ground of one's belonging is a matter, in the end, of grace. So it felt for Styron. But grace, as Norman Maclean has put it (words I've lived by without understanding quite how much they meant), "comes by art, and art does not come easy."

And my art has not come easy these past years—neither the art of living nor the art of writing, which had, till now, been a world of wilderness and play, a deep consolation I could find without working too hard for it. It is a myth, I think, that artists prosper on adversity. More truthful are Kyo Maclear's words in *Bird Art Life*:"A mind narrows when it has too much to bear." Writing these words, for example, has not come easy; writing poetry over the past two years has seemed almost to cost me myself. But I know the only worse thing would have been not to write them at all.

If it was hard to make, at least it got made, and I am recharged in the process—and perhaps, who knows, others will find some healing in the reading. Writing to the young poet, Rilke says that only poetry that comes hard, poetry that had to be made, is worth a damn. Or words to that effect."Hold to what is difficult," Rilke also said. And I've held.

Most of the time, these past years, my mind has run like Elizabeth Bishop's sandpiper:

> He runs, he runs to the south, finical, awkward,
> in a state of controlled panic, a student of Blake . . .
>
> . . . Looking for something, something, something.
> Poor bird, he is obsessed!

Too often, these past years, my days have felt as I describe them in "When the Panic":

> When the silence grows shrill in you and won't be said;
> When the sadness grows deep in you, like winter, but will

Not well; when the panic rises, like the past, and won't
Be shaken; when five years of untaken sleep become

A nightmare of doubt, a life in drought; when the fear
Wakes before you with the scissors in its hands; when

Hope becomes a harder case than you know how to make;
When the floor drops from under everything you thought

You were and meant and knew; when the world shrinks
Back to shibboleth and nothing peaceful anywhere knows

The letters of your name . . .

Such is the perpetual slow-burning emergency of the unhoused self. And this is the cruel truth: the stillness of mind that art requires for its making is never harder to achieve than in those times when you most need to make the art. A poem is hard to make in catastrophe and hyper-vigilance, but the best way back to the quietness art requires is art itself. The making. And making poems under the weight of despair requires the will, a blind faith, and more courage than you feel. You must sometimes force yourself there, and open the space, and swim against the tide of panic. Remembering my children has fired my flagging will. The thought of them has sometimes brought enough stillness to raise a poem and bring the calm it requires for its making.

Most of the time, I have lived these past few years out of step "with all that escapes me," as Seamus Heaney puts it in *Squarings*. Making poetry, though (and sometimes taking a walk, and sometimes receiving love), has from time to time led me back into the lyric of everything else I am, which poetry overhears. It is my blessing that poetry, a poetry of necessity, has kept insisting upon itself, waking me hard from the dread lethargy of depression.

Art—letting rhythm and metaphor rock me back to the world beyond my head—can become a hearth you can dwell by, a tent and a fireplace under stars, while you wait your homelessness out.

One Saturday morning in August, staying in a friend's spare room, a cabin set down like a Japanese temple in a water garden, a poem came, "Morning Doves, Zen Garden." And writing it, sitting outside, carried me back toward the grace the poem describes:

At a certain point,

If you can't forget, you can't get by; remember instead:
The music of the mind of things—birdsong, frog plunk, cloud
        Shadow. Lines that hold; children who grow; things as they are. Leaves
Have fallen like pirate pieces on the pebbles by the pond. Something is strong in you
            and won't stop: water
                    on stone, summer holed up inside the fall.

6.

The science of psychology is beginning to acknowledge the role of poetry, reading it and writing it, in helping sufferers survive their depression and remake meaning. A search under "poetry therapy" in Google will yield a wealth of research literature—most of it unreadable. There is even a *Journal of Poetry Therapy*. A poem, Robert Carroll writes in one paper, "gets into us and plays through our psycho/neuro/immune-sensory selves." There is some sense in this literature that the shaping of traumatic experience into the sculpture of voice that is a poem, and the way a poem engages musical and linguistic brain functions at once, reconciling the two hemispheres, have something to do with a poem's power to heal. Poetry orders the chaos of experience into lyric sense; it even pieces our minds together again. Russell Meares has a wonderful book on this subject, *The Poet's Voice in the Making of Mind*, which argues that the metaphoric mode poetry employs, the play it makes in and with language, the leaps of connection it allows, distinguish poetry making and reading as essential in the making of a mind, and in the remaking of the broken self.

Perhaps that's why God spoke to Job the way He did, in metaphor and meter.

Gregory Orr writes beautifully on this in his book *Poetry as Survival*. As a boy, Orr shot his brother dead in a hunting accident. He found his way out of despair, his parents and all those around him being utterly unable to comfort him, when a local librarian suggested he read some poetry.

"We often experience the world as confusing and chaotic, especially during crises. This confusion can be outside us, in the objective conditions of our social and political lives, or it can be inside us. . . . Our day to day consciousness can be characterized as an endlessly shifting, back-and-forth awareness of the power and presence of disorder in our lives and our desire or need for a sense of order," and "in certain existential crises disorder threatens to overwhelm us entirely." "Human culture," Orr concludes, "'invented' or evolved the personal lyric as a means of helping individuals survive the existential crises represented by extremities of subjectivity and also by such outer circumstances as poverty, suffering, pain, illness, violence or the loss of a loved one."

That survival happens in two ways in the making of a poem, Orr writes: first we shift the experience a "bearable distance" from us into the world of language; second, the poet has "made and shaped" her experience into a form, has brought order to disorder, rather than "passively" enduring it. As Shakespeare puts it, the poet gives to "airy nothings" (not so airy, sometimes) "a local habitation and a name." Poems make places out of emotions and ideas. Though it's made of breath and words and implications, a poem is an architecture, and it will hold you. A poem is a garden that will tend you.

7.

And why, among the many forms of utterance, literature, and the other arts, does poetry have this special power? Form is a large part of the answer, and also the depths and breadths to which poetic form and structure make our thinking and our speaking run. We are linguistic beings, as Hinton puts it. To find oneself again through language, in thought and feeling rightly voiced, is to truly home oneself again.

Poetry can make one's suffering habitable.

To make a poem is to escape your head; thinking alone won't get a poem made. Poetry is what happens when we ask more of language; it is what happens (to language and to a poet and to her readers and to the world). Poetry liberates language from writing, as Robert Bringhurst puts it: it gives language back to speech and to all that speaking implies (of self and place and moment) beyond what it says. In poetry, form and discipline let language do its other work: hymning, singing, incanting, invoking. Jane Hirshfield puts it this way: "Every good poem begins in language awake to its connections." Verdi defined music as noise organized by wisdom; but that is even truer of poetry. And much of the wisdom that organizes it belongs to a mind wider and wiser and wilder than one's own.

Making or reading a poem, we can be reawakened, through wakeful language, to all the rest of what we've forgotten we're connected to, inside ourselves and beyond. Poetry can do this because it refuses, as Seamus Heaney has put it, "the intellect's eagerness to foreclose." Through metaphor and rhythm, through trimness and the refusal of cliché, poetry invites more world into our heads and onto our tongues than ordinary thought and most prose permit.

Through giving ourselves over to language that leads us beyond where language normally takes us—and sometimes leaves us for dead—poetry can make a hearth we can share with all the rest of who we are.

8.

"Mythologies that shape primal cultures," as David Hinton puts it in *Hunger Mountain*, "typically embody a sense of deep kinship with landscape." This is true of the indigenous cultures of the traditional peoples of the continent I inhabit, and it is true of first peoples around the world, a wisdom we are learning to acknowledge even as we risk wiping that knowing from the face of the deep. Poetry has never forgotten our kinship with the rest of the more-than-merely-human world.

Dualistic Western thought has manufactured a breach "between consciousness and the empirical landscape." It has orphaned us, culturally, from the family of all things and banished our minds from the wisdom embodied in places and the natural order of the cosmos. We live in our heads; we inhabit, we are, our thoughts. We can't easily access, indeed we feel excommunicated from, the wisdom inherent in places—the wisdom beyond language that will earth us in our lives again.

"For the ancients, the elemental silence of things is the perfect wisdom that we, as linguistic beings, have lost," Hinton writes. And it is that silence, that deep knowing, classical Chinese poetry, and all lyric poetry in all traditions, seeks to utter. This is a paradox, of course—to seek silence through utterance. But as Jane Hirshfield writes in *Nine Gates*, poetry practices in language what meditation practices in silence. Poetry is a broad church in which many things are told and sung. But to all lyric poets, in particular the Chinese classical poets Hinton studies and translates, and to me, poetry is "nothing less than a sacred medium . . . capable of bringing us as close to that lost wisdom as language can."

Two small poems I've written recently almost carry me out of my head and sit me in that silence on the hearth of all things.

The first is a sijo, a Korean form, in spirit and shape and spiritual aspiration, kin to the poems Hinton loves.

> Under a thin crescent moon,   I walk the mangroves with my friend
> At dusk. A single heron stalks the flats,   and bats stream above
> The river into town. After years,   at last, my heart's at peace.

The second, "Freeway Pastoral," is a poem in a Chinese style, written— paradoxically—in my head, as I drove the freeway north.

> A dozen (free range) cattle were re-arranging
>   Twilight into a perfect asymmetry beside

The freeway north, as I drove it toward
                The city to meet my love, and day died
Back among the Picton Hills.
                            The dams were over-
        Brimming after weeks of autumn rain; black
Ducks, out late, fretted the silver shallows,
                And not a keystroke
        Out the window was out of place.
    In my heart, too,
The weather was still and the night swelled. Later,
        We'd take this road together homeward
In the dark, and the new moon would fish
        A thousand stars like supper from the stream.

❖

Chinese is a pictographic system, of course, language made of visual metaphor. In it, the characters that combine to say *poetry*—what it is and
what it does—are "Temple" and "Word." Poetry makes of speech a prayer,
as Hinton figures it—for that is how the ancient Chinese poets understood their art: a bowing into the unknown, into the holiness of things,
into the incomprehensible coherence that we have the privilege, living,
to dwell among. Poetry makes a small temple, in which the cosmos we
inhabit, in its and our apparent confusion, is gathered into holy order
for a while. A poem is a place of pause. A belonging together again in the
eternal and unsayable scheme of things.

Every good poem means what the cosmos means, a small piece of it
anyway, and it stands you back inside it.

Poetry is divination: it is a *hearth*, a holiness made by *art*, a voicing
that *hears* the *earth* and puts it back in our *hearts* again. A poem rests our
sorrows in the silence of all that passes away and all that is and was and
will be again.

9.

It is the disciplines involved in making a poem—disciplines like those involved in love and prayer and meditation, of cooking and pilgrimage, but more so—that help one break clear of the clutter of thought, while putting to work the gifts of apprehension, of patternmaking and utterance that distinguish us human beings, perhaps uniquely, from many other beings. Poetry can't make do with reason; it won't work if thinking is all it does. But it won't work either if one particular mind—a memory and an ecology of sense and feeling and emotion and utterance—is not at play, if someone is not turning, with the help of some learning about what it takes to make a poem, inarticulate conceits and concepts and dumb feltsense into lines, and lines into those small rooms that stanzas are, and making of those rooms a home where all of us can dwell, forgiven.

A good poem says more than a poet could possibly know—and certainly mean—because poetry insists that the poet gives her mind and speech over, for once, not merely to what she wants to say, but to what wants to be said.

Language is wiser than we know and capable of saying more than we can think; and form, as James Galvin said to me once, is the way we plug into language and what it knows (and we do not). Form pushes ego aside; it walks thinking outside. The disciplines of prosody help the poet escape Job-like loops of self; those disciplines act, when one cannot seem to act on one's own, to set one's finical thinking aside and get some listening done and something said beyond the noise in one's head.

The disciplines of grace a poem entails work the way God finally works on Job—to let the world back into one's head and the landscape and the sky back into one's sense of self. Poetics are the fire on the hearth that turns soul into breath, self into Self, the personal into the human, and makes of a plaint a prayer, in which all of us are given back to our fortune (both our sorrows and our joys). In a good poem, the saying says what we too often forget—that we belong to each other and to all things, and that some of all that is known is known in us, and some of what is beautiful is beautiful in us, and some of the integrity of the cosmos coheres in us, notwithstanding the turmoil in our heads.

The waters of the lake lie wide awake and worry
            the wind at dusk; like the feathers
Of the wood duck, they fret a rising easterly, which deepens their brown
To gray. These are captured waters, backed up behind the weir;
                they spread across the flats, and I sit beside them
As if beside my self (*all by my own*, as my daughter said
                   when she was young), and wonder where
The past has been, and I've been, all these passing
Years, pent up here this feather moment at the close of day.

I've come to the reservoir to be among kin,
               to sit and forget myself in birdsong. I've come
To the reservoir to sink: my hope is to slide from a mind
Shrill with hopeless schemes
        to put right everything that cannot be. I've had to let a life go,
Which had taken a lifetime to catch, and it helps
              to watch the kingfishers tie their flies
And wait. Hope is their knack, and I'd like to catch it if I could . . .
                   —from "The Reservoir"

10.

To be found again and happy and at home is to know yourself and to be able to live, at least from time to time, as Hinton puts it, outside the merely "human realm of words and concepts, outside the self to which a name refers." To feel healthy, whole, and maybe even wise, one needs to understand one's self as a small part of what the world knows and loves.

One poet who seems to have managed that, at least in his poetry, was known as Thatch-Hut. The Chinese character that names him so, *Thatch-Hut*, includes a half roof, a hut open to the weather downwind, a kitchen vessel, and a tiger—an animal the ancients "revered," writes David Hinton, "for the spontaneous power of its movements, the clarity and immediacy of its mind." A poem is "a tiger that lives in the everyday world," a wildness domesticated; it is a household inhabited by the nature of the place. It is the outside come on in; it is the inside opened out.

The kind of dwelling a poem is, that practice of belonging, is a hard place to find and to hold. And it's easy enough to lose, as Job lost it, when the self is disordered by trauma. But since it's performed in poems, reading is a way of remembering. Writing is another. Each poem, even if only in the making, is a house, a thatched hut, that holds you and pieces you together again, and reminds you that who you are is much more than you seem.

11.

There is a risk, in a spiritual crisis, of making poems in which we "order our speech by reason of darkness," as God warns Job. There must be room in a poem for the whole of which one's suffering is only a part; there must be light. A bird or two. Space. Speaking all one's grief may be useful therapy, but often makes bad poetry. The challenge is to let the poem lead you out of your mind—to wonder and wander in the world, sometimes by dropping you deep down below the hell you sometimes inhabit. Despair is a place to start—the only poems that count, as Rilke says, are those made from necessity—but it is not a place to stop. The thatched hut is open to the world.

> At close of day I watch an egret
> nail a soft landing in a ploughed field and earth
> The shallow sky. The ground is scoured where she falls, a soul
> Turned, like a pocket, inside out, and the bird wanders
> the black rows, scoring them loosely with its one bright note.
>
> She makes an inverse music, it seems to me,
> plucking the furrows
> For what they may yield, an improvised notation

That erases itself writing itself down, singing the earth back silently

> Into the belly of a bird, a reverie

In negative, which wakes the dawning dark

> all the way back to its beginning again.

> —from "Egret in a Ploughed Field"

Nonetheless, it is astonishing the consolation the most agonized poems—which as they plunge, also fly—can bring. I think as I speak this of Gerard Manley Hopkins's "No Worst, There Is None":

O the mind, mind has mountains; cliffs of fall
Frightful, sheer, no-man-fathomed. Hold them cheap
May who ne'er hung there. Nor does long our small
Durance deal with that steep or deep. Here! creep,
Wretch, under a comfort serves in a whirlwind: all
Life death does end and each day dies with sleep.

The consolation, the cosmos, that gets in, is not in the anguish the poet speaks, but in the work beyond language that the metaphors and rhythms, the sound-world of the poem, divine. Such a poem holds all suffering and gives it form, an aspect of all Creation again.

12.

Depression, unhearthing, though one would wish it on no one, has, if you can survive it, its uses. "There is a way of passing away from the personal, a dying," writes Rumi, "that makes one plural," and poetry is a way of doing that. And that dying and coming back with a pen in your hand leaves traces. Depression teaches compassion. In finding one's way back from it, you find your way deeper into communion with all beings, especially your fellow women and men. Depression endured makes one plural.

Poems, handholds in a plunge, or momentary stays against confusion, as Frost put it, may save other lives, for each of us is likely to end up in some version of the trouble Job found himself in, and I did too. My sense is that poetry stays some of the confusion, orders some of the chaos, of existence, into which all of us may enter at some point, even if no one much reads the poems—though it's better if they do. The coherence of the world wants saying, it seems, if it is to stay coherent, and we are to stumble well enough among it. So poetry needs making, even if the world shouts it out and mostly turns the other way.

Poetry in the West, while more marginal to the discourses of daily life perhaps than ever, remains vital, as restless in its hunger, as generative as the cosmos itself. Poetry will always be made; the challenge is to remind enough of those we teach and love and raise to read it—and, if they will, to make it. For, as Richard Rohr put it recently in an interview, it is hard to heal and stay healed in a narcissistic world without much of an ear for poetry. It is hard to stay whole and make healing in a world that doesn't know how to slow, in a world that is as broken as Job or any of us—anxious, fractured, scattered like the sandpiper.

The world needs the weary of spirit strong. It needs especially the seers—those who can apprehend and value all that is lost sight of in commercial and political and academic discourses—to feel at home in their lives and capable. It needs them well enough often enough to tend the hearth that homes the world.

As William Carlos Williams famously wrote:

It is difficult
    to get the news from poems,
            yet men and women die miserably
for lack
    of what is found there.

May poetry, even just the fact that it exists and seems insistent to be made, remind us that we are clothed, like Job, in everyday beauty, that the world is in us, and that we are called to do justice however we can with our lives.

Note:

WHEN GOD WANTED finally to cut Job a break, He gave him a natural history lesson, and he gave it to him in poetry. This, according to Mary Catherine Bateson, whom I heard on an episode of the *On Being* podcast, is what Gregory Bateson's father used to tell young Gregory.

From Home to Cosmos

Mary Evelyn Tucker

The autumn equinox has passed, filled with afternoon rain. A patch of blue breaks through at dusk, surrounded by a sea of clouds that catches the glow of sunset and warms my heart with joy. Some deep resonance of light and color lingers in the sky, commingling with my skin and reflecting off the rainwater gathered on each drying leaf. I am drenched with sunset. I sink into the dance of autumn—geese overhead, lingering insect song, the careful movement of a doe with two young ones through the bush. I am held by the maples and birch longing for more rain. The dry creek is straining for the rush of water. The massive elm stumps circling the fire pit are cracking with brittleness. This outdoor hearth of the fire pit is mirrored by an inner hearth around a fireplace in our living room. Both hearths provide a place of grounding where family, friends, and ancestors gather to celebrate life.

I am at home near these fireplaces, waiting and expectant, hoping to renew myself—to find centering in the moment of transition between seasons. Late summer is molting into autumn. Colors blaze anew. I yearn for the great turning, lighting incense, bowing in all the directions, and calling on the ancestors to join me in this journey through the seasons.

Only with the arrival of the intricately woven Persian carpet handed down over seven decades did our house become fully home. From my grandmother, Evelyn Carroll Hayes, it passed to my mother, Mary Elizabeth Hayes Tucker, and now to me, Mary Evelyn Carroll Tucker. It moved from 117th Street in New York City where my mother's parents lived, to their vast living room at Jericho Farm in upstate New York, then to the high-ceiling living room in Pelham, New York, where I grew up, and now to my home in the country of Lewisburg, Pennsylvania. Through the decades, it has provided our family with the glowing centering of home—rhythms of blessed assurance even in times of uncertainty.

The luminous colors in the carpet are like stained glass windows reflecting light from the floor up to the ceiling. Deep turquoise blue provides a serene grounding for the swirl of flowers and vines curling around my feet. This rug gives homage to the endless images of creativity in nature. The floral designs are contained within borders, amplifying the center's explosive power yet binding in and turning back tangled torrents of botanical energy. When I step gently on the colors—the dark turquoise, the sky blue, the soft doe brown, the deep salmon maroon—I feel dynamic energy filling the room, a garden of delight, still flowing from the imaginations of weavers in the ancient Iranian city of Esfahan.

This Persian carpet, the heart of my hearth, weaves me into a longer ancestral heritage—biological lineage, and even a geological and a cosmological one. These floral patterns emerged within the deep time of evolution that is manifest in the complex patterns of nature itself. Each one of these shapes of flowers and plants reflect the long journey of life unfolding toward complex forms. Such beauty arose in the fiery burst of stars where carbon atoms first emerged that eventually gave rise to carbon-based life that evolved over billions of years on this volcanic planet. Finally they burst forth in the explosion of diverse life forms in the last sixty-five million years of the Cenozoic era.

So it is here in my home hearth that I sense how we humans participate in ever-expanding dynamic circles of connectivity. Like the plants and flowers, we have evolved out of geological and biological changes during billions of years of Earth's evolution. Even earlier, stellar explosions formed the carbon that gave rise to life, including the carbon in our bodies. This is a cosmological context that we are only now beginning to absorb. Our identity is not just local or national. We are Earth-born beings made from cosmic stardust. Thus the stars are our ancestors. Deep time is our birthplace.

Our consciousness is changed as we realize we belong to the Earth and the universe together. We share the same atoms. This change of consciousness gives rise to an even broader shift of conscience as we come to recognize that our relatives are not only family and other humans but every life form that has evolved with us. We are kin to all life, even to the prelife in the stars. How much our genuine identify shifts—from isolated economic beings in a hypermodern society to interdependent members of an Earth community.

Thus our role as humans is to be more than simply consumers; we are meant to be participants and transformers. Human creativity needs to be aligned with Earth's creativity. When that happens, mutually enhancing human-Earth relations will be expressed in a variety of forms: eco-economics, alternative energies, green politics, environmental education, ecospiritualities, and other creative practices we have not yet imagined. With this basis of deep time and aligned creativity we might find our way forward amid forces that are both life-destroying and life-enhancing. This is not simply a process of romantically harmonizing with nature, but seeing the dynamic unfolding of Earth processes as part of a larger evolutionary whole. Just as evolution moves between forces of chaos and creativity, so, too, does human culture. We are at a critical moment in finding our way forward while also staying grounded. T. S. Eliot described this creative tension in the Four Quartets: "To be still and still moving." Our hearth is our home in ever-expanding dynamic circles of connectivity—local, bioregional, continental, planetary, solar, galactic, and cosmic.

In some senses this interconnected cosmological and ecological context is new for contemporary humans. But this integrated perspective of concentric circles is part of earlier traditions as well. For example, in Chinese Confucian thought the human person is not an isolated individual, but someone deeply held within the family and society, and also within the creative processes of the universe and Earth. Indeed, these creative processes are like parental forces that give birth to humans and all species. In Chinese thought the cosmos is termed "Heaven" in a metaphorical sense referring to the celestial systems overhead, while Earth is that body where all the myriad life-forms arise—"the 10,000 things." Heaven is also understood to be a creative guiding force of the cosmos, while Earth is a generative nurturing force of life.

The eleventh-century, neo-Confucian philosopher Zhang Zai articulated this perspective with his notable "Western Inscription," which he wrote on the western wall of his study: "Heaven is my father and Earth is my mother and even such a small creature as I finds an intimate place in their midst. Therefore that which extends throughout the universe I regard as my body and that which directs the universe I regard as my nature. All people are my brothers and sisters, and all things are my companions." The identity of one's body with the universe is part of Chinese

Confucianism in micro-macrocosmic relations. The nurturing of the life force of one's own nature and that of the cosmos is what is to be cultivated.

Although Zhang Zai's inscription was written one thousand years ago, modern Chinese still recognize and acknowledge its implications for the ongoing connection to all life. While these verses were intended metaphorically, we now know that their truth can be scientifically verified. Life arises from the generative dynamics of stars and from the intricate matrix of ecosystems. So hearth, in a traditional Chinese context, is the nested creativity of the cosmos and Earth into which humans are born. Humans complete this creativity, for they are regarded in Chinese Confucianism in the "Doctrine of the Mean" as cocreators with the "transforming and nourishing powers" of nature. Indeed, we affect and are affected by these great processes of nature. The question for the Confucians is how we might resonate with these processes in mutually enhancing ways. It is our question today as well.

In Chinese philosophy humans are seen as the mind and heart of Heaven and Earth. There is only one Chinese character (hsin) for this thinking/feeling dimension of the human. No division, no dualism. In this context humans are considered to be both the consciousness and the conscience of the universe. As the reflective/emotive component of the universe we complete the dynamic unfolding of Heaven and Earth. This is both a given and an achievement through study and self-cultivation. Through such self-realization of our full nature we form a triad with the cosmological and ecological dimensions of reality. In this sense humans are meant to contribute toward the common good, namely the flourishing of nature and the well-being of society. That is the aim of Confucian education—to create ethical, caring humans who foster harmonious, productive societies through humane government. The Confucian literati and scholar-officials studied history and the classics so as to be moral leaders in education, culture, and politics. They tried to encourage humaneness, namely, greater compassion for all living things. While not always realized due to historical distortions, societal disruptions, and gender limitations, these ideals aimed to inspire a generosity of spirit for a public good. Such ideals need further articulation and adaption to modern circumstances.

From ancient Chinese cosmology to contemporary scientific

cosmology we may rediscover where we come from and how we belong. This Persian carpet is the result of the botanical images and interwoven cosmologies across the Silk Road from China. It is part of the great exchange of cultures and artistic creativity through the ages from China to Persia and on to Rome. This exchange continues today across Eurasia and beyond, resulting in the ongoing transformation of peoples and places. Our destiny now is to find our role as hearth makers and community creators amid the great fecundity and diminishment of life—cultural and biological.

When I am held by the heart of my hearth I know it is possible to rediscover historical relationships that reweave cultural resonances. And I realize, too, that our hearths are interconnected at every level of reality. My hearth rug is a symbol of the ever-expanding hearth—weaving us into a local bioregional sense of place, a continental sense of place, a planetary sense of place, a solar sense of place, and a galactic sense of place. Our living-room rug is part of a living Earth and universe that holds all of us in an embrace of deep time and vast space. It is the garden where our ancestors gathered and planted their life dreams. It is where we now cultivate the hopes and dreams of those who will come after.

The Other House

W. S. MERWIN

I come back again to the old house
that I thought I knew for most of a lifetime
the house I reclaimed from abandon and ruin
and that I called my home at times when I was here
and at times when I was somewhere far from here
this time I have not come to reclaim anything
but to move nothing and to touch nothing
as though I were a ghost or here in a dream
and I know it is a dream that has no age
in this dream the same river is still here
the house is the old house and I am here in the morning
in the sunlight and the same bird is singing

from *Garden Time* (Copper Canyon Press, 2016)

Works Cited

1 W. S. Merwin, "Rain Light" from *The Shadow of Sirius*. Copyright © 2009 by W. S. Merwin. Reprinted with the permission of The Permissions Company, Inc., on behalf of Copper Canyon Press, www.coppercanyonpress.org.

59 From *The Poetic Edda* by Carolyne Larrington (Oxford: Oxford University University Press, 2014). Reprinted with permission from Oxford University Press.

69 From *The Neolithic of Mainland Scotland*, ed. Kenneth Brophy, Gavin MacGregor, Ian Ralston (Edinburgh: Edinburgh University Press, 2016).

159–172, 252 From *Genesis* by Sebastião Salgado and Lelia Wanick Salgado (Cologne, Taschen, 2013). Used with permission from Amazonas Images.

228 Excerpt from *Crediting Poetry: The Nobel Lecture* by Seamus Heaney. Copyright © 1995 by the Nobel Foundation. Reprinted by permission of Farrar, Straus and Giroux.

230 From *Hunger Mountain* by David Hinton (Shambhala Publications, 2012). Reprinted with permission from David Hinton.

231 Tredinnick, Mark. "Frog Nocturne," first published in *The Lyrebird & Other Poems*, Picaro Press, Newcastle, 2011. Used with permission from the author.

232 Excerpts from "Sandpiper" from *Poems* by Elizabeth Bishop. Copyright © 2011 by the Alice H. Methfessel Trust. Publisher's Note and compilation copyright © 2011 by Farrar, Straus and Giroux. Reprinted by permission of Farrar, Straus and Giroux.

232 Tredinnick, Mark. "When the Panic," first published in *The Lyrebird & Other Poems* (2e), Ginninderra Press, Port Adelaide, 2017. Used with permission from the author.

235 From *Poetry as Survival* by Gregory Orr (Athens: University of Georgia Press, 2002). Reprinted with permission from the University of Georgia Press.

236 "The Fire" from *The Lives of the Heart* by Jane Hirshfield. Copyright © 1997 by Jane Hirshfield. Reprinted by permission of HarperCollins Publishers.

242 Tredinnick, Mark. "Egret in a Ploughed Field," *Egret in a Ploughed Field*, the Chinese University Press, Hong Kong, 2017.

243 By William Carlos Williams, from *The Collected Poems: Volume II, 1939–1962*, copyright © 1944 by William Carlos Williams. Reprinted by permission of New Directions Publishing Corp.

250 W. S. Merwin, "The Other House" from *Garden Time*. Copyright © 2016 by W. S. Merwin. Reprinted with the permission of The Permissions Company, Inc., on behalf of Copper Canyon Press, www.coppercanyonpress.org.

Notes on the Photographs

160 *Botswana. January 2008.* The healing or trance dance is the San's most import-ant mystical ritual. As the women sing and clap, the men dance around them. During this dance, medicine men lay their hands on everyone present to draw out the "arrows of sickness." Dried seed pods are filled with small stones and, when tied to the legs of medicine men, rattle loudly as they dance. The frenzy of their trance, the San people believe, marks their entry into the world of spirits.

162 *Kamchatka. Russia. September and October 2006.* The Kamchatka Peninsula stretches 780 miles (1,250 kilometers) south of the Russian mainland, with ocean on either side. This photograph shows the Karimsky Volcano, which currently rises to a height of 4,800 feet (1,468 meters) and is the most active on the Peninsula. More than 100 times per day, it expels a plume of gas and ash several hundred meters into the air and sends boulders careening down its steep slopes. Karimsky's last big eruption was in 2003.

164 *South Georgia. November and December 2009.* A colony of black-browed alba-trosses (*Thalassarche melanophris*) on the archipelago of Willis Islands; in the background one can see Trinity and Bird Island.

166 *Ethiopia. October and November 2008.* A Christian worshiper leaves the church of Makina Lideta Maryan. This church is inside a grotto, at an altitude of 9,646 feet (2,940 meters).

168 *Yamal Peninsula. Siberia. Russia. March and April 2011.* These caravans of sledges carry all the belongings of the families in the group. Usually the men take care of the reindeer, herding them with smaller sledges and sometimes with snowmobiles; the women and children ride on the caravans, which may be composed of as many as ten sledges tied to each other, with one woman in charge.

170 *Amazonas, Brazil. May 2009.* The Anavilhanas, the name given to around 350 forested islands in Brazil's Rio Negro, form the world's largest inland archipel-ago. Covering 390 square miles (1,000 square kilometers) of Amazonia, they start 50 miles (80 kilometers) northwest of Manaus and stretch some 250 miles (400 kilometers) up the Rio Negro, as far as Barcelos. Their formation dates back to the last Ice Age. Since water levels change with the seasons by as much as 65 feet (20 meters), the Anavilhanas are themselves ever-changing.

Editors

Co-Editor Susan O'Connor is an environmental and arts advocate. She has served on the boards of several art museums, including the Menil in Houston, Texas. She has also been a board member of the Orion Society and the American Prairie Reserve. She cofounded several nonprofits including Pacific Writers Connection, Ala Kukui: Hana Retreat, Ohana Makamae, and Families First both in Boston and Missoula. She is a coeditor, with Annick Smith, of *The Wide Open: Prose, Poetry, and Photographs of the Prairie*, which included such notable writers as Peter Matthiessen, Richard Ford, Gretel Ehrlich, and James Harrison with photographic portfolios by Lee Friedlander, Lois Conner, and Geoffrey James. She presently lives in Missoula, Montana with her husband Roy and three black Labradors.

Co-Editor Annick Smith is the author of *Homestead, In This We Are Native, Big Bluestem*, and *Crossing the Plains with Bruno*. She produced the prize-winning feature *Heartland*, and was a founding board member of Robert Redford's Sundance Institute. Her travel and nature writing, short stories, and essays have appeared in *Audubon, Outside, Islands, Travel + Leisure, Orion, The New York Times, Story*, and *National Geographic Traveler*, and have been widely anthologized. In 1989 she was coeditor with William Kittredge of *The Last Best Place: A Montana Anthology*. She was also coeditor with Susan O'Connor of *The Wide Open: Prose, Poetry and Photographs of the Prairie*. She lives on a homestead ranch in Montana's Blackfoot River Valley.

Consulting Editor Helen Whybrow is a freelance writer and editor, and Editor at Large for *Orion* Magazine. For many years she was the publisher and editor-in-chief of Countryman Press, an imprint of W. W. Norton. She is the editor of the anthology *Dead Reckoning: Great Adventure Writing 1800–1900* (Norton/Outside) and author of the biography *A Man Apart: Bill Coperthwaite's Radical Experiment in Living* (Chelsea Green). She lives in Vermont, where she and her family run an organic farm and a retreat center for social justice activists.

Consulting Poetry Editor Sandra Alcosser is a poet whose work has appeared in the *New Yorker*, the *New York Times*, *Paris Review*, *Ploughshares*, *Poetry*, and the Pushcart Prize Anthology. She received two individual artist fellowships from NEA and her books of poetry, *A Fish to Feed All Hunger* and *Except by*

Nature, received the highest honors from National Poetry Series, Academy of American Poets, and Associated Writing Programs. She was the National Endowment for the Arts' first Conservation Poet for the Wildlife Conservation Society and Poets House, New York, as well as Montana's first poet laureate. She founded and directs San Diego State University's Creative Writing MFA each fall.

Project Manager Minette Glaser spent twenty years building unique partnerships to restore native wildlife to the prairies and forests of the West, including peregrine falcons, black-footed ferrets, buffalo, swift foxes, wolves, and grizzly bears. She has worked for the National Audubon Society, Peregrine Fund, Hornocker Wildlife Institute, and Defenders of Wildlife. At the Ocean Conservancy, she organized the contributions of specialists from around the world to create a global strategy for marine biodiversity conservation, which was published by Island Press.

Contributors

Sara Baume is the author of *A Line Made by Walking*, which was shortlisted for the Goldsmiths Prize, and *Spill Simmer Falter Wither*, which received the Geoffrey Faber Memorial Prize, was shortlisted for the Costa First Novel Award, and was longlisted for, among others, the Warwick Prize for Writing, the Guardian First Book Award, and the Desmond Elliott Prize. Her short fiction and essays have been published in anthologies, newspapers, and journals including the *Irish Times*, the *Guardian*, the *Stinging Fly*, and *Granta*. She is a graduate of the International Writing Program run by the University of Iowa and the recipient of a Literary Fellowship from the Lannan Foundation. She lives in Cork, Ireland.

Alok Bhalla is a widely published critic, translator and poet. A retired professor, he has been a Fellow at the Institutes of Advance Study at Nantes (France), Bellagio (Italy), Shimla and Gandhi's Sabarmati Ashram (India). His books include *Stories About the Partition of India* (4 volumes), *Partition Dialogues* (interviews with major Indian and Pakistani writers) and *Life and Times of Saadat Hasan Manto*; translations of Intizar Husain's *A Chronicle of the Peacocks*, *Story is a Vagabond*, and *Day and Dastan*. He was elected to the Executive Council of the Sahitya Akademi (India's Academy of Letters), and lives in India.

Tony Birch is the author of several novels and collections of short stories, including *Ghost River*, which received the Victorian Premier's Literary Award for Indigenous Writing; *Blood*, which was shortlisted for the Miles Franklin Award; and, most recently, *Common People*. He is the first indigenous writer to receive the Patrick White Award. A regular guest on ABC local and national radio, Birch has been a longtime lecturer at Victoria University, where he is now the first recipient of the Dr. Bruce McGuinness Indigenous Research Fellowship. He lives in Melbourne, Australia.

Boey Kim Cheng is the author of five collections of poems, a travel memoir entitled *Between Stations*, and a novel about the life of the Tang Dynasty poet Du Fu, *Gull Between Heaven and Earth*. He is also the editor, with Adam Aitken and Michelle Cahill, of *Contemporary Asian Australian Poets*. A recipient of the National Arts Council's Young Artist Award, Boey emigrated from Singapore to Australia in 1997 and taught creative writing at the University of Newcastle before joining Nanyang Technological University in Singapore.

Victoria Cribb spent many years travelling, studying and working in Iceland before becoming a full-time translator in 2002. She has translated more than 25 novels by Icelandic authors including Arnaldur Indriðason, Ragnar Jónasson, Sjón and Yrsa Sigurðardóttir. In 2017 she received the Orðstír honorary translation award for services to Icelandic literature. She lives in Cambridge, UK.

Angie Cruz is the author of two novels, *Soledad* and *Let It Rain Coffee*, a finalist for the International IMPAC Dublin Literary Award, and her essays and short fiction have appeared in *The New York Times*, *Gulf Coast*, *Callaloo*, and elsewhere. Her writing and teaching has been supported by numerous grants and residencies, including from the New York Foundation of the Arts, the Pittsburgh Foundation of the Arts, Ledig House, Yaddo, and the MacDowell Colony. The founder and editor of *Aster(ix)*, a literary/arts journal, she is Assistant Professor of English at the University of Pittsburgh.

Geffrey Davis is the author of *Night Angler* and *Revising the Storm*, winner of the A. Poulin Jr. Poetry Prize and a finalist for the Hurston/Wright Legacy Award. Other honors include a Cave Canem fellowship, the Anne Halley Poetry Prize, the Dogwood First Prize in Poetry, the Wabash Prize for Poetry, and the Leonard Steinberg Memorial Prize from the Academy of American Poets. His work also appears in *The New York Times Magazine*, *The New Yorker*, *Ploughshares*, *New England Review*, and *PBS Newshour*. A native of the Pacific Northwest, Davis serves as poetry editor of *Iron Horse Literary Review* and teaches in the MFA program at the University of Arkansas in Fayetteville.

Debra Magpie Earling is Bitterroot Salish and a member of the Flathead Nation. She is the author of the novels *Perma Red*, which received the American Book Award, and *The Lost Journals of Sacajewea*. Her work has also appeared in *Ploughshares* and *Northeast Indian Quarterly* as well as several anthologies, including *Talking Leaves: Contemporary Native American Short Stories* and *Montana Women Writers: A Geography of the Heart*. The recipient of fellowships from the National Endowment for the Arts and the Guggenheim Foundation, she is now the Director of Creative Writing at the University of Montana in Missoula.

Gretel Ehrlich is the author of fifteen books, including *The Solace of Open Spaces*, a record of her first years living on the Wyoming range, cowboying, and herding sheep; and *A Match to the Heart*, a memoir about being hit by lightning on her ranch. Her most recent book, *Facing the Wave*, received the

PEN Award for Nonfiction and was nominated for the National Book Award. The recipient of a Guggenheim Fellowship, a Whiting Award, three National Geographic Expedition grants, and an award from the American Academy of Arts and Letters, Ehrlich has traveled by dogsled with subsistence Inuit hunters at the top of Greenland for twenty years, and as a result has written extensively about climate change.

Alisa Ganieva is an author, journalist, and literary critic from Dagestan. Her controversial debut novel, *Salaam, Dalgat!* was published under a male pseudonym and received the prestigious Debut Prize—Ganieva revealed her true identity only at the award ceremony. *The Mountain and the Wall*, published in Russia in 2012 (*Праздничная гора*), was recently released in the US; her follow up, *The Bride and the Bridegroom* (*Жених и невеста*), has been shortlisted for the Russian Booker Prize. In 2015, the *Guardian* named Ganieva one of Moscow's "30 Under 30." She works as an editor in the *Nezavisimaya Gazeta* newspaper's book review supplement and is a TV presenter on a Russian independent channel, where she interviews experts in politics, economics, and culture. She lives in Moscow, Russia.

Sarah Hedden is a conservationist and architectural designer. Born in the Utah desert and raised in a climate of aridity, the lessons she learned in this distinctive landscape have informed her sense of urgency, wonder, and devotion. As a designer and curator of sacred space, her work is born out of her own search for stillness in a loud and unsettled world; becoming a student of Tea Ceremony is part of that search. Hedden received her Masters in Architecture from the University of California, Berkeley.

Jane Hirshfield is the author of eight collections of poems, including *Come, Thief; After*, which was shortlisted for the T.S. Eliot Prize; *Given Salt*, a finalist for the National Book Critics Circle Award; and, most recently, *The Beauty*, a finalist for the National Book Award. She is also the author of *Ten Windows: How Great Poems Transform the World* and *Nine Gates: Entering the Mind of Poetry*. A recipient of fellowships from the Guggenheim and Rockefeller foundations, and the National Endowment for the Arts, Hirshfield is a chancellor of the Academy of American Poets. While never a full-time academic, she has taught at UC Berkeley, Bennington, the Bread Loaf Writers' Conference, and Stanford University. She lives in the San Francisco Bay Area.

Intizar Husain (1923–2016) has been called one of the greatest writers in the Urdu language, and Pakistan's preeminent chronicler of change. His voice of compassion and insight is much needed, not only in his troubled homeland but wherever English-speaking readers know about Pakistan only through the mass media. Born in 1925 in Dibai, India, Husain migrated to Pakistan in 1947. His epic novel of the Partition, *Basti*, was shortlisted for the 2013 Man Booker International Literary Prize and was recently republished in the New York Review of Books Classics series. His honors include the 2014 French Officier de L'Ordre des Arts et des Lettres and the Lifetime Achievement Award presented by the 2012 Lahore Literary Festival. He passed away in Pakistan in 2016.

Ameena Hussein is a sociologist, writer, and editor. She is the author of the novel *The Moon in the Water*, which was longlisted for the Man Asia Literary Prize and the Dublin IMPAC; as well as the short story collections *Fifteen* and *Zillij*, winner of the State Literary Prize. Hussein was also an editor of *Sometimes There is No Blood*, a survey of research on violence against women in rural areas by the International Centre of Ethnic Studies in Colombo. In addition to editing several collections of stories for children and adults, Hussein is cofounder of the Perera Hussein Publishing House, known for publishing cutting-edge Sri Lankan fiction. She lives in Sri Lanka.

Pico Iyer is the author of two novels and ten works of nonfiction, ranging in subject matter from revolutionary Cuba to the Fourteenth Dalai Lama to Islamic mysticism, including *Video Night in Kathmandu*, *The Lady and the Monk*, *The Global Soul*, and most recently, *The Art of Stillness*. His work has been translated into twenty-three languages, and he has been a constant contributor for more than twenty years to the *New York Review of Books*, *Harper's*, *The New York Times*, *Granta*, and elsewhere. Iyer's three TED *Talks*—on movement, stillness, and the limits of knowledge—have now been viewed more than seven million times. Since 1992, he has been based in suburban western Japan, while traveling widely from North Korea to Easter Island and from Yemen to Tibet.

Dr. Pualani Kanaka'ole-Kanahele is a great-grandmother, photographer, dancer, teacher, author, researcher, adventurer, activist, chanter, and believer of things Hawai'i; her vast reservoir of knowledge ranges from ethno-astronomy to volcanism. She retired from the University of Hawai'i and the community college system in 2013 after forty years of service; she also served in leadership roles, including as President, for the Edith Kanakaʻole Foundation for twenty-four years. After being involved in hula since infancy, she also retired as kumu hula, or dance teacher, of the Hawaiian traditional dance in 2011. Pualani Kanakaʻole-Kanahele is of pure Hawaiian ancestry and is passionate about being Hawaiian and living on these islands; this passion has only increased since her retirement. "I am Hawaiʻi, this I know! Ua ʻike au!"

William Kittredge is the author of numerous books of fiction and nonfiction, including the memoir *Hole in the Sky*; three collections of essays, *Owning It All*, *Who Owns the West*, and *Balancing Water*; as well as the novel *The Willow Field*. With Annick Smith, Kittredge coedited *The Last Best Place: A Montana Anthology* and coproduced the Academy Award-winning film *A River Runs Through It*. For his work Kittredge has received the Montana Governor's Award for the Arts, the Robert Kirsch Lifetime Achievement Award from the *Los Angeles Times*, a Lifetime Achievement Award from the Western Literature Association, and was cowinner of both the Montana Governor's Award for the Humanities and the National Endowment for the Humanities' Charles Frankel Award, awarded by President Clinton. He lives in Montana.

Gerður Kristný is among the leading contemporary writers of Iceland. She has written nonfiction, fiction, children's books, and six volumes of poetry, which have been translated into more than thirty languages. *Blóðhófnir* (*Bloodhoof*), her poetic rewriting of Norse myths, received the Icelandic Literature Award and was nominated for the Nordic Council Literature Prize; her biography *Myndin af pabba—saga Thelmu* (A Portrait of Dad—Thelma's Story) received the Icelandic Journalism Award; and *Garðurinn* (*The Garden*) received the West-Nordic Children's Literature Prize. Kristný has participated in numerous international festivals and residencies, including the Ingmar Bergman residency and the International Writing Program's Fall Residency at the University of Iowa. She lives in Reykjavík, Iceland.

Andrew Lam is a former Vietnamese refugee and now lives in San Francisco. He is the author of the short story collection *Birds of Paradise Lost*, which received the PEN Oakland/Josephine Miles Literary Award and was a finalist for the California Book Award, as well as the essay collections *Perfume Dreams: Reflections on the Vietnamese Diaspora*, which received the PEN Open Book Award, and *East Eats West: Writing in Two Hemispheres*. In 2004, Lam was the subject of a PBS documentary that aired nationwide. He has held teaching fellowships at San Jose State University and Stanford University. The recipient of support from Creative Work Fund to write a series of stories exploring the lives of those who've crossed borders in the 21st century and the relationship between Vietnam and California, Lam writes a regular column for *Shanghai Daily* and contributes regularly to the *Los Angeles Times*, the *San Francisco Chronicle*, *Boom California*, *Al Jazeera*, and *Huffington Post*.

Barry Lopez is the author of sixteen works of fiction and nonfiction, including *Arctic Dreams*, recipient of the National Book Award, and *Of Wolves and Men*, a finalist for the National Book Award. His essays are collected in *Crossing Open Ground* and *About This Life*. His most recent books are the collections of short stories *Resistance* and *Outside*. Lopez's shorter work appears regularly in a wide range of journals, including *Harper's*, *Granta*, *Freeman's*, *Orion*, and the *Georgia Review*. The recipient of numerous cultural and literary awards, he has received Guggenheim and Lannan fellowships, and awards from the American Association of Geographers, the Academy of Television Arts & Sciences, and the New York Public Library. Since 2000, he has served as a Visiting Scholar at Texas Tech University, where his papers are archived in the Sowell Family Collection in Literature, Community and the Natural World. In 2002, he was elected a Fellow of the Explorers Club in recognition of his international fieldwork and travel to Antarctica and more than ninety countries. He lives with his wife in the Cascade Mountains of western Oregon, his home since 1970.

Bill McKibben is an author and environmentalist who in 2014 was awarded the Right Livelihood Award, sometimes called the "alternative Nobel Prize." His 1989 book *The End of Nature* is regarded as the first book for a general audience about climate change, and has appeared in twenty-four languages; he has gone on to write a dozen more books. He is a founder of 350.org, the first planet-wide grassroots climate change movement, and *Foreign Policy* named him to their inaugural list of the world's 100 most important global thinkers. The Schumann Distinguished Scholar in Environmental Studies at Middlebury College and a fellow of the American Academy of Arts and Sciences, he was the 2013 winner of the Gandhi Prize and the Thomas Merton Prize, and holds honorary degrees from eighteen colleges and universities. A former staff writer for the *New Yorker*, he writes frequently for a wide variety of publications around the world, including the *New York Review of Books*, *National*

Geographic, and *Rolling Stone*. He lives with his wife in the mountains above Lake Champlain, where he spends as much time as possible outdoors.

Christopher Merrill has published six collections of poetry, including *Brilliant Water* and *Watch Fire*, for which he received the Lavan Younger Poets Award from the Academy of American Poets. He has also edited many volumes and books of translations, as well as six works of nonfiction, among them, *Only the Nails Remain: Scenes from the Balkan Wars*; *Things of the Hidden God: Journey to the Holy Mountain*; *The Tree of the Doves: Ceremony, Expedition, War*; and *Self-Portrait with Dogwood*. His writing has been translated into over thirty languages, his journalism appears widely, and his honors include a Chevalier from the French government in the Order of Arts and Letters. Merrill serves as director of the International Writing Program at the University of Iowa, on the US National Commission for UNESCO, and in April 2012 President Obama appointed him to the National Council on the Humanities. He lives in Iowa.

W. S. Merwin, a former US Poet Laureate, is one of America's most widely read and revered poets. He is also an accomplished translator, gardener, and environmental activist. His collections of poems include *The Carrier of Ladders*, winner of the Pulitzer Prize; *The Shadow of Sirius*, again winner of the Pulitzer Prize; *Migration: New & Selected Poems*, winner of the National Book Award; *Present Company*, winner of the Bobbitt Prize from the Library of Congress; and, most recently, *The Moon Before Morning* and *Garden Time*. He has received numerous awards for his work and translations, including the Ruth Lilly Poetry Prize, the PEN Translation Prize, the Wallace Stevens Award, the Harold Morton Landon Translation Award from the Academy of American Poets, and the Lannan Lifetime Achievement Award, as well as fellowships from the Guggenheim Foundation, the National Endowment for the Arts, and the Rockefeller Foundation. Merwin has lived in Majorca, London, France, and Mexico, as well as in Boston and New York. He now lives in Maui, Hawai'i and for the past thirty years has painstakingly restored his land into one of the most comprehensive palm forests in the world.

Mihaela Moscaliuc was born and raised in Romania and came to the United States in 1996. She is the author of *Father Dirt*, which won the Kinereth Gensler Award, and *Immigrant Model*; translator of Carmelia Leonte's *The Hiss of the Viper*; and editor of *Insane Devotion: On the Writing of Gerald Stern*, among other books. She has also published articles and book chapters on Romanis/

Gypsies, exophony and code-switching, and literature. She received two Glenna Luschei Prairie Schooner Awards, an Individual Artist Award from the New Jersey State Council on the Arts, and a Fulbright Scholar award. She is assistant professor of English at Monmouth University and adjunct professor in the MFA Program in Poetry and Poetry in Translation at Drew University. She resides in Ocean, New Jersey.

Kavery Nambisan was born in Kodagu district, Karnataka, in South India. After obtaining her surgical degree, she chose to work in the villages and has served as a governing council member of the Association of Rural Surgeons of India. She started to write fiction while practicing as a surgeon and has published seven novels, six of them with Penguin India. *The Story That Must Not Be Told* was shortlisted for the Man Asian and the South Asian Literature awards. She lives with her husband in Lonavla, India.

Chigozie Obioma was born in Nigeria. A recipient of Hopwood Awards in fiction and poetry, his work has appeared in *Virginia Quarterly Review, Transition*, and the *Guardian*, among others. His debut novel, *The Fisherman*, was published in 2015 and is being translated into twenty-three languages. The novel was the winner of the inaugural FT/Oppenheimer Award for Fiction and the NAACP Image Awards for Debut Author, and was a finalist for the Man Booker Prize 2015 and the Guardian First Book Award. He lives in Lincoln, Nebraska, where he is a professor of literature and creative writing at the University of Nebraska–Lincoln.

Yvonne Adhiambo Owuor is a Kenya-born prizewinning author. Her most recent work, *Dust*, won the Jomo Kenyatta Prize, Kenya's most prestigious literary prize, and was shortlisted for the Folio Prize. Owuor also won the Caine Prize in 2003 for her short story, "Weight of Whispers." Her travel and landscape writing focuses on the African continent and highlights its liminal spaces, people, and experiences. In 2010, along with eleven other writers from Africa, she participated in the Chinua Achebe Center's "Pilgrimages" project and went to Kinshasa. Owuor graduated Kenyatta University and holds an MPhil in Creative Writing from the University of Queensland, Australia. She lives in Nairobi, Kenya.

Carl Safina is a writer and educator. His work has been recognized with MacArthur, Pew, and Guggenheim Fellowships, and his writing has won Orion, Lannan, and National Academies literary awards. He is the Endowed

Professor for Nature and Humanity at Stony Brook University, where he formerly cochaired the Alan Alda Center for Communicating Science. In addition, he runs the not-for-profit Safina Center. Safina's books include *The View from Lazy Point* and *Beyond Words: What Animals Think and Feel*, among others, and his writing appears in the *New York Times*, *Audubon*, and *National Geographic News*. He lives on Long Island, New York with his wife.

Sebastião Salgado was born in Brazil and began his career as a professional photographer in Paris in 1973, working with photo agencies such as Magnum Photos. In 1994, he and Lélia Wanick Salgado formed Amazonas Images. He has travelled in over 100 countries for his photographic projects. He is a UNICEF Goodwill Ambassador, an honorary member of the Academy of Arts, a member of the Académie des Beaux-Arts of Institut de France, and a Chevalier (Knight) de la Légion d'Honneur, France. Lélia and Sebastião have worked since the 1990s on the restoration of a section of the Atlantic Forest in Brazil. In 1998 they succeeded in turning this land into a nature reserve and created the Instituto Terra. Salgado lives in Paris.

Frank Stewart is the editor *of Manoa: A Pacific Journal of International Writing*. He is also the author of four books of poetry and a history of environmental writing and has edited numerous literary and natural history anthologies concerning Hawai'i, the Pacific, and Asia. His essays, poetry, and translations have been widely anthologized. His awards include the Whiting Award for his poetry, the Elliot Cades Award, and the Hawai'i State Writers Award. He is president of the Manoa Foundation and a professor of English at the University of Hawai'i.

Zoë Strachan is an author and creative writing teacher at the University of Glasgow. Her most recent novel, *Ever Fallen in Love*, was shortlisted for the Green Carnation Prize and nominated for the London Book Awards. Her debut, *Negative Space*, won a Betty Trask Award and was shortlisted for the Saltire First Book of the Year Award. She was the coeditor of New Writing Scotland, and edited *Out There*, the first anthology of LGBT writing from Scotland in twenty years. She has held residencies as UNESCO City of Literature writer-in-residence at the National Museum of Scotland, a Hermann Kesten Stipendiaten, a Hawthornden Fellowship, a British Council visiting fellowship at the University of Iowa, and won a Robert Louis Stevenson Award. She has also written short stories, essays, plays, and operas. She lives in Glasgow with her partner.

Mark Tredinnick is a celebrated Australian poet, essayist, and writing teacher, whose books include *Almost Everything I Know, Bluewren Cantos, Fire Diary, The Blue Plateau,* and *The Little Red Writing Book.* His honors include the two Premiers' Literature Awards, the Montreal and Cardiff Poetry Prizes, and the Calibre Essay Prize. His latest book is *Egret in a Ploughed Field;* two new poetry collections, *Walking Underwater* and *A Beginner's Guide,* will be published in 2018–19. He is at work on the memoir *Reading Slowly at the End of Time* and *The Divide,* a work in poetry and prose on the Great Dividing Range of Eastern Australia. Mark is the father of five children; he lives in Picton, southwest of Sydney, and he teaches at the University of Technology, Sydney.

Natasha Trethewey is a poet and teacher who served two terms as the nineteenth Poet Laureate of the United States (2012–2014). She is the author of four collections of poetry, *Domestic Work, Bellocq's Ophelia, Native Guard*—for which she was awarded the 2007 Pulitzer Prize—and *Thrall.* Her book of nonfiction, *Beyond Katrina: A Meditation on the Mississippi Gulf Coast,* was published in 2010. She is the recipient of fellowships from the Guggenheim Foundation, the National Endowment for the Arts, the Rockefeller Foundation, the Beinecke Library at Yale, and the Radcliffe Institute for Advanced Study at Harvard. A fellow of the American Academy of Arts and Sciences, she is Board of Trustees Professor of English at Northwestern University.

Mary Evelyn Tucker is codirector of the Forum on Religion and Ecology at Yale, where she teaches in the joint MA program between the School of Forestry & Environmental Studies and the Divinity School. She coedited *Confucianism and Ecology, Buddhism and Ecology,* and *Hinduism and Ecology.* With her husband, John Grim, she has authored *Ecology and Religion* and edited Thomas Berry's books, including *Selected Writings.* With Brian Swimme, she wrote *Journey of the Universe* and is the executive director of the Emmy-award-winning film *Journey.* With Grim, she organized ten conferences on World Religions and Ecology at Harvard, and coedited the ten resulting volumes. She served on the International Earth Charter drafting committee and was a member of the Earth Charter International Council. She lives with Grim in Connecticut.

Luis Alberto Urrea was born in Tijuana, Mexico. Extensively published in fiction, nonfiction, and poetry, his work has won the American Book Award, the American Academy of Arts and Letters Fiction Award, and the Lannan Literary Award. He has also has been a finalist for the Pulitzer Prize and the PEN-Faulkner Award, and was voted into the Latino Literature Hall of Fame. He is the author of sixteen books, among them *The Devil's Highway, The Hummingbird's Daughter, Into the Beautiful North, The Water Museum,* and the recent poetry collection, *The Tijuana Book of the Dead.* Urrea lives with his family in Naperville, Illinois.

Terry Tempest Williams is the author of seventeen books focusing on an ethic of place, including the classic in environmental literature *Refuge: An Unnatural History of Family and Place.* Her most recent book is *The Hour of Land: A Personal Topography of America's National Parks.* Williams has received a Lannan Literary Fellowship in creative nonfiction and a John Simon Guggenheim Fellowship, and her work has been anthologized worldwide. She is currently writer-in-residence at the Harvard Divinity School. She lives in Castle Valley, Utah, with her husband.

Dr. Nishat Zaidi is a scholar, critic, and translator from New Delhi. Her recent publications include *Day and Dastan*, a translation with Alok Bhalla of Intizar Husain's two novellas; *Story is a Vagabond: Fiction, Essays and Drama* by Intizar Husain, a collection which she coedited; and Makers of Indian Literature: *Agha Shahid Ali.* Zaidi lives in New Delhi, where she is a professor in the Department of English at Jamia Millia Islamia.

milkweed
editions

Founded as a nonprofit organization in 1980, Milkweed Editions
is an independent publisher. Our mission is to identify, nurture
and publish transformative literature, and build
an engaged community around it.

milkweed.org

Interior design & typesetting by Mary Austin Speaker
Typeset in Adobe Jenson

Adobe Jenson was designed by Robert Slimbach for Adobe
and released in 1996. Slimbach based Jenson's roman styles
on a text face cut by fifteenth-century type designer Nicolas Jenson,
and its italics are based on type created by Ludovico Vicentino
degli Arrighi, a late fifteenth-century papal scribe
and type designer.